Presented pursuant to the GRA Act 2000 c.20, ‹

Ministry of Defence
Annual Report and Accounts

including the Annual Performance Report and
Consolidated Departmental Resource Accounts

2003/04

(For the year ended 31 March 2004)

Laid in accordance with the Government Resources and Accounts Act 2000

Ordered by the House of Commons to be printed
12 October 2004

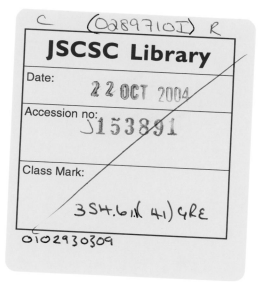
London: The Stationery Office
HC 1080

12 October 2004
£32.75

Contents

Foreword by the Secretary of State

In my foreword to last year's Annual Report and Accounts, I said that 2002/03 had been an extraordinarily demanding year for our Armed Forces and civilian staff. This remained the case throughout 2003/04. And our people continued to meet the challenges, from the front line wherever that lay in the world, to the offices and workshops of the United Kingdom. As Secretary of State for Defence, it is my privilege to work with them. I continue to admire their professionalism, determination and commitment. In particular, we all owe a continuing debt of gratitude and thanks to those who gave their lives during the year in the service of our country and to make the world a better place.

Rt. Hon. Geoff Hoon MP, Secretary of State for Defence

Defence business during the year was inevitably dominated by Iraq. UK Forces continued to serve there with distinction, often supported by civilian colleagues. But we should not forget how many other places they were operating. As this Report sets out, during the year, the Armed Forces were working in Afghanistan, the Balkans, Cyprus, and west and central Africa, as well as in the Middle East. And they were busy at home – in Northern Ireland, in providing emergency fire cover, and on more routine activities.

At the same time we have been working to ensure that that we will continue to have Armed Forces of the right size and shape, with the right equipment, to meet the challenges of the future. In December 2003, we published a White Paper, *Delivering Security in a Changing World* setting out our assessment of the future security environment. Against this baseline, in July 2004, we published a further White Paper, *Delivering Security in a Changing World: Future Capabilities*, that set out the capabilities and reformed force structure we need to meet the changes in international security requirements.

We have also been working to ensure that the Ministry of Defence is properly configured to support our Armed Forces as efficiently and effectively as possible. We have been pursuing a major programme of reform and efficiency for some time. This is necessary to enable us to build for the future, and the Annual Report shows the good progress we have been making. This work also formed the basis of the MoD's contribution to the cross-Government Lyons and Gershon Reviews, and of our Spending Review Settlement in July. Building on the programmes set out in this Report, our challenge over the next three to four years is to complete the changes we have set out. I do not underestimate the size of the challenge. But I am confident that we can succeed.

Overall, this Report shows that the Armed Forces and the Ministry of Defence have delivered, are delivering, and will continue to deliver what they are required and resourced to do, often in the face of considerable challenges. I particularly welcome the fact that, for the first time, the Comptroller and Auditor General has this year approved the MoD's accounts without qualification. This is very significant achievement we have been working towards for several years.

The high operational tempo we have maintained in recent years is a demonstration of the Armed Forces' and Department's success in delivering what is required of them. At the same time, we are embarked on a major programme of modernisation and reform. And as the Report makes clear, they are making significant contributions to delivery of the wider Government agenda. We continue to ask a lot of all our people, military and civilian. I and my colleagues remain committed to ensuring they have the support they need and deserve to deliver on this ambitious programme of operational activity and organisational reform. I am confident that they will continue to meet the challenges and help make the world a safer place.

Geoffrey Hoon

Introduction

Introduction

1. This year, the Ministry of Defence has again combined its Annual Performance Report and its Departmental Resource Accounts into one document: the MoD Annual Report and Accounts. Overall, it provides a comprehensive and clear record of the Department's performance during 2003/04. Section 1 sets out overall performance, beginning with a summary of progress against our Spending Review 2002 Public Service Agreement (PSA) objectives and targets. Section 2 contains the Departmental Resource Accounts. Additionally, the Report contains a series of Annexes offering background departmental information, including a list of further sources of information.

Section 1

2. Section 1 is structured along the same lines as the Balanced Scorecard, through which the Department's performance is reported internally. The Defence Balanced Scorecard encapsulates the Defence Management Board's key objectives and priorities over the whole range of MoD business. In the Report, these objectives are grouped into the four chapters (or 'perspectives'), shown below, of: Outputs and Deliverables, Resource Management, Enabling Processes and Building for the Future. Within these perspectives, the main section headings correspond to high-level Scorecard objectives (i.e. Operations, Effectiveness, Policy, etc.).

Figure 1: Defence Balanced Scorecard 2003

Are we delivering what the Government expects?

OUTPUT AND DELIVERABLES

A. OPERATIONS: To achieve success in tasks we undertake.
B. EFFECTIVENESS: To be ready to respond to what might arise.
C. POLICY: To help to build a safer world.

How well are we planning and managing our resources?

RESOURCE MANAGEMENT

D. FINANCIAL RESOURCES: To control and make best use of the Department's resources.
E. PEOPLE: To achieve broad manning balance within each Service and recruit and retain sufficient Civil Servants.
F. DEFENCE INFRASTRUCTURE: To have infrastructure of the right size and quality, effectively and efficiently managed.
G. REPUTATION: To enhance our reputation among the UK public and internally.

BATTLE WINNING DEFENCE CAPABILITY

ENABLING PROCESSES

H. TRAINING: To provide improved individual and collective training to support operational needs.
I. PROCUREMENT: To improve the procurement of equipment and infrastructure.
J. LOGISTIC SUPPORT: To provide more responsive, integrated and efficient logistic support.
K. MANAGEMENT: To improve management, accountability and efficiency across the Department.

Are we organised as well as we can be?

BUILDING FOR THE FUTURE

L. PERSONNEL STRATEGY: To invest in military and civilian personnel and develop them for the future.
M. MODERNISING DEFENCE: To modernise defence to meet future military requirements.
N. TECHNOLOGY AND EQUIPMENT: To invest in technology and develop equipment capability for the future.

Are we developing our people and organisation for the future?

Performance Against PSA Objectives and Targets

3.   The MoD's progress against its PSA objectives and targets is addressed throughout this Report, and the Department's performance against its current (SR 2002) PSA objectives is published quarterly on the Treasury and MoD websites. A summary of progress against SR 2002 PSA objectives and targets for 2003/04 to 2005/06 is set out at the front of the Report. A final assessment of progress against the MoD's SR 2000 PSA objectives and targets for 2001/02 to 2003/04 is at Annex B, together with the top level targets for 2005/06 to 2007/08 agreed this summer in SR 2004. Of the 16 individual targets in the 2002 Spending Review, the MoD is ahead on 1 target, on course to meet a further 10, and is showing slippage on 4. One more is yet to be assessed. Of the 25 SR 2000 individual targets, 16 were met in full, 2 were met with some slippage, 2 were partly met, 1 (which has been carried forward to SR2002) is on course, 3 were not met and 1 has not yet been finally assessed.

Section 2

4.   Under the Government Resources and Accounts Act 2000, the Department is required to prepare resource accounts for each financial year, to conform with Treasury direction, detailing the resources acquired, held, or disposed of during the year and the use of resources by the Department during the year. The Permanent Head of the Department, as Accounting Officer of the Department, is responsible for preparing the Department's accounts and for transmitting them to the Comptroller and Auditor General. In preparing the accounts, the Accounting Officer is required to comply with the Resource Accounting Manual, prepared by the Treasury.

5.   The resource accounts are prepared on an accruals basis and must give a true and fair view of the state of affairs of the Department, the net resource outturn, resources applied to objectives, recognised gains and losses, and cash flows for the financial year. The Departmental Resource Accounts for 2003/04 are set out in Section 2, together with the Comptroller and Auditor General's certification and report to the House of Commons.

Further Information

6.   Other sources of detailed information relevant to the MoD's performance are identified throughout the report, and listed in Annex F.

Section 1

Performance Report

Summary of Performance Against SR2002 Public Service Agreement Objectives and Targets

Aim: to deliver security for the people of the United Kingdom and the Overseas Territories by defending them, including against terrorism, and act as a force for good by strengthening international peace and security.

Table 1: Performance Against Public Service Agreement Targets for 2003/04 to 2005/06			
PSA Target	Supporting Performance Indicator (where relevant)	Assessment at 1 April 2004	Report Paragraphs
Objective I – Achieve success in the military tasks that we undertake at home and abroad.			
1. Achieve the objectives established by Ministers for Operations and Military Tasks in which the UK's Armed Forces are involved, including those providing support to our civil communities. **Overall Assessment: On Course**		**On Course** The Armed Forces achieved a high degree of success against the policy and military objectives set for all Operations overseas, including in Iraq, Afghanistan, the Balkans, Sierra Leone, and the Democratic Republic of Congo. Continuing support was provided to the civil authorities at home	7-28
2. Improve effectiveness of the UK contribution to conflict prevention and management as demonstrated by a reduction in the number of people whose lives are affected by violent conflict and a reduction in potential sources of future conflict, where the UK can make a significant contribution. JOINT TARGET WITH DfID AND FCO. **Overall Assessment: Not yet assessed**		Data on performance against the PSA target is not yet available. The cross-departmental programme continued to develop over the year, with MoD developing and refocusing defence relations programmes and initiatives, working to support conflict prevention initiatives across Africa, the Middle East, Europe, Central America and Asia, and undertaking wider-ranging conflict prevention work under the Defence Diplomacy Programme.	48-50
Objective II – Be ready to respond to the tasks that might arise.			
3. By 2006 ensure that a minimum of 90% of high-readiness forces are at their required states of readiness with no critical weakness. (As set out in MoD's 2002/03 Annual Report and Accounts, from 1 April 2003, reporting against this target covers all forces, not just those at high readiness.) **Overall Assessment: On Course**		**On Course** The proportion of units with no critical weaknesses reported by their military commanders increased steadily over the year from 77% in the first quarter to 93% in the fourth quarter.	32-36

Table 1 (continued): Performance Against Public Service Agreement Targets for 2003/04 to 2005/06

PSA Target	Supporting Performance Indicator (where relevant)	Assessment at 1 April 2004	Report Paragraphs
Objective II (continued) – Be ready to respond to the tasks that might arise.			
4. Recruit, retain and motivate the personnel needed to meet the manning requirement of the Armed Forces, so that by the end of 2004, the Royal Navy and RAF achieve, and thereafter maintain, manning balance, and that by the end of 2005, the Army achieves, and thereafter maintains, manning balance. (Manning balance is defined as between −2% and +1% of the requirement, and is measured against the target prevailing at the time. Since the total manning requirement of whole Service manning is dynamic, this target will itself fluctuate over the PSA period.) **Overall Assessment: On Course**	Achieve manning balance.	**On Course** The trained strength of the Navy was 96.8% at end year, remaining just below manning balance over the year. The trained strength of the Army was 97.2% at end year, having made significant progress towards manning balance over the year. The trained strength of the RAF was 98.5% at end year, having remained within target over the year. Some improvement in critical shortage groups, but progress slow. Continuing shortages in all three Services.	73-75
	Achieve single Service guidelines for deployed separated service. **Royal Navy/Royal Marines:** No more than 660 days separated service over 3 years for Able Seaman within TOPMAST; no more than 60% of time away from base port over 2 years for non-TOPMAST personnel. **Army:** Tour lengths should be not more than 6 months, with 24 month average tour intervals. **Royal Air Force:** no more than 6% of personnel with more than 140 days detached duty over 12 months and 4% with more than 280 days detached duty over 24 months.	**On Course** **RN:** Average separated service for Able Ratings 169 days over 3 year period. **Army:** Average tour interval 23.3 months, but with variation. Royal Armoured Corps 14 months, Infantry and Royal Artillery 18 months. **RAF:** 5.4% of personnel more than 140 days detached duty over 12 months and 2.4% of personnel more than 280 days detached duty over 24 months.	160
	Improve the living conditions of Service personnel and their families.	**On Course** 3,347 new-build Single Living Accommodation bedspaces delivered and 1,402 Service family houses upgraded in 2003/04.	96-97
5. Strengthen European security through an enlarged and modernised NATO, an effective EU military crisis management capacity and enhanced European defence capabilities. JOINT TARGET WITH FCO. **Overall Assessment: On Course**		**On Course** Good progress made: NATO has enlarged by seven members and is modernising its capabilities and reforming its structures to adapt to the new threats and challenges we face. We continue to be at the forefront of developing European defence capabilities that will strengthen both NATO and the EU. The UK is working effectively to ensure coherence between the two organisations.	43-47

Table 1 (continued): Performance Against Public Service Agreement Targets for 2003/04 to 2005/06

PSA Target	Supporting Performance Indicator (where relevant)	Assessment at 1 April 2004	Report Paragraphs
Objective III – Build for the future.			
6. Develop and deliver to time and cost targets military capability for the future, including battle-winning technology, equipment and systems, matched to the changing strategic environment. (All assessments subject to NAO validation). **Overall Assessment: Slippage**	On average, in-year slippage of equipment in-service dates of fewer than 10 days for new major projects, to be attained during 2003/04 and maintained throughout the PSA period.	**Slippage** 2.2 months average slippage for new projects in 2003/04.	123
	On average, in-year slippage of equipment in-service dates of fewer than 4 weeks for existing major projects, to be attained during 2003/04 and maintained throughout the PSA period.	**Slippage** 2.8 months average slippage for existing projects in 2003/04.	123
	97% of customers' key requirements attained during 2003/04 and maintained throughout the PSA period.	**On Course** 98.8% of customers' key requirements met in 2003/04.	123
	On average, no real terms increase in major project costs, to be attained during 2003/04 and maintained throughout the PSA period.	**Slippage** 2.7% average increase in costs measured against project approvals in 2003/04.	123
Value for Money			
7. Increase value for money by making improvements in the efficiency and effectiveness of the key processes for delivering military capability. Year-on-year output efficiency gains of 2.5% will be made each year from 02/03 to 05/06, including through a 20% output efficiency gain in the DLO. **Overall Assessment: On Course**	Reduce the per capita cost of successfully training a military recruit by an average of 6% by April 2006.	**On Course** 4.2% average reduction in cost of successfully training military recruit by April 2004 against end-year target of 4%.	110
	Achieve 0% average annual cost growth (or better) against the Major Equipment Procurement Projects.	**Slippage** 3.1% average increase in costs measured against estimated cost at beginning of year.	123
	Reduce by 20% (relative to April 2000) the output costs of the DLO, while maintaining support to the Front Line.	**On Course** 6.8% cumulative reduction in Logistics costs against end-year target of 6%.	138
	Reduce MoD Head Office and other management costs by 13%.	**On Course** 10.6% cumulative reduction in Head Office costs against end-year target of 9%.	184
	Identify for disposal land and buildings with a Net Book value of over £300m.	**Ahead** Cumulative value of £230M land and buildings identified for disposal by April 2004 against end-year target of £134M.	101

Output and Deliverables

Operations

Objective

To succeed in the tasks the MoD undertakes.

Public Service Agreement Target (SR2002 MoD Target 1)

- Achieve the objectives established by Ministers for Operations and Military Tasks in which the United Kingdom's Armed Forces are involved, including those providing support to our civil communities.

Performance Measures and Assessment

Achieve operational success for operations and other Ministerially directed tasks:

- *The Armed Forces achieved a high degree of success against the policy and military objectives set for all operations overseas, including in Iraq, Afghanistan, the Balkans, Sierra Leone, and the Democratic Republic of Congo;*

- *A minimum nuclear deterrent capability was maintained throughout the year;*

- *The security of the UK's Overseas Territories, including Cyprus, the Falkland Islands, and Gibraltar, was maintained;*

- *Continuing support was provided to the civil authorities at home, including in Northern Ireland, in civil emergencies (particularly the provision of emergency fire cover across the UK until June 2003), in the routine provision of Search and Rescue and of Fisheries Protection services, and in the investigation and disposal of suspected explosive devices.*

Other Measures

Monitor the proportion of the Armed Forces, including Reserves, involved in the prosecution of contingent and enduring operations and other Ministerially directed tasks:

- *The proportion of regular forces deployed on Operations and other Military Tasks declined from a peak of about 35% overall in the first quarter of the year (including about 47% of the Army), to about 20% overall (including about 23% of the Army) across the remainder of the year;*

- *Some 4,000 Reservists, about 9% of total Reserve Forces, have been involved in Op TELIC since the end of the main conflict phase.*

Further Sources of Information

- Quarterly PSA reports to HM Treasury
  www.hm-treasury.gov.uk/performance/MoD.cfm and www.mod.uk;

- *Operations in Iraq: First Reflections;*

- *Lessons for the Future* (assessment of performance on Operation TELIC);

- MoD Evidence to the House Of Commons Public Accounts Committee on Operation TELIC – *United Kingdom Military Operations in Iraq (HC 60);*

- MoD Evidence to the House of Commons Defence Committee on *Lessons of Iraq (HC 57);*

- *Delivering Security in a Changing World* (Defence White Paper and supporting essays);

- *UK Defence Statistics 2004.*

Figure 2: Principal Deployments of the Armed Forces on 1 April 2004

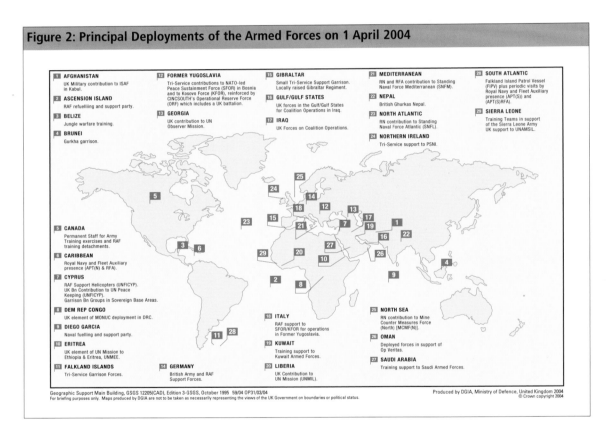

Iraq

7. The main warfighting phase of Operation TELIC ended in May 2003. The Department's initial report – *Operations in Iraq: First Reflections* – setting out the role of the UK Armed Forces during the main period of hostilities in Operation Telic and drawing early conclusions, and a subsequent, more comprehensive analysis – *Operations in Iraq: Lessons for the Future* – are available at www.mod.uk, together with a range of further information on ensuing activity in Iraq.

The MoD also cooperated closely with the House of Commons Public Accounts and Defence Committees and with the National Audit Office during their own enquiries into the earlier phases of Operation TELIC. Copies of their reports are available at www.parliament.the-stationery-office.co.uk/ and www.nao.org.uk/publications/vfmsublist/index.asp.

Warrior armoured vehicles of the Princess of Wales Royal Regiment prepare for a patrol in southern Iraq.

8. The UK continued to work throughout the year for a stable, united, law-abiding Iraq, at peace with its neighbours and enjoying representative government. Over 30 nations contributed troops to operations in Iraq, while many others pledged aid. United Nations Security Council Resolution (UNSCR) 1483, adopted on 22 May 2003, acknowledged the status of UK and US Forces as Occupying Powers in Iraq. The UK commanded Multinational Division South East, covering the provinces of Al-Basrah, Al-Muthanna, Dhi Qar and Maysan. In October 2003, UNSCR 1511 authorised the Multinational Force to undertake stabilisation tasks. On 15 November 2003, the Iraqi Governing Council set out a political timetable, leading to the assumption of authority by a sovereign Iraqi government by the end of June 2004. Following the end of warfighting, some 18,000 UK forces remained in Iraq (from a peak of some 46,000 personnel). This reduced to 9,500 by August 2003 and remained at roughly that level throughout the rest of the year.

A soldier attached to the Cheshire Regiment mans an observation post in Basrah.

9. Early successes included the construction of a water pipe-line from Kuwait to Umm Qasr in the first week of April 2003, delivering up to two million litres of drinking water daily. The Umm Qasr Water

Treatment Plant was also operational by the first week of April 2003, treating up to three million litres a day. Humanitarian and reconstruction work continued throughout the year, with UK forces delivering a number of small-scale "Quick Impact Projects" that significantly and speedily improved the quality of life for many ordinary Iraqis. Projects included assistance to schools, hospitals and to the Marsh Arab community. Army engineers also helped with the restoration of power, water and infrastructure throughout Multinational Division South East. UK Forces have worked hard throughout the year to develop the capacity of Iraqis to provide security in their own country. Joint patrols by Iraqi police and UK Forces began in mid-April 2003. By 1 March 2004, there were some 75,000 Iraqi police in Iraq, with over 12,000 of those recruited in the UK area. UK Forces were training six battalions of the Iraqi Civil Defence Force and led the development of the Iraqi Coastal Defence Force (ICDF), training 10 of its officers at Dartmouth in the UK. The Ministry of Defence Police also has around 20 officers in Iraq, where they play a key role in the development of the Iraqi Police Service. The range and quality of the work of UK Forces in Southern Iraq has been recognised by several independent bodies, including the House of Commons Defence Committee, while UNOPS and UNICEF have praised UK Forces for the humanitarian help they have given local people in tackling the long-standing problem of unexploded ordnance left by Saddam's wars.

Troops from the Cheshire Regiment support an Iraqi police patrol in southern Iraq.

10. Reserve Forces made an invaluable contribution to this work. By the start of March 2004, almost 10,000 Reservists (out of a total Reserve Force of just under 45,000) had been involved in Operation TELIC, with over 4,000 involved in the post-conflict phase. Their military contribution has ranged from the provision of complete reserve units, including medical units, to the reinforcement of regular units and formations of all the Services. In addition, using their wide range of individual skills and experience, Reserve personnel have been able to participate in peace support activities in such areas as local government development, education and economic reform. At the same time, Reserves continued to contribute on a voluntary basis to other operations around the globe. Their versatility and commitment continue to prove their worth and demonstrate that the 1997 Strategic Defence Review's aspiration for a useable, relevant and integrated Reserve Force is working successfully in practice.

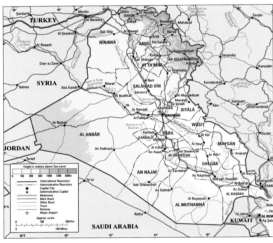

South Eastern Iraq.

Other Overseas Operations

Afghanistan

11. UK Armed Forces continued to play an important role in Afghanistan, helping the Afghan Transitional Authority (ATA) and the Afghan people to rebuild their country. Our largest single contribution during the year and since has been to the NATO-led International Security and Assistance Force (ISAF). This comprises around 300-350 troops in Kabul contributing to the maintenance of security across the capital, at the international airport and in the ISAF Headquarters as part of the Kabul Multinational Brigade. Additionally, since March 2003 we have been carrying out a very successful local training programme for Junior Non-Commissioned Officers for the Afghan National Army and in July 2003, we deployed a Provincial Reconstruction Team (PRT) of 100 troops to the northern city of Mazar-e-Sharif and its surrounding provinces. This was followed by the deployment of a second PRT of some 30 troops to the city of Meymaneh, also in North West Afghanistan. These PRTs play an important role in helping the ATA extend its capacity and its reach, and assist in developing a secure and stable environment and in stimulating security sector reform and reconstruction. Although military-led, key parts of the PRTs are provided by representatives from the Foreign and Commonwealth Office and Department for International Development. In June 2004, we transferred both PRTs to the ISAF as part of our commitment to the expansion of the Force. We also contributed the bulk of the troops needed for a new Forward Support Base and Quick Reaction Force, both based in Mazar-e-Sharif, and we currently have about 260 troops deployed in North West Afghanistan. A further 190 personnel from several other nations, including Afghans, are also serving as part of the ISAF in the region.

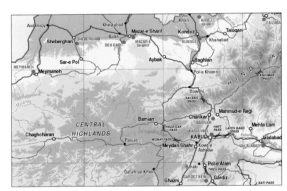

Northern Afghanistan.

The Balkans

12. During the year, the UK provided a reduced, but still significant, contribution in both Bosnia and Kosovo, and one of the four Battalions of the NATO Balkans-wide Operational Reserve Force (ORF). Additionally, the UK has been involved in a number of conflict prevention programmes across the Balkans, including supporting the EU's Op CONCORDIA in the former Yugoslav Republic of Macedonia. Following

progressive stabilisation over the last 10 years, NATO announced at the Istanbul Summit in June 2004 that the NATO Stabilisation Force (SFOR) operation in Bosnia and Herzegovina will now conclude at the end of 2004. NATO and the EU are now working together to deploy a new and distinct follow-on EU mission to the country, including a military component under the Berlin Plus arrangements. The UK will provide the initial lead of the EU Mission. This will work in close partnership with a limited continuing NATO Headquarters in Sarajevo.

13.　NATO's review of operations in the Balkans in 2003 set out a regional approach to security operations. This change in operational concept enabled a reduction of about 40% (from around 18,600 to 11,200) in the number of troops deployed under SFOR in **Bosnia and Herzegovina**, with the UK's contribution falling by about 20% (from around 1,200 to 960). SFOR continued its successful peace stabilisation operation and assisted international work to normalise the country. Between November 2003 and March 2004, the UK Battle Group in Multinational Task Force (North West) was central to operations recovering illegal arms and ammunition: over 115 tonnes of weapons were seized from 32 caches. The MoD also led the foundation of a multinational Peace Support Operations Training Centre to train young Bosnian officers from both entities in peace support operations, helped the International Organisation for Migration to provide de-mobilised soldiers with assistance in starting their own business, offered advisory support to the Office of the High Representative, and continued to support the International Criminal Tribunal for the Former Yugoslavia (ICTY) through detention of indicted war criminals.

Balkans.

14.　In **Kosovo**, the UK contribution to the NATO Kosovo Force (KFOR) mission dropped from a battalion to a smaller but highly effective contribution of around 200 troops, retaining the capability to deploy across the whole of Kosovo. In addition, around 70 Ministry of Defence Police officers are stationed in Kosovo, working with the UN Interim Administrative Mission and the Kosovo Police Service on a wide range of international policing tasks, operational to administrative, including responding to the challenges posed by the outbreak of violence in March 2004. Following the outbreak of violence, the Operational Reserve Force was also used to good effect to help restore a safe and secure environment. Lead elements of the Ready Battalion (1st Battalion, The Royal Gloucestershire, Berkshire and Wiltshire Regiment) began deploying to Kosovo on 18 March 2004 within 24 hours of NATO's Activation Order, returning to the UK 30 days later after the situation had been stabilised. MoD involvement with the Kosovo Protection Corps (KPC) continued with the provision of a serving UK 2* officer as the KPC Co-ordinator to assist the KPC in fulfilling its mandated role of civil emergency activity and "train the trainer" de-mining programmes.

15.　In **Macedonia**, Op CONCORDIA ran from 31 March to 15 December 2003 and successfully provided security for international monitors who were overseeing the re-entry of Macedonian security forces into former crisis areas. This was the first European Union military operation conducted under the European Security and Defence Policy, and drew on NATO assets and capabilities under the Berlin Plus arrangements. The UK contributed 2 staff officers to HQ Op CONCORDIA and 1 watchkeeper. The Operation's success was demonstrated by the replacement of military support with a civilian police mission in December 2003.

Sierra Leone

16.　As part of the United Nations Mission in Sierra Leone (UNAMSIL), the UK has provided 22 personnel, comprising a Headquarters contingent of 7 (including the key posts of Chief of Staff Force and Chief of Staff Observers) in the capital Freetown, and 15 United Nations Military Observers deployed throughout the country. UNAMSIL's main objectives are to assist the Government of Sierra Leone to extend its authority, restore law and order and stabilise the situation progressively throughout the entire country, and to promote a political process leading to a renewed disarmament, demobilisation and reintegration (DDR) programme and the holding of free and fair elections. Significant progress has been made, enabling local government elections in May 2004, and handing back primacy in the Northern and Southern regions to the Government on 10 June 2004 on conclusion of the DDR programme. However, recognising that the Government of Sierra Leone is not yet in a position to take over full control of the country without international support, the United Nations has extended UNAMSIL in a reduced form until June 2005, with the United Kingdom's contribution reducing to 13 posts.

Sierra Leone.

17. In addition to this UK operational commitment to the UN, MoD is closely involved in the process of Security Sector Reform in Sierra Leone. The UK-led International Military Advisory and Training Team (Sierra Leone) (IMATT(SL)) currently comprises 98 UK personnel and 12 internationals. IMATT(SL)'s role is to develop the Sierra Leone Armed Forces (RSLAF) into an effective and democratically accountable armed force capable of carrying out the defence missions and tasks assigned to it by the Government of Sierra Leone. HMG has made the commitment that IMATT(SL) will remain in some form until at least 2010. The current campaign plan aims to have reduced the team to a strength of 25 by the end of 2009.

18. Commander IMATT(SL) is also responsible for Op VOSPER, an Information Operation using selected military activity (ship visits, exercises and training teams). This supports the capacity-building activities with the RSLAF and demonstrates UK commitment to supporting the stability of Sierra Leone.

Democratic Republic of Congo

An RAF Hercules Transport at Entebbe Airport, supporting the EU Stabilisation Force deployed to Bunia in the Democratic Republic of Congo.

19. Operation ARTEMIS (July-September 2003) was launched as the first EU military operation without recourse to NATO assets. Based around a major French contribution, the EU deployed over 2,000 troops, including 94 from the UK, to Bunia in the Democratic Republic of Congo in response to a UN Security Council Resolution to establish an interim emergency multinational force. The Operation successfully stabilised the security conditions and improved the humanitarian situation, pending the deployment of a reinforced UN Mission.

Democratic Republic of Congo.

Other Military Tasks

Independent Nuclear Deterrent

20. Throughout the year, the UK's Trident submarine force maintained an independent nuclear deterrent capability at sea in support of NATO's strategy of war prevention and as the ultimate guarantee of our national security.

Security of Overseas Territories

21. In **Cyprus**, UK Forces maintained important military facilities within the Sovereign Base Areas of Akrotiri and Dhekelia. Both UK and US Forces used RAF Akrotiri extensively as a forward-mounting base in support of operations in Iraq. UK Forces based in the **Falkland Islands** continued to demonstrate the Government's commitment to the security of that territory, including South Georgia and the South Sandwich Islands. **Gibraltar**-based UK Armed Forces continued to provide valuable support, logistic, communications and training facilities in support of UK operations.

Search and Rescue

22. The Royal Navy and Royal Air Force maintained a year-round 24-hour search and rescue helicopter service, based at eight locations around the British Isles and also on Cyprus and the Falkland Islands. Other Service assets, in particular the Royal Air Force's Mountain Rescue Service and Nimrod maritime patrol aircraft, were also used for search and rescue. The Armed Forces' rescue services were called out on 1,772 occasions in 2003/04 (compared with 1,670 in 2002/03) and assisted a total of 1,317 people, including 103 military personnel.

Military Aid to the Civil Authorities

23. Overall responsibility for security and civil emergencies within the UK rests with the Home Office. Responses to specific incidents are managed by lead government departments, the emergency services, the devolved executives, and a wide range of other civil authorities (for details see www.ukresilience.info). MoD provides Military Aid to the Civil Authorities by drawing almost exclusively on resources designed and funded for other Defence tasks.

24. By far the largest category of requests for Military Aid is for investigation of suspected explosive devices. The Police outside London rely on the MoD to provide this support, which is partly funded by the Home Office. Support from bomb disposal teams was requested on 675 occasions in 2003/04, compared with 431 occasions in 2002/03 and 957 in 2001/02. Other aid is generally small-scale with the Police being the source of the majority of the requests. We estimated in February 2003 that we were receiving 30 to 40 such requests per annum (*Official Report*, 25 February 2003, Column 444W) with the number increasing. Government and local authority investment in civil response (for instance in flood prevention and defences) is, however, showing some signs of reducing the number of 'no-notice' requests for assistance.

Military Aid to the Civil Power in Northern Ireland

25. The Armed Forces continued to play an important role in supporting the Police Service of Northern Ireland in maintaining law and order, especially in the face of the threat from dissident republican groups. Military patrols supported the Police in searching for and capturing terrorists, their weapons and other equipment, and in dealing with serious public disorder. As part of our normal process of keeping force levels under review in consultation with the Chief Constable of the Police Service of Northern Ireland, we were able to reduce the number of Service personnel committed over the year, from 14,320 on April 1 2003 to 14,030 on April 1 2004. We also continued to rationalise the Defence estate in Northern Ireland, including vacating a number of bases and installations across the Province.

Op FRESCO

26. The settlement of the national fire dispute meant that it was possible to stand down the 11,000 personnel committed to the provision of emergency fire cover in June 2003. Although it was recognised that there was no alternative but to provide emergency fire cover, the commitment had a significant impact on the Armed Forces. Subsequent contingency planning for provision of emergency fire cover by the Armed Forces has drawn on lessons learned from the dispute. In parallel, however, the Office of the Deputy Prime Minister's framework for the modernisation of the fire service recognises that Armed Forces' support should not be taken for granted in future.

Fisheries Protection

27. The Fishery Protection Squadron of the Royal Navy's Portsmouth Flotilla delivered 908 Fisheries Patrol Days from 1 April 2003 to 31 March 2004, made 1,710 boardings (an increase of 28% over the previous year), and identified 4,076 fishing vessels and 84 infringements. In fulfilment of the MoD's agreement with the Department of the Environment, Food and Rural Affairs, 23 vessels were detained.

The Royal Navy now delivers the majority of the Fisheries Patrol Days required, using the 3 recently commissioned ships of the new River Class Offshore Patrol Vessels – HMS TYNE, HMS SEVERN and HMS MERSEY. These capable ships are leased by the Royal Navy under innovative, and to date very promising, arrangements with Vosper Thorneycroft.

Counter-Drugs Operations

28. The Armed Forces provided valuable assistance to HM Customs and Excise and other anti-narcotics agencies around the world. In particular, units deployed to the Caribbean continued to undertake patrols and joint operations with the US Coast Guard and drug-enforcement agencies. For instance, during a six-week period from November 2003 to January 2004, UK Forces facilitated the disruption of 14 tonnes of cocaine and the arrest of 13 traffickers.

Activity Levels of the Armed Forces

29. With the end of war-fighting operations in the Gulf, activity levels, as measured by the numbers of personnel deployed on Operations or other Military Tasks, for all three Services declined from the high levels seen in 2002/2003, with Royal Navy activity in particular depressed during the middle of the year as units recuperated, ships underwent maintenance and personnel took leave. Sustaining commitments in Iraq at the same time as in Northern Ireland, the Balkans, Afghanistan and other theatres meant however, that demands on the Army remained high. The Royal Air Force flew a total of 48,550 hours on operations, including 29,000 on Operation TELIC.

30. As set out in Supporting Essay 2 to the Defence White Paper *Delivering Security in a Changing World*, published in December 2003, our planning assumptions have developed to reflect the level and frequency of

Table 2: % of Trained Strength of Regular Forces Deployed on Operations and other Military Tasks								
	2002/2003				2003/2004			
	Quarter 1	Quarter 2	Quarter 3	Quarter 4	Quarter 1	Quarter 2	Quarter 3	Quarter 4
Royal Navy/Royal Marines	17.5%	13.0%	16.5%	28.5%	18.7%	12.8%	14.0%	17.7%
Army	24.6%	23.9%	32.5%	55.6%	46.9%	23.2%	22.9%	22.6%
Royal Air Force	12.6%	10.9%	19.1%	21.8%	16.5%	13.0%	12.9%	12.1%

Notes
(1) Percentages exclude those either preparing for, or recovering from, deployments and are quarterly averages. Figures are based on man-day equivalents and cannot be compared across the Services. A list of Military Tasks can be found on the Department's website (www.mod.uk).
(2) This data is collected through Service personnel management systems and local command reports.

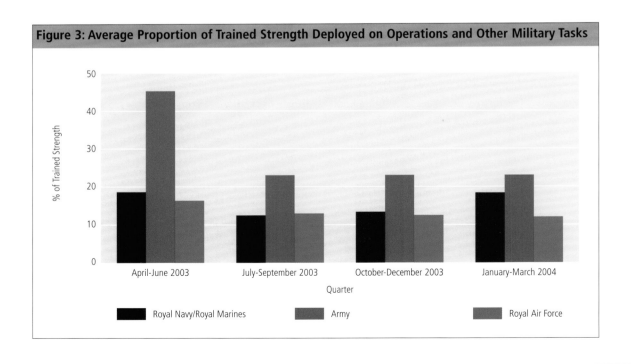

Figure 3: Average Proportion of Trained Strength Deployed on Operations and Other Military Tasks

deployments for the more complex and demanding pattern of operations now necessary. We therefore now plan:

- that as a norm and without creating overstretch, we should be able to mount an enduring Medium Scale (MS) peace support operation simultaneously with an enduring Small Scale (SS) peace support operation and a one-off Small Scale intervention operation;

- that we should be able to reconfigure our Forces rapidly to carry out the enduring Medium Scale peace support operation and a Small Scale peace support operation simultaneously with a limited Medium Scale intervention operation; and

- that, given time to prepare, we should be capable of undertaking a demanding one-off Large Scale (LS) operation while still maintaining a commitment to a simple Small Scale peace support operation.

Additionally, we must also take account of the need to meet standing commitments with permanently committed forces, such as Quick-Reaction Alert Aircraft designed to maintain the integrity of UK airspace.

31. These assumptions set out what we plan to be able to achieve. In reality, we would expect to face periods where we are operating both above and below these levels. Our ability to sustain operations in excess of these assumptions will depend on a variety of factors including the nature and duration of the operations themselves. Figure 4 below sets out in broad terms the concurrency levels of the operations and other Military Tasks in which the Armed Forces have been engaged from 1999 to 2003. It is not definitive, but gives a general indication of the scale of military activity over this period.

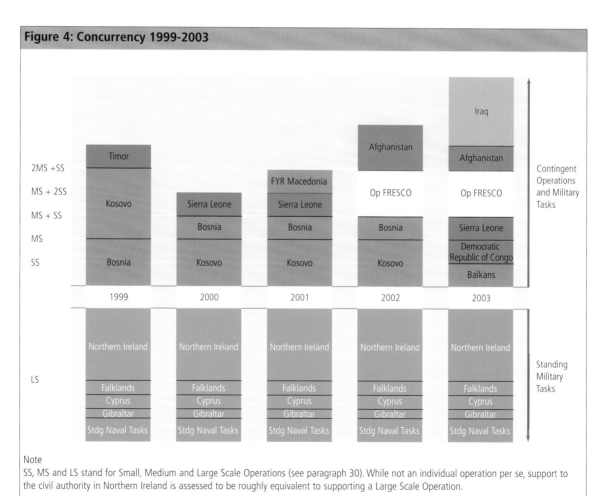

Figure 4: Concurrency 1999-2003

Note

SS, MS and LS stand for Small, Medium and Large Scale Operations (see paragraph 30). While not an individual operation per se, support to the civil authority in Northern Ireland is assessed to be roughly equivalent to supporting a Large Scale Operation.

Effectiveness

Objective:

To be ready to respond to what might arise.

Public Service Agreement Target (SR2002 MoD Target 3)

- By 2006 ensure that a minimum of 90% of high-readiness forces are at their required states of readiness with no critical weakness.

Performance Measures and Assessment

All Force Elements to meet planned readiness targets with no critical or serious weaknesses:

- *The proportion of Force Elements with no critical weaknesses reported by their military commanders increased steadily over the year from 77% in the first quarter to 93% in the fourth quarter.*

Other Measures

Assess our ability to generate and deploy, sustain and recover UK Armed Forces as required:

- *Operations in Iraq and elsewhere during the year effectively demonstrated our ability to deploy and sustain forces on operations and recover them thereafter, but highlighted a number of shortfalls. Some of these have already been addressed and we are looking carefully at how we can improve our ability to prepare in advance of commitment to specific deployments.*

Further sources of information

- Quarterly PSA reports to HM Treasury;

- MoD Evidence to the House Of Commons Public Accounts Committee on *Operation TELIC – United Kingdom Military Operations in Iraq (HC 273);*

- MoD Evidence to the House of Commons Defence Committee on *Lessons of Iraq (HC 57)* and Government Response (HC 635);

- *Operations in Iraq: First Reflections;*

- *Lessons for the Future* (assessment of performance on Operation TELIC);

- *Delivering Security in a Changing World* (Defence White Paper and supporting essays).

Readiness

32. The Armed Forces undertake operations and other Military Tasks as required by the Government. A system of graduated readiness ensures that the right Force Elements (e.g. a Royal Navy ship, an Army brigade, or Royal Air Force aircraft and crew) are ready to deploy when they are needed. Each Force Element is set a planned and funded 'readiness target'. Performance against these targets is then used as a measure of whether the Armed Forces are achieving the level of military capability for which they are resourced. In previous years, we reported on the readiness of rapidly deployable Force Elements only. As noted in the *Annual Report and Accounts 2002/03,* this did not provide a complete picture of overall military capability. In order to give a better picture of the ability of the Armed Forces to cope with the levels of operational activity currently undertaken, readiness reporting since 1 April 2003 has therefore covered all Force Elements at readiness. Force Elements are deemed to be 'ready' only if they achieve their required states of readiness – i.e. they meet the appropriate levels of collective performance, manning and equipment for that readiness state – and have sufficient logistic support to maintain that state of readiness for a period thereafter. Force Elements on operations may be deemed 'ready' where they could in principle be redeployed in their primary role within required readiness times.

33. There was steady improvement over the year in the proportion of Force Elements with no critical weaknesses as reported by military commanders (see Figure 5 below). The relatively low readiness levels at the beginning of the year reflect the inevitable impact of Operation TELIC and Operation FRESCO on the Armed Forces' capability; the steady improvement thereafter reflects the process of subsequent recuperation (see paragraphs 34 to 36 below). By the fourth quarter of the year (January to March 2004), 93% of Force Elements were meeting their planned and funded readiness levels with no critical weaknesses reported. The Armed Forces continued to meet their operational commitments and Military Tasks throughout the year.

34. Following the drawdown of the maritime component in the Gulf region in the early part of the year, the **Royal Navy** went through a period of recuperation with many ships requiring unscheduled upkeep, notably those of the Royal Fleet Auxiliary. This period included post-operation leave for many personnel and resulted in a diminished level of readiness. Towards the end of the year, levels recovered as units regenerated to their required readiness. Readiness was further affected by a shortage of trained personnel in some critical skills, mitigated in part by the use of full-time Reservists.

35. As anticipated, readiness levels in the **Army** fell during the first half of the year while forces recuperated from the Large Scale war-fighting operation in Iraq. In the second half of the year, effective recuperation produced a continuing improvement in readiness levels.

36. Following the end of offensive operations in Iraq, there was a significant reduction in the number of **Royal Air Force** personnel and Force Elements deployed on operations. Since their return from the Gulf, these forces have been recuperating, with readiness levels steadily improving as a result. However, there are concerns about the dilution of the balance of experience on frontline RAF squadrons and equipment shortages in some areas.

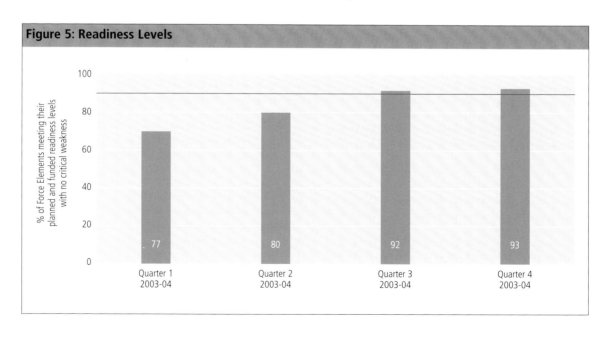

Figure 5: Readiness Levels

Sustainability and Deployability

37. The Armed Forces are funded routinely to achieve the peacetime readiness states described above and to fulfil a range of standing Military Tasks. Additional funding is required to prepare for contingent operations, deploy forces into theatre, and sustain and then recover them.

38. The deployment of the Armed Forces on operations involves the preparation, mounting and movement of personnel and equipment, together with large quantities of containerised supplies through air and sea ports. This demanding task requires the reinforcement of UK military assets with strategic airlift and sealift assets from both military allies and the commercial market, particularly at the most demanding scales of effort. The Defence Transport and Movements Agency's strong commercial position enables it to secure assets to meet planning timelines. In addition, in order to secure access to additional assets to reinforce dedicated RO-RO shipping and strategic transport aircraft, the UK has joined several multinational strategic lift initiatives.

39. Some supplies that could not easily be obtained within anticipated warning times need to be maintained against the levels of effort and the concurrency assumptions set out in the Defence White Paper *Delivering Security in a Changing World: Future Capabilities*. The demands of operations in Iraq and elsewhere during the year effectively demonstrated our ability to do this. Inevitably, there will be a variance between what we plan for and what we find we need for a specific operation.

40. We are looking carefully at how we can improve further our ability to prepare in advance of a commitment to specific operational deployments. In particular, the Department is examining ways of engaging industry earlier in the preparation period to increase the likelihood that urgently purchased equipment and modifications are delivered to the frontline in good time. However, the speed with which the Department is able to apply lessons, such as the introduction of an effective consignment tracking system, depends upon a number of factors including the complexity of technical solutions and competing demands for resources.

Joint Rapid Reaction Forces (JRRF)

41. The JRRF are a pool of highly capable Force Elements, maintained at high readiness and trained to the required joint standards. In practice, the operational tempo over the year exceeded the previous JRRF planning requirement (to be able to mount and sustain a single, non-enduring, medium-scale war-fighting operation, in addition to a medium-scale peacekeeping operation by March 2005). Some 46,000 personnel (including 5,000 Reservists), built mainly upon the JRRF, deployed to the Middle East on Op TELIC at the peak of activity there, and a medium-scale commitment of around 9,000 personnel, drawn in part from the JRRF pool of high-readiness forces, remains in the region. Simultaneously, 19,000 Service personnel (many drawn from high-readiness forces) participated in fire-fighting duties on Op FRESCO, whilst others contributed to concurrent operations in Afghanistan, the Balkans and Sierra Leone. We have therefore already demonstrated the level of capability required, but have also identified continuing shortfalls in certain specialist areas. Action is in hand to address these. As set out in the Defence White Paper *Delivering Security in a Changing World*, we are looking further in light of experience in Iraq and elsewhere at the forces assigned to the JRRF to reflect the increased frequency of Small and Medium Scale operations.

Delivery of Medical Support

42. Following the Deployable Medical Capability Study (completed in April 2004), we have concluded that we require 400 beds to support a focused intervention at Medium Scale, with an overall requirement of 600 beds (a reduction of 200 from our previous assessment) to support up to three concurrent operations (Medium/Medium/Small). We plan to achieve the capability by 2006 using modules containing the medical consumables and medicines needed to deploy state-of-the-art medical equipment to field hospitals.

Policy

Objective:

To help build a safer world.

Public Service Agreement Targets (SR2002 MoD Targets 2 and 5):

- Improve the effectiveness of the UK contribution to conflict prevention and management as demonstrated by a reduction in the number of people whose lives are affected by violent conflict and a reduction in potential sources of future conflict, where the UK can make a significant contribution (Joint target with DfID and FCO);

- Strengthen European Security through an enlarged and modernised NATO, an effective EU crisis management capacity and enhanced European defence capabilities (Joint target with FCO).

Performance Measures and Assessment:

Shaping NATO and the EU in line with wider UK interests:

- *Bulgaria, Estonia, Latvia, Lithuania, Romania, Slovakia and Slovenia acceded to NATO. The UK continued to provide them with practical assistance;*

- *NATO Response Force reached interim operational capability;*

- *Further streamlining of NATO command structures;*

- *Further progress towards coherent NATO/EU institutional architecture enabling flexible responses to crises. Articles in EU Constitutional Treaty ensuring European Security and Defence Policy consistent with NATO;*

- *Creation of European Defence Agency, progress in addressing identified European capability shortfalls, and development of EU Battle Groups Concept;*

- *Successful EU military missions in Macedonia and Congo.*

UK military contribution:

- *The UK continued to commit almost all its forces, including nuclear forces, to NATO. Contribution of equipment and personnel for interim air policing in the Baltic States. Considerable forces offered for initial rotations of the NATO Response Force.*

Effective Defence policy on conflict prevention:

- *Development and refocusing of defence relations programmes and initiatives. Cross-Whitehall conflict pools enhanced and put to good use;*

- *Significant progress on verification and disarmament of Libya's WMD programmes, and programmes for destruction of Russian chemical weapons;*

- *Support to international efforts for collection, stockpile management & destruction of surplus Small Arms and Light Weapons. Completion of negotiations on Protocol on Explosive Remnants of War;*

- *UK/US agreements on framework for missile defence cooperation and arrangements for the upgrade of radar at RAF Fylingdales. UK Missile Defence Centre established;*

Effective Defence participation in the Government's long-term strategy for countering terrorism;

- *Continuing development of capabilities identified in SDR New Chapter. Development of collective NATO and EU Chemical, Biological, Radiological and Nuclear defence capabilities;*

- *Strengthened defence capability to respond to the threat of international terrorism overseas and at home, including creation of Civil Contingencies Reaction Forces.*

Further Sources of Information

- Quarterly PSA reports to HM Treasury;

- MoD Evidence and Government Response to the House of Commons Defence Committee on *The Defence White Paper 2003* (HC 465 and HC 1048);

- MoD Evidence and Government Response to the House of Commons Defence Committee on *Arms Control and Disarmament (Inspections) Bill* (HC 321 and HC 754);

- MoD Evidence and Government Response to the House of Commons Defence Committee on *The Government's Proposals for Secondary Legislation under the Export Controls Act* (HC 620 and Cm 5988);

- MoD Evidence and Government Response to the House of Commons Defence Committee on *Strategic Export Controls: Annual Report for 2001, Licensing Policy and Parliamentary Scrutiny* (HC 474 and Cm 5943) and MoD Evidence on *Strategic Export Controls: Annual Report for 2002* (HC 390);

- MoD Evidence and Government Response to House of Commons Defence Committee on *A New Chapter to the Strategic Defence Review* (HC 93 and HC 975);

- MoD Evidence and Government Response to the House of Commons Defence Committee on the *Draft Civil Contingencies Bill* (HC 557 and Cm 6078);

- MoD and FCO Evidence to the House of Commons Defence Committee on *European Security and Defence* (HC 1165);

- *Istanbul Summit Communiqué, issued by the Heads of State and Government participating in the meeting of the North Atlantic Council, 28 June 2004* http://nato.usmission.gov/News/ISUM_Communique_ 062804.htm;

- *Council Joint Action 2004/551/CFSP of 12 July 2004 on the establishment of the European Defence Agency,* http://ue.eu.int/uedocs;

- *European Council NATO-EU Planning, Consultation and Operations Document SN 307/03 of 11 December 2003,* http://ue.eu.int/uedocs;

- *Treaty establishing a Constitution for Europe,* http://ue.eu.int/igcpdf/en/04/cg00/cg00087.en04.pdf;

- *Delivering Security in a Changing World* (Defence White Paper and supporting essays);

- *Delivering Security in a Changing World: Future Capabilities;*

- *The G8 Global Partnership: Progress Report on the UK's Programme to Address Nuclear, Chemical and Biological Legacies in the Former Soviet Union,* published jointly by FCO, DTI and MoD in November 2003, www.dti.gov.uk/energy/nuclear/fsu/news/First_annual_report.pdf;

- Papers for the 2004 NPT Prepcom, www.fco.gov.uk;

- Papers for the 2003 CWC Review Conference, www.opcw.org;

- *Protocol V on Explosive Remnants of War,* www.gichd.ch/ccw;

- *November 2002 Missile Defence public discussion paper,* www.mod.uk/issues/cooperation/missile_defence.htm;

- *Draft Civil Contingencies Bill,* http://www.ukresilience.info/ccbill/index.htm;

- *UK Defence Statistics 2004.*

NATO and European Defence

43. The MoD and the Foreign and Commonwealth Office contributed to good progress over the year in strengthening NATO and developing the European Union's European Security and Defence Policy. The accession to NATO on 29 March 2004 of Bulgaria, Estonia, Latvia, Lithuania, Romania, Slovakia and Slovenia brings the Alliance to 26 members, strengthening security for all in the Euro-Atlantic area. The MoD played an important part in helping these Allies to prepare for membership by providing practical help including English language training, secondment of UK advisers to Defence Ministries and staff training in the UK. We have continued to construct a coherent institutional architecture that allows flexible responses to crises by a NATO operation, an EU operation with recourse to NATO assets under Berlin Plus arrangements, or an autonomous EU operation as appropriate.

44. During the year, the UK supported NATO in taking key steps to streamline its Command Structure. Allied Command Operations is now the single strategic command with operational responsibilities. Allied Command Transformation, as the other strategic command, takes responsibility for overseeing the transformation of Allied forces and capabilities. We also helped deliver the NATO Response Force (NRF), which will provide Allies with a flexible, deployable, technologically advanced and interoperable force. An interim operational capability

for the NRF was achieved in October 2003 and the full capability is expected by October 2006.

45. The UK continued to commit almost all its combat forces to NATO, in addition to our nuclear forces and the majority of our support and enabling capabilities. We contributed equipment and personnel to NATO's interim air policing solution in the Baltic States, implemented on their accession. The UK has led the way in Europe in providing truly deployable capability and maintaining significant forces at very high readiness. We have offered considerable forces for initial rotations of the NRF, including a deployable maritime component command, the deployable land component command (the Allied Rapid Reaction Corps) and the UK's Joint Force Air Component Command Headquarters. Recognising the vital role envisaged for the NRF, the UK intends to continue to support future requests to generate forces.

46. The UK continued to pursue practical improvements to Europe's military capabilities that will benefit both NATO and the EU. We have been instrumental in the creation of a European Defence Agency to oversee and drive forward capability improvements, and have continued to push forward the European Capabilities Action Plan to address capability shortfalls against the Helsinki Headline Goal. We have also worked with partners to outline a new Headline Goal for ESDP (Headline Goal 2010), reflecting the changing strategic environment and the need for the EU to be able to respond more quickly to crises. The importance of rapid response is also behind the EU's Battle Groups Concept, which we originally developed with France and Germany. It looks to EU Member States to provide a number of very high-readiness force packages (of around 1,500 personnel each) designed principally for use in response to requests from the UN.

47. Two EU military missions were successfully completed in 2003/04: Operation CONCORDIA in the Former Yugoslav Republic of Macedonia and Operation ARTEMIS in the Democratic Republic of Congo. These demonstrated that the EU is able to conduct crisis management operations both within Europe and further afield. Building on this, the UK will command an EU military operation in Bosnia from the end of 2004. This operation, conducted with recourse to NATO planning facilities as agreed under Berlin Plus arrangements, will support the EU's wider civil objectives in Bosnia. The strategic partnership between the EU and NATO will be further strengthened by improved liaison arrangements now agreed between the EU Military Staff and NATO. Also, the EU's ability to predict and react to emerging crises using its range of security tools will be enhanced by the creation of a Civil-Military Cell with the ability to set up an ad hoc Operation Centre in certain limited circumstances if other operational headquarters are not available. The UK negotiated defence articles in the EU Constitutional Treaty ensuring that the European Security and Defence Policy continues to develop in an open, flexible and militarily robust way consistent with our commitment to NATO.

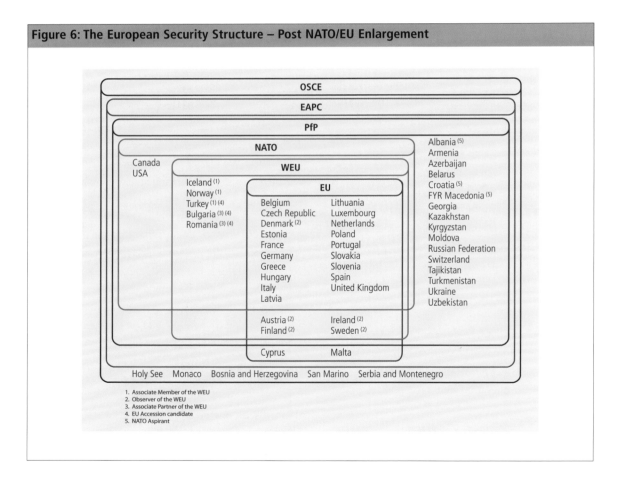

Figure 6: The European Security Structure – Post NATO/EU Enlargement

1. Associate Member of the WEU
2. Observer of the WEU
3. Associate Partner of the WEU
4. EU Accession candidate
5. NATO Aspirant

Defence Diplomacy and Conflict Prevention

48. We currently have 22 military observers and 434 troops on UN operations, who represent 1.07% of UN military manpower. The majority of these are in Cyprus, where the UK has continued to support the United Nations Force In Cyprus (UNFICYP) mission, providing over 400 troops (out of an overall force of about 1,250 personnel), predominantly in the Nicosia area. Their duties include patrolling the buffer zone between the Greek and Turkish Cypriot communities and providing reassurance. The period between December 2003 and April 2004 saw intense diplomatic efforts by the United Nations, supported by the Guarantor Powers and the European Commission, to achieve a solution to the Cyprus problem. On 24 April 2004, referendums were held on both sides of the island. The referendum in the Turkish Cypriot community was carried (65% voted yes), but in the Greek Cypriot community, the settlement proposals were opposed by a large majority (76% voted no). Accordingly, the Annan Plan, which was designed to be self-executing in time for a reunited island to enter the EU on 1 May, became null and void. The UK's offer of territory from the Sovereign Base Areas, which was an integral part of the Plan, also became null and void. Cyprus joined the EU on 1 May as a divided island, with the acquis suspended in northern Cyprus. In light of this outcome, the UN Secretary General subsequently undertook to conduct a review of UNFICYP's mandate, force levels and concept of operation. Other current commitments include contributions to UN Mission in Sierra Leone (see paragraph 16 above) and to the Verification and Monitoring Team in Sudan.

49. During the year, the MoD created a new grouping of Defence Relations directorates in order to improve the strategic direction, management and delivery of the UK's defence relations activities overseas both within and outwith the Conflict Prevention Pools, and to link our bilateral activities to defence policy, through regional strategies and country objectives. Further details are set out in the Defence White Paper *Delivering Security in a Changing World* and its supporting essays, available at www.mod.uk. Good progress on the UK's main defence relations programmes and initiatives was maintained over the period. The *Russian Resettlement Programme* continues to be a model programme – the principles of which have been used in the last year to scope projects for Ukraine, Georgia and Moldova. MoD has worked closely with Serbia and Montenegro to prepare for a resettlement programme to begin in late 2004. The *Junior Staff Officers Course* in Slovakia, developed from a UK/Netherlands initiative, to prepare students from NATO and partner countries to take part in multinational operations, became fully operational with the first course in early 2004, and, combined with the output of the British Military Training team based in the Czech Republic, represents a significant contribution towards developing the operational capability of allies and partner nations. The civilian MoD Police (MDP) also provide around 100 officers – mainly constables and sergeants – on overseas missions in a number of locations. These are mainly in Kosovo (see paragraph 14) and Iraq (see paragraph 9), where they are recognised as doing a good job in difficult circumstances, but also include Kenya and Pitcairn Island (in the South Pacific). The MDP has been recognised as a Centre of Excellence for international policing and undertakes pre-deployment training for its own officers and those from Home Department Police Forces.

50. The Global and Africa Conflict Prevention Pools continued to promote a coherent cross-Whitehall approach in HMG efforts to prevent, contain and manage conflict. The innovative inter-departmental approach allows the UK to improve its response to conflict, both in the short and longer term, by combining skills and expertise across Whitehall. At the end of March 2004, the Global Pool was funding 15 strategies relating to conflict prevention, divided between regional and country strategies and 'themed' strategies (such as Security Sector Reform). These have ranged from rapid support in immediate post-conflict situations (e.g. Afghanistan, Iraq), to long-term stability and confidence-building work in intractable problem areas such as the Middle East and the frozen conflicts in the Former Soviet Union. The Africa Pool has been successful in providing an effective joined-up UK contribution to African peacekeeping operations in Burundi, Côte d'Ivoire and Liberia, as well as playing a significant role in peace processes in Sudan and the Democratic Republic of Congo. The latter have been achieved while maintaining a high level of ongoing programme engagement in a range of other countries, particularly in respect of creating African capability and capacity for regional peace support operations. Defence Advisory Team activity and commitment continued to broaden over the period to cover the full ambit of Security Sector Reform. Recognition both in Whitehall and abroad of the Team's expertise, capabilities and contribution to structural reform overseas is reflected in the growing and increasingly diverse portfolio of its engagements. The team has been particularly effective in providing assistance to countries in Central and Eastern Europe, the Middle East, South and South East Asia, Africa, the Caribbean and Central and South America.

Counter-Terrorism

51. The MoD has continued to work closely with other Government Departments on developing the UK's broader response to the threat we face from international terrorism. While there is no specific military solution to this problem, the Armed Forces have an important contribution to make to each of the four strands of the UK's counter-terrorist strategy. Conflict prevention, peace-support operations, and defence diplomacy can all assist in prevention by tackling some of the underlying causes of terrorism. The military can play an important role in pursuing terrorists and those who support them. And the Armed Forces are able, through long-standing and well-practised arrangements, to respond to requests from the civil authorities for help in protecting the public and preparing to handle the consequences. We continue to develop the capabilities that the SDR New Chapter identified as necessary for the military to play their full part in this broad spectrum of activity. In addition to the continuing operations to ensure security in Iraq and to assist in rebuilding Afghanistan (as set out in paragraph 11 above), the Armed Forces have been engaged in maritime interdiction operations in the Mediterranean and Arabian Seas and in the crucial task of building the counter-terrorist capacity of other nations.

Counter Proliferation and Arms Control

52. The Department continued to make a major contribution to the UK's arms control and counter-proliferation activities during 2003-2004. International treaties form the basis of the UK's efforts in arms control. Defence officials participated actively within UK delegations in a number of international meetings during the year, including the Preparatory Committee for the 2005 Nuclear Non-Proliferation Treaty Review Conference (for which the MoD produced a working paper on the verification of the dismantlement of nuclear warheads and their components) and the first Review Conference of the Chemical Weapons Convention (for which the MoD drafted nine major papers).

53. UK conventional arms control activities continued to contribute to conflict prevention and stability across the OSCE area through inspections, evaluations and confidence and security building measures. Under the terms of three key treaties (Conventional Forces in Europe (CFE), Vienna Document 1999 (VD99), and Open Skies (OS)), the UK received 19 inbound inspections or evaluations (including five on British Forces Germany), and conducted 14 outbound inspections or evaluations on non-NATO signatories. The UK also initiated a joint OS mission with the Russian Federation over Georgia in February 2004, which was the first of its kind and an all-round success. Conventional arms control policy focused on the adapted CFE, which will move the treaty from a bloc-based to a state-based treaty once the Russian Federation meets its Istanbul 1999 commitment to withdraw its forces from Georgia and Moldova, enabling the treaty to be ratified. Details of UK holdings declared under the CFE Treaty can be found in *UK Defence Statistics 2004*, available at www.mod.uk.

54. Significant progress was made in helping Russia destroy its stockpiles of chemical weapons (CW). Following completion of the UK's first project in early 2003, our second project – the procurement of equipment for an electricity substation at Shchuch'ye – is now well under way, jointly funded by UK, Norway, the EU and the Czech Republic. The UK signed a Memorandum of Understanding with Canada in November 2003, under which Canada will make a grant of some C$33M for the UK to implement on its behalf the construction of a railway to support the Shchuch'ye CW destruction facility. Further details of the MoD assistance programme are available at www.dti.gov.uk/energy/nuclear/fsu/mod.shtml.

55. The MoD has also continued to contribute to international consideration of conflict-related humanitarian concerns. Negotiations on the new legally binding Protocol V (to the Geneva Convention) on Explosive Remnants of War (ERW) were successfully concluded in November 2003. The Protocol contains new provisions that will offer significant humanitarian benefit to those in areas affected by ERW, making clearance of unexploded ordnance quicker and more effective. The UK fully supports the aims of Protocol V and intends to ratify it later this year.

56. The MoD is one of the major advisory Departments on implementation of Export Controls, which changed significantly during the year with the implementation of the Export Control Act 2002, and contributes actively to the development of various international Export Control regimes.

57. Together with FCO and DfID, the MoD is also contributing towards collection, stockpile management and destruction of surplus Small Arms and Light Weapons, with a focus on Man-Portable Air Defence Systems, which pose a significant threat to military and civilian aircraft, particularly in terrorist hands.

Proliferation Security Initiative

58. In May 2003, President Bush launched the Proliferation Security Initiative (PSI). Under this, nations are striving to establish a more co-ordinated and effective basis to impede and stop states and non-state actors of proliferation concern from trafficking in WMD and delivery systems. The UK has taken a leading role in the development of the PSI. The MoD hosted and chaired two of the six Operational Expert Meetings, and led an air-interception Command Post Exercise.

Chemical, Biological, Radiological and Nuclear Defence (CBRN Defence)

59. Unfortunately, it remains the case that international arms control and non-proliferation efforts do not preclude the possibility that Chemical, Biological, Radiological or Nuclear weapons might in some circumstances be used against us or our Allies, whether by states or terrorists. The UK therefore continues to develop its ability to counter the threat posed by CBRN weapons. Working with NATO and EU allies, we have sought to build collective CBRN defence capabilities. This has culminated in the development of the NATO Multinational CBRN Defence Battalion. The UK contributes forces to this specialist unit designed to help protect deployed NATO forces from CBRN attack. A similar EU initiative is also progressing well, as part of the Equipment Capabilities Action Plan.

Missile Defence

60. We also continue to consider the wide range of issues relating to defending against ballistic missiles, and to work on these in international forums, in particular within NATO structures. NATO has completed a feasibility study assessing Active Layered Theatre Ballistic Missile Defence, and is studying the viability of territorial missile defences. Work is in hand to determine how NATO might acquire active theatre missile defence by 2010, through a mixture of national and common capabilities. In June 2003, we signed a UK/US Memorandum of Understanding outlining the framework for future co-operation on missile defence activities, and agreed an Annex in December 2003 detailing arrangements for the upgrade of the ballistic missile early warning radar at RAF Fylingdales, for use as part of the US ballistic missile defence system. In addition, the UK Missile Defence Centre was established and opened by the Minister for Defence Procurement on 18 July 2003. The Centre is jointly resourced by Government and industry and provides the primary technical interface between the UK and US Governments on strategic missile defence.

Civil Emergency Response

61. The MoD played a significant supporting role in the development of the overall civil emergency mechanism. We were, for instance, involved in the development of the Civil Contingencies Bill prior to the public consultation process that commenced in June 2003. The Bill is currently before Parliament. Enhancements in our ability to co-ordinate a response to civil emergencies, identified as part of the New Chapter of the Strategic Defence Review, were also taken forward. Joint Regional Liaison Officers were appointed for each of the MoD's eleven regions, working within the Army's regional brigade structure, but acting on behalf of all three Services. This mechanism allows us to co-ordinate our activity with the civil authorities in the regions, through the Regional Resilience Forums introduced by the civil authorities in 2003, Local Resilience Forums and other contacts.

62. The fourteen Civil Contingencies Reaction Forces, identified as a means of providing additional MoD support, were also formed during 2003, achieving full operational capability at the end of the year. The Civil Contingencies Reaction Forces are drawn from the Armed Forces' Reserves. Their formation will enable the Reserves to play a full role in the response to major emergencies, on the same basis as the rest of the Armed Forces, but also drawing on the strong regional presence of the Reserves across the UK. They are already playing a role in the exercise programme organised by the civil authorities in the regions, reflecting the MoD's longstanding engagement in the civil exercise programme.

Essay: Defence White Paper

In December 2003, the Ministry of Defence published its once-a-Parliament White Paper, *Delivering Security in a Changing World.* It provides an updated assessment of the security environment, and serves as a policy baseline against which the Department will make the decisions to provide the Armed Forces with the structures and capabilities they require to carry out the operations they can expect to undertake. It represents an evolution of the expeditionary strategy articulated in the 1998 Strategic Defence Review (SDR), and builds on the conclusions of the SDR New Chapter of 2002 and recent operational experience.

The White Paper identifies the three key challenges to our peace and security that now confront us: international terrorism, the threat associated with the proliferation of weapons of mass destruction, and the challenges posed by failed and failing states.

In response, it makes the case for a rebalancing of the UK's Armed Forces. In addition to our standing Military Tasks and overseas commitments, our Armed Forces must be optimised to conduct three concurrent Small and Medium Scale operations, at least one of which is an enduring peace support operation. This reflects our experience of the pattern of operations since the SDR, and is what the Department judges the trend to be for the foreseeable future. These forces must also be capable of rapidly projecting military effect further afield than the core regions set out in the SDR (Europe, the Middle East and the Mediterranean) to encompass sub-Saharan Africa and South Asia, and to meet the wider threat from international terrorism on a global basis. Key to this will be our ability to exploit successfully the benefits to be derived from advances in technology, in particular those associated with "networked enabled capability" (NEC).

In building this into our plans, the Armed Forces must, of course, retain the ability to adapt at longer notice for the less frequent, but more demanding, Large Scale operations. The policy set out in the White Paper seeks to strike this balance. We will plan to maintain a broad spectrum of capabilities to ensure that we are able to conduct limited national operations, or be the lead or framework nation for coalition operations at Small to Medium Scale. But we do not envisage needing to replicate the same range of capabilities at Large Scale, given that it is inconceivable that the most demanding of operations could be undertaken without the involvement of the United States (either leading a coalition or as part of NATO).

In planning for the future, the Department will concentrate on enhancing our ability to deliver military effects, and continue the move away from assessing military capability by the numbers of platforms and personnel in the inventory. This will require considerable change – in mindsets as well as force structures and operational planning. As the Secretary of State said in his statement to the House of Commons on 11 December 2003, "Resources must be directed at those capabilities that are best able to deliver the range of military effects required, whilst dispensing with those elements that are less flexible". This will mean reductions in some of the older surface vessels, heavy armour and single-role fast jets, to enable further investment in today's highest priorities – medium-weight forces, precision strike, logistics and NEC – to enable us to deliver ever more precise and rapid military effect.

In setting the policy context, the White Paper will determine the shape of our Armed Forces for many years to come. Following its publication last December, the Department constructed a thorough examination of its capabilities and overheads in order to establish the precise nature of an appropriate force structure and future equipment programme to support the policy set out in the White Paper. This will ensure that we have the right capabilities we need for the challenges ahead, and that we are spending our resources in the best possible way. A further White Paper, *Delivering Security in a Changing World: Future Capabilities* (Cm 6269), published in July 2004, detailed the force structure changes emerging from that examination.

Resource Management

Annual Budget

Objective

* To control expenditure within budgeted limits.

Performance Measure and Assessment

Defence budget not overspent:

* *Net resource expenditure of £34,651M against resources voted by Parliament of £35,653M;*

* *Additional operational expenditure of £1,493M during 2003/04, against Estimates provision of £1,748M;*

* *Resource DEL outturn £30,033M against provision of £30,902M;*

* *Capital DEL outturn £5,648M against provision of £6,088M;*

* *Combined DEL outturn £35,681M against provision of £36,990M.*

Further Sources of Information

* *UK Defence Statistics 2004;*

* MoD Evidence to the House of Commons Defence Committee on *Annual Report and Accounts 2002/2003* (HC 589-i);

* *Central Government Supply Estimates 2003/04 Main Supply Estimates (HC 648);*

* *Central Government Supply Estimates 2003/04 Spring Supplementary Estimates (HC 350);*

* *Ministry of Defence Departmental Resource Accounts 2003/04.*

Defence Budget and Spending

63. For the first time this year, the Ministry of Defence achieved an unqualified opinion from the Comptroller and Auditor General (C&AG) that the Departmental Resource Accounts in Section 2 of this report give a true and fair view of the state of affairs of the Department and of its net resource outturn, recognised gains and losses and cashflows for the year. This is a significant achievement towards which the Department has been working since publishing its first full Departmental Resource Accounts, for 1999/2000.

64. Table 3 compares performance against the estimates approved by Parliament. Request for Resources 1 (RfR 1) covers the Departments day-to-day running costs. Request for Resources 2 (RfR 2) covers the net additional cost of operations (see paragraph 66 below). Request for Resources 3 (RfR 3) covers war pensions and allowances. MoD expenditure in 2003/04 was contained within voted provision, with an overall Net Resource[1] underspend of £1,002M or just over 2.8%. The underspend against RfR 1 was mainly the result of lower than expected asset depreciation and cost of capital charges following management action to reduce holdings of obsolete assets. In addition, following the Quinquennial review of fixed assets in 2002/03, there were fewer downward valuations of assets than had been anticipated.

65. 2003/04 was the first year of managing the Defence budget under Stage 2 of the Resource Accounting and Budgeting regime, and the MoD was not initially subject to a cash Departmental Expenditure Limit (DEL). The Department's estimated cash requirement for the year was derived from its resource plans and was consistent with the overall resource control totals and standard commercial accounting practice. However, during the year, the MoD was asked to constrain its cash spending. This did not change the overall defence budget, which remained exactly as set out in the 2002 Spending Review settlement, but it did require action to constrain activities which generated cash expenditure in year.

66. The Department is voted additional resources (RfR 2) to cover the net additional costs of Operations. No formal budget is set. The Department's performance against the estimate included in the Spring Supplementary Estimates, including for capital expenditure, is set out in Table 4 below. Overall expenditure in 2003/04 was £1,493M, about 85% of the provision, including £1,311M for operations in Iraq, £104M for operations in the Balkans (Bosnia, Kosovo and the Former Yugoslav Republic of Macedonia), £36M for operations in Afghanistan, and £1.7M for operations in Africa (Democratic Republic of Congo and Sierra Leone)[3]

67. Details of how the MoD's expenditure for 2003/04 is broken down in respect of the three primary objectives of our Public Service Agreement are set out in detail in Schedule 5 and Note 26 to the Departmental Resource Accounts, and summarised in Table 5 below.

Table 3: 2002/03 Parliamentary Controls (£M)[2]

	Final Voted Provision	Departmental Resource Accounts	Variation
Request for Resources 1	33,082	32,302	-780
Request for Resources 2	1,414	1,233	-180
Request for Resources 3	1,158	1,116	-42
Net Resources	**35,653**	**34,651**	**-1,002**
Net Cash Requirement	30,087	29,338	-749

Table 4: Net Additional Costs of Operations against Spring Supplementary Estimates (SSE) 2003/04 (£M)[4]

	DEL	Outturn	Variation
Resource DEL (RfR2)	1,414	1,233	-180
Capital DEL	334	260	-74

Table 5: Resources by Departmental Objectives 2003/04 (£M)[4]

		Net
Objective 1:	Achieving success in the tasks we undertake	3,481
Objective 2:	Being ready to respond to the tasks that might arise	26,777
Objective 3:	Building for the future	3,156
(Total RfRs 1 & 2)		**33,415**
Paying war pensions and allowances (RfR3)		1,116
Total		**34,531**

[1] Including both cash and non-cash items.

[2] Includes Resource Departmental Expenditure Limit and Annually Managed Expenditure, less Resource Appropriation-in-Aid (e.g. profit/loss on disposal of capital items and stock).

[3] Details set out in Note 27 to the Departmental Resource Accounts 2003/04.

[4] Excludes £120M for excess Appropriation-in-Aid and Consolidated Fund Extra Receipts included in total outturn of £34,651M in Table 3 (see Note 7 to the Defence Resource Accounts 2003/04).

68. In addition to the Parliamentary control totals set out above, against which Departmental expenditure is presented in the Departmental Resource Accounts and audited by the National Audit Office, the Treasury issues separate Departmental Expenditure Limits covering both the majority of the Department's operating costs (excluding some non-cash costs specifically relating to nuclear provisions) and capital expenditure. In 2003/04, MoD expenditure was contained within the DELs for both its capital and its resource expenditure, with an overall underspend of £1,309M, or 3.5%. As noted above, the resource underspend was primarily caused by lower than expected non-cash depreciation and cost of capital charges. The capital underspend arose from the end year accounting for the value of assets transferred to contractors under PFI projects. This underspend has been carried forward to 2004/05 as agreed under standard end year flexibility rules. Detailed figures by Top Level Budget Holder are set out in table 6 below.

Table 6: Defence Budget Outturn against Departmental Expenditure Limits (DEL) 2003/04 (£M)		
	DEL	**Outturn**
Combined DEL	**36,990**	**35,681**
Resource DEL[5]	**30,902**	**30,033**
Allocated to TLBs:		
Commander-in-Chief Fleet	3,281	3,242
General Officer Commanding (Northern Ireland)	657	649
Commander-in-Chief Land Command	5,166	5,079
Commander-in-Chief Strike Command	3,753	3,385
Chief of Joint Operations	497	524
Chief of Defence Logistics	8,054	7,836
2nd Sea Lord/Commander-in-Chief Naval Home Command	691	693
Adjutant General	1,718	1,720
Commander-in-Chief Personnel and Training Command	1,025	995
Central	2,642	2,695
Defence Procurement Agency	2,895	2,875
Corporate Science and Technology	423	420
Departmental level accounts adjustments[6]		-81
Capital DEL[7]	**6,088**	**5,648**
Allocated to TLBs:		
Commander-in-Chief Fleet	36	37
General Officer Commanding (Northern Ireland)	40	43
Commander-in-Chief Land Command	172	21
Commander-in-Chief Strike Command	43	40
Chief of Joint Operations	32	22
Chief of Defence Logistics	1,274	1,210
2nd Sea Lord/Commander-in-Chief Naval Home Command	29	28
Adjutant General	26	41
Commander-in-Chief Personnel and Training Command	20	18
Central	-27	-96
Defence Procurement Agency	4,309	4,296
Corporate Science and Technology	0	0
Departmental level adjustments[6]		-12

Notes:

(5) Includes all operating costs in RfR1 less items accounted for as Annually Managed Expenditure, such as nuclear provisions. Excludes expenditure on Conflict Prevention activities (See Table 4)

(6) Departmental adjustments not apportioned to TLBs

(7) Includes all expenditure on fixed assets, less the income from the sale of such assets. Excludes expenditure on Conflict Prevention activities (See Table 4)

Losses and Write-Offs

69. Details of the losses reported are set out in Note 29 to the Departmental Resource Accounts (pages 161-165 below). £423M (over 90%) of the losses reported in 2003/04 arose from five cases. Of these, the write down of £287M in the assessed value of the submarine facility at Devonport (in essence a technical accounting adjustment), the write-off of £48M development costs following withdrawal from the MRAV project and the write-off of £18M equipment in Northern Ireland all reflect changes in the Department's planning assumptions and requirements in light of the changing security environment. The abandoned claim of £39M for project VIXEN represents the final closing of the books on a project cancelled in February 1997. The £31M write down for the Astute Class Training Service PFI is required by accounting rules following slippage to the planned In Service Date of Astute to reflect the reduced use the Department will in practice now derive from the contract.

70. The Departmental Resource Accounts also identify further write-offs that have not yet been brought to completion and will be formally incorporated in future years' accounts. A significant proportion of these relate to procurements already reported on in detail to Parliament. These include £205M for Chinook Mk3 Helicopters, £118M for the Defence Stores Management System and £75M for Nimrod MRA4. Several of these projects have also been examined in detail by the National Audit Office. In addition, £314M arises from our withdrawal from the multinational Long Range TRIGAT project in 1995, and our decision not to proceed to production of Medium Range TRIGAT in 2000. Under the terms of the Memorandum of Understanding governing these projects, we cannot close these transactions until all work is complete and all intergovernmental transactions finalised. Inevitably, it takes time formally to close the books in these often complex cases, but we are working to reduce this as far as possible.

71. The changes envisaged in the Defence White Paper *Delivering Security in a Changing World* of December 2003 and set out in the *Future Capabilities* paper of July 2004, combined with the significant organisational efficiencies and rationalisations included in the Department's SR2004 efficiency programme following the Lyons and Gershon Reviews, will generate further write-offs over the next ten years as force structures are adjusted to meet changing circumstances.

72. Further information on the financial performance of the Department can be found in the Departmental Resource Accounts at Section 2 of this publication.

Manning Levels

Objective

To achieve broad manning balance within each Service (headline numbers and mix) and to recruit and retain sufficient MoD civil servants.

Public Service Agreement Target (SR2002 MoD Target 4)

- Recruit, train, motivate and retain the personnel needed to meet the manning requirement of the Armed Forces, so that by the end of 2004 the Royal Navy and the RAF achieve, and thereafter maintain, manning balance, and that by the end of 2005, the Army achieves, and thereafter maintains, manning balance. *(Manning balance is defined as between -2% and +1% of the requirement, and is measured against the target prevailing at the time).*

Performance Measures and Assessment

Trained strength of forces between -2% and +1% of the overall requirement by 31 December 2004 (RN and RAF) and by 31 December 2005 (Army):

- *As of 1 April 2004*
  - *RN trained strength of 37,470, or 96.8% of overall requirement (compared to 97.6% on 1 April 2003);*
  - *Army trained strength of 103,770, or 97.2% of overall requirement (compared to 95.5% on 1 April 2003);*
  - *RAF trained strength of 49,120, or 98.5% of overall requirement (compared to 98.5% on 1 April 2003);*

- *Substantial mobilisation of Reserves in-year for operations.*

Critical shortage groups:

- *Some improvement in critical shortage groups, but shortages remain in all three Services;*

- *Reduction in overall shortfall in medical personnel from 26% to 23%.*

Enhanced Diversity:

- *Progress made on implementing MoD's Race Equality Scheme and introducing our Unified Diversity Strategy. All three Armed Services and the MoD named in the top ten public sector ethnic minority employers;*

- *Overall Service ethnic minority strength of 4.9% (including Commonwealth recruits), just short of overall goal of 5% ethnic minority representation. UK ethnic minority intake 2.1% RN (target 2.5%), 2.8% Army (target 2.9%), 1.8% RAF (target 2.6%);*

- *As at 1 April 2004, women comprised 8.9% of UK Regular Forces (8.7% on 1 April 2003), and 11.6% of the total 2003/04 intake (12.3% in 2002/03);*

- *Civilian diversity targets exceeded for disabled personnel in MoD Senior Civil Service and Band D, and women in Band B. Targets just missed for women in Band D and disabled and ethnic minority personnel in Band B. Significantly below target for women and ethnic minority personnel in MoD Senior Civil Service and ethnic minority personnel in Band D.*

Reduce number of Service personnel medically downgraded and level of civilian absence:

- *Enhanced Regional Rehabilitation Units produced quicker return of referred personnel to active service;*

- *Increase of 1,120 (6.1%) in number medically downgraded result of improved application of revised procedure and stringent requirements for operational deployments;*

- *Average civilian sick absence 7.6 days (previous year 7.6 days, PSA target 7.0 days, public sector average 8.9-10.6 days).*

Further Sources of Information

- *Quarterly PSA reports to HM Treasury;*

- *MoD Evidence to HCDC on 2002/03 Report & Accounts (HC589-i);*

- *Delivering Security in a Changing World (Defence White Paper and supporting essays);*

- *Unified Diversity Strategy;*

- *Race Equality Scheme (RES) 2002-2005*
  www.mod.uk/linked_files/racial_equality.pdf;

- *RES first progress report*
  www.mod.uk/linked_files/issues/personnel/2003_race_equality_report.pdf;

- *CRE Partnership Agreement;*

- *The Defence Health Programme 2003/2007;*

- *CIPD survey: Employee Absence 2004: A Survey of Management Policy and Practice (The CIPD headline absence rates were 9.1 working days lost per employee overall and 10.7 days for the public sector) www.cipd.co.uk/subjects/hrpract/absence/empabs04.htm;*

- *CBI survey: Room for Improvement: CBI Absence and Labour Turnover 2004, in association with AXA, copies available from TSO (The CBI figures were 7.2 working days lost per employee overall and 8.9 days for the public sector);*

- *Naval Manning Agency Annual Report and Accounts 2003/04;*

- *Army Personnel Centre Annual Report and Accounts 2003/04;*

- *RAF Personnel Management Agency Annual Report and Accounts 2003/04;*

- *Defence Dental Agency Annual Report and Accounts 2003/04;*

- *UK Defence Statistics 2004.*

Service Manning Levels

73. At the end of 2003/04, the **Royal Navy and Royal Marines** had a shortfall of some 1,250 personnel against the trained strength requirement (a deficit of 3.2%). This is a slight increase from the position at the beginning of the year when the deficit was 2.4%. During the year, there was continued pressure on the requirement and reductions in wastage rates during initial training. However, reduced inflow and high outflow of RN Ratings have offset these gains. Shortages in some branches remain a concern, including engineering trades, Warfare Leading Hands and Petty Officers, Submarine Leading Hand Communicators, Royal Marine Other Ranks and Medical Assistants (Submarines).

74. As at 1 April 2004, the **Army** had a shortfall of 2,960 personnel against the requirement (a deficit of 2.8%), representing a continuing trend of improvement from the deficit of 4.5% of last year.

This was primarily due to strong recruiting and inflow to trained strength, and good levels of retention. Premature Voluntary Retirement (PVR) rates for non-commissioned ranks improved, from 5.5% to 5.3%, while for Officers there was a marginal deterioration from 3.4% to 3.7%. Manning shortages exist within 26 Army trade groups in the Royal Logistics Corps, the Royal Electrical and Mechanical Engineers, the Royal Signals, the Royal Engineers, the Intelligence Corps and the Army Medical Services. These 'pinch point' trades are being targeted with a package of financial and other measures to alleviate the high levels of operational commitment experienced by the individuals within the groups.

75. The manning position in the **Royal Air Force** remained fairly stable during 2003/04 with the overall manning deficit being around -1.5%. Shortages in certain key branches and trades, such as medical officers and junior officer navigators remain a concern. The average number of exits from the Service through PVR remains constant at 2.1% for officers and down from 3.9% to 3.7% for airmen.

Table 7: Strength and Requirements of Full Time UK Regular Forces, Full Time Reserve Service (FTRS) and Gurkhas

	Royal Navy/Royal Marines			Army			Royal Air Force		
	2002	2003	2004	2002	2003	2004	2002	2003	2004
Trained Requirement	39,180	38,510	**38,720**	106,970	106,980	**106,730**	49,990	49,640	**49,890**
Trained Strength	37,490	37,600	**37,470**	100,420	102,120	**103,770**	49,200	48,900	**49,120**
Variation	-1,690	-910	**-1,250**	-6,560	-4,850	**-2,960**	-790	-750	**-770**
Untrained Strength	4,860	4,960	**4,500**	14,380	14,880	**13,650**	4,120	4,700	**4,650**
Total UK Regular Forces	42,350	42,560	**41,970**	114,790	117,000	**117,420**	53,320	53,600	**53,770**

Notes:

Figures are rounded to the nearest ten and may not sum precisely to the totals shown. Figures include UK regular forces, trained Gurkhas, full time Reserve personnel and Nursing Services Personnel.

Figure 7: Service Manning Surplus/Deficit

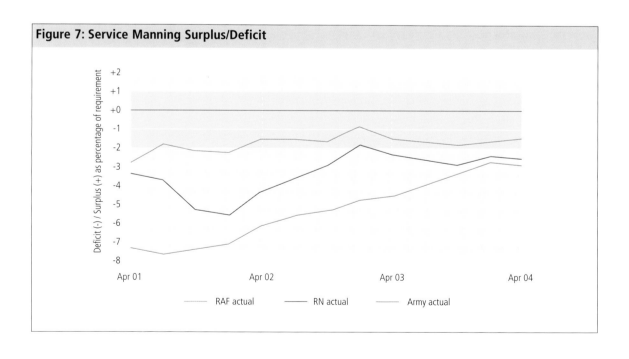

Table 8: Intake to UK Regular Forces from Civilian Life

	Royal Navy/Royal Marines			Army			Royal Air Force		
	01/02	02/03	03/04	01/02	02/03	03/04	01/02	02/03	03/04
Officer intake	410	420	**340**	820	900	**880**	450	460	**520**
Other rank intake	4,600	4,800	**3,780**	14,030	15,710	**14,310**	3,340	3,990	**3,640**
Total intake	5,010	5,220	**4,120**	14,850	16,610	**15,190**	3,780	4,450	**4,160**

Notes:

Figures do not include full time Reserve personnel, Gurkhas or the Home Service battalions of the Royal Irish Regiment. Figures are rounded to the nearest ten and may not sum precisely to the totals shown.

Table 9: Outflow of UK Regular Forces

	Royal Navy/Royal Marines			Army			Royal Air Force		
	01/02	02/03	03/04	01/02	02/03	03/04	01/02	02/03	03/04
Officer outflow	530	510	**470**	1,070	970	**950**	670	580	**620**
Other rank outflow	5,270	4,780	**4,300**	13,290	13,580	**13,640**	3,860	3,670	**3,410**
Total outflow	5,800	5,300	**4,770**	14,360	14,550	**14,600**	4,530	4,250	**4,040**

Notes:

Figures include outflow from the untrained strength. They do not include full time Reserve personnel, Gurkhas or the Home Service battalions of the Irish Regiment. Figures are rounded to the nearest ten and may not sum precisely to the totals shown.

Defence Medical Services (DMS)

76. Recruitment into the DMS has improved and a number of actions are in hand to improve retention. In January 2004, the shortfall of medical officers stood at 20%, compared with 24% in January 2003. The overall position for the DMS has also improved across the same period, with a shortfall of 23% (not including those in training), compared with 26% the previous year. In January 2004, there were around 350 more fully trained medical personnel than there had been in 1999, with over 500 more in the training pipeline. Around 40 consultants are due to be accredited over the next four years. As at March 2004, 7 consultants and 13 vocationally trained GPs had joined the DMS under the "Golden Hello" scheme. Nevertheless, shortfalls remained in critical specialties, including general surgeons, orthopaedic surgeons, anaesthetists and A&E and ITU nurses; sustaining a high operational tempo within harmony and clinical governance remains challenging. Despite these difficulties, DMS personnel have successfully supported deployed operations in Iraq, Bosnia, Kosovo, Afghanistan, and Sierra Leone during the year, and as of 10 May 2004, 414 Regular and Reserve personnel from the DMS were deployed overseas.

Medical teams prepare to receive casualties flown to a Field Hospital by an RAF Chinook.

77. The requirement for military medical manpower is driven by the need to support deployed operations. The Deployable Medical Capability Study examined what is required to support Defence Planning Assumptions and concluded that it was possible to adjust the balance of Regular and Reserve personnel, and thereby reduce the number of Regular personnel required at high-readiness. This should reduce the overall shortfall in Regular medical personnel against requirement to about 10% by August 2004, although shortages will remain in some critical specialties.

Reserves

78. The role of the Reserves is to reinforce and support the regular Armed Forces in time of crisis. The Reserve Forces continue to play a vital role in support of expeditionary operations, for which they have been providing between 10 and 15% of total UK Forces. During 2003/04, Reservists continued to be mobilised for Operation TELIC in Iraq, contributing some 25% of the land force in the early stages of peace support operations in late 2003. Reservists were also mobilised for operations in the former Yugoslavia, for the International Security Assistance Force in Afghanistan and in support of operations against international terrorism. Additionally, Reservists contributed training time in support of the Armed Forces' efforts to maintain fire emergency cover in the UK during Operation FRESCO. A breakdown of Reserve manpower strengths is shown in Table 10. Lessons drawn from the mobilisation of Reserves in support of operations in Iraq will inform restructuring of all Reserve Forces in order to maximise the support they provide to operational capability. The support given to Reservists called out for operations and their families has also been the subject of surveys, which will inform future work.

79. In support of the defence and security of the UK, Civil Contingency Reaction Forces achieved full operating capability on 31 December 2003. These are based upon the command and control structure of Territorial Army units and include volunteers from all the Volunteer Reserve Forces. They are designed to support the national emergency services in the full range of emergency events which may require the deployment of a large disciplined manpower component.

Volunteer Reserve Forces (VRF)

80. Approximately one fifth of the Armed Forces' Reserves are volunteers from the general public, who undertake paid training and accept a liability for call out for permanent service in an emergency. The training given to volunteer Reservists helps to develop leadership, team working and communication skills, as well as offering the opportunity to acquire a variety of other skills such as driving and first aid. In addition, the training builds self-confidence, self-reliance and physical fitness. It is the view of the Department that these skills and personal qualities are as vital to the success of UK firms and organisations as they are to the Armed Forces. In times of shortages of regular manpower, the Armed Forces are increasingly able to make use of Reservists, including volunteer Reservists, to undertake periods of full time service which are of benefit to the Regular Forces, to the volunteer's reserve unit and to the individual volunteer.

81. All Services have reviewed and enhanced their recruiting efforts for the Volunteer Reserve Forces in order to maintain their trained strengths. The Department recognises that the ability to mobilise and deploy Reserves depends upon the three-way relationship between the MoD, the Reservist and the employer. The SaBRE (Supporting Britain's Reservists and Employers) Campaign continues to offer advice and support to employers during the mobilisation process. During the year, it became a condition of enlistment or re-engagement into the Volunteer Reserves for Reservists to agree to their membership being disclosed to their employer.

Table 10: Strength of the Reserve Forces at 1 April 2004 [1]

	Regular Reserves			Volunteer Reserves		
	RN/RM	**Army**	**RAF**	**RN/RM**[2]	**Army**[3]	**RAF**[4]
Strength	10,700	31,200	9,500	3,800	38,300	1,600
of which mobilised	–	100	–	–	2,900	–
Individuals liable to recall	12,000	110,700	27,100	*	*	*
TOTAL	**22,700**	**141,900**	**36,600**	**3,800**	**38,300**	**1,600**

Notes:

(1) Figures exclude FTRS personnel

(2) Excludes University Royal Navy Unit personnel

– denotes zero or rounded to zero

(3) Includes Officer Training Corps and non-regular permanent staff

(4) Excludes University Air Squadron personnel

* denotes not applicable

Sponsored Reserves (SR)

82. Sponsored Reserves (SR) are members of the workforce of a civilian contractor providing specialist support to the Armed Forces in peacetime and during operations. When the reservists are called out to support operations, they come under military authority. There are five active SR contracts, four of which were called upon (some individual Sponsored Reservists more than once) to support operations during 2003/04:

- A contract for strategic sealift with AWSR Consortium provides the Royal Navy with Ro-Ro ships and 156 personnel as crews. 64 were mobilised during the year.

- A contract with Vosper Thorneycroft provides a full time civilian systems engineer to maintain and support the complex, predominantly commercial off-the-shelf, survey system aboard each of the 2 new hydrographic survey vessels HMS ECHO and ENTERPRISE. A total of 5 personnel are involved to support a watch rotation cycle, although none was mobilised during the year.

- The Army's Heavy Equipment Transporter programme contracts a third of the required total of vehicles and crews from Fastrax Consortium and is fully integrated into Army units in the UK and Germany. It was successfully deployed on Operation TELIC in Iraq. 23 Sponsored Reserves were mobilised during the year.

- An arrangement with the Meteorological Office provides the RAF with the Mobile Meteorological Unit of up to 53 personnel. They continue to be heavily tasked in support of operations in Iraq and in the former Yugoslavia. 101 Sponsored Reserves were mobilised during the year.

- Engineering support for communications aircraft of 32 Squadron RAF is provided by Serco Aerospace (up to 16 personnel). They were mobilised for the first time in support of Operation TELIC. 31 Sponsored Reserves mobilised during the year.

Civilian Manning Levels

83. The Department employed 109,000 Full Time Equivalent civilian staff on 1 April 2004[9]. This was an increase of 1,470 over last year's figure of 107,530 Full Time Equivalent staff. The figures for UK-based staff have decreased slightly with the bulk of the increase being attributable to locally engaged civilians supporting our operation in Iraq, which grew by 1,430 Full Time Equivalents during the year. An increasing number of civilian staff now deploy to operational theatres alongside their uniformed colleagues. Some work alongside key military commanders as Policy Advisers to provide accurate and timely policy advice on the full range of political, legal and presentational issues. Some provide local contractual, secretariat and financial advice to deployed forces. Lists are maintained of civilian staff prepared to deploy overseas at short notice, or available for augmentation duties in the UK to allow 'round the clock' manning in the event of a crisis.

The secretariat team of MoD civil servants deployed with the UK military logistic headquarters during the campaign against Iraq.

Diversity

84. The MoD Diversity Panel was established nearly two years ago. It meets twice a year and is chaired by the Permanent Secretary and Chief of the Defence Staff. The Panel comprises senior MoD personnel and 9 external members, representing different strands of society, who bring a wealth of experience to help MoD take forward departmental diversity objectives. This year the Panel produced a Unified Diversity Strategy for MoD staff, service and civilian, which is encouraging a more consistent approach to diversity across the Department.

[9] The civilian workforce numbers quoted in this report are against the new Civilian Workforce Level 0 definitions that were changed following the public consultation in line with the National Statistics Protocols (see www.dasa.mod.uk for more information).

Table 11: Civilian Recruitment[1]

	2001/02		2002/03		2003/04	
	Non-Industrial	Industrial	Non-Industrial	Industrial	Non-Industrial	Industrial
Total number of staff recruited[2]	4,754	1,848	4,399	1,119	4,397	1,279
Number and percentage of women recruited	2,473 (52%)	455 (24.6%)	1,979 (45%)	256 (23%)	2,172 (49%)	300 (23%)
Number and percentage of ethnic minorities recruited[3]	165 (3%)	20 (1%)	145 (3%)	21 (2%)	144 (3%)	21 (2%)
Number and percentage of people with disabilities recruited[3]	116 (2%)	21 (1%)	68 (2%)	20 (2%)	77 (2%)	25 (2%)
Appointments of less than 12 months in respect of those posts specified in Annex A of the CSCRC.	0	0	0	0	0	0
Extensions up to a maximum of 24 months, of appointments originally made for a period of less than 12 months (with reasons).[4]	9	29	15	4	21	1
Recurrent short term appointments.	0	0	0	0	21	40
Short term appointments where highly specialised skills are required.[5]	3	13	0	0	4	0
Appointments under Government programmes to assist the long term unemployed.[6]	4	0	8	0	5	0
Secondments.[7]	11	0	13	1	20	1
Extensions to secondments (with reasons).[8]	3	0	2	0	1	0
Re-appointments of former civil servants.	88	17	102	35	110	11
Transfers of staff with their work (not under TUPE).	0	0	0	0	28	3
Transfers of staff from other public services without work (excluding public bodies staffed exclusively by civil servants).[9]	13	0	38	2	95	0
Appointments of surplus acceptable candidates to shortage posts.	0	0	0	0	7	0
Appointments of disabled candidates under modified selection arrangements.	4	1	17	0	9	1
Supported employment appointments.	0	0	0	0	0	3
Number of exceptions reserved for the Commissioners' use.	0	0	0	0	0	0
Any appointments exceptionally approved by the Commissioners under the Orders in Council, outside the terms of the Code.	0	0	0	0	0	0

Notes:

(1) Figures in this table differ from those published in UK Defence Statistics 2004 because of definitional differences including those described in the notes below.

(2) Figures for 2001/02 exclude recruitment to Trading Fund Agencies. Figures for all years exclude Locally Employed Civilians and Royal Fleet Auxiliary. The exception categories reflect the information required to be published in the revised Civil Service Commissioners Recruitment Code. Historical data is provided where possible.

(3) Figures are compiled from questionnaires returned by individual recruits.

(4) The majority of these extensions were to meet short-term requirements whilst permanent replacements were sought. Fair and open competition has been used wherever possible.

(5) This shows the number of staff recruited where the requirement was short term and required specialist skills and where holding an open competition would not have identified any further candidates.

(6) An exception approved by the Commissioners following the launch of the Government's Welfare to Work – New Deal Programme. Figures exclude those New Deal candidates recruited through normal open and fair competition.

(7) Excludes other Government Departments, but includes for example, local authorities, hospitals, etc.

(8) Extensions owing to a requirement to utilise one individual's knowledge of PPP/PFI.

(9) Figures for 2002/03 include 32 MD Police officers transferred from Home Office Police Forces. Figures for 2003/04 include 82 MD Police officers transferred from Home Office Police Forces.

Race Equality Scheme

85. The MoD's Race Equality Scheme (RES), which encompasses the Armed Forces, the MoD Civil Service and the MoD Police, was published in May 2002. It covers the period 2002-2005 and confirms the Department's continuing commitment to promote equality of opportunity and good relations between people from all ethnic groups. Specifically, it records how the Department intends to fulfil its obligations under the Race Relations (Amendment) Act 2000. We are working towards full implementation of the Scheme and the first progress report was published in January 2004. We participated again in the Business in the Community Race for Opportunity scheme, and all three Armed Services and the MoD were named in the top ten public sector ethnic minority employers.

86. Although there is still much to be done, particular achievements included provision of translation and interpretation services for housing, welfare and pay enquiries, changes to the Armed Forces' clothing policy to take account of cultural and religious differences, and provision of special operational ration packs for those with particular dietary requirements. On the civilian side, a pilot junior development scheme for ethnic minority staff received positive feedback and is being run again. Good progress has been made towards building relevant race equality considerations into the Department's procurement processes, and work continues to introduce race equality into day-to-day business, including the development of a process for checking all relevant policies for compliance with race and other diversity legislation.

Service Equal Opportunities and Diversity

87. The Armed Forces continued to work closely with the Commission for Racial Equality under the terms of a second Partnership Agreement, signed in July 2003. This focuses on progress against expected outcomes in relation to recruitment, retention, career progression, cultural change, complaints procedures, leadership accountability and implementing race equality policies. Ethnic minority representation in the Armed Forces continued to increase. At 1 April 2004 it stood at 4.9% (9,320) of trained strength including Commonwealth recruits, just short of our overall 2004 goal of 5% ethnic minority representation. The individual Services' achievements against their 2003/04 targets for recruitment of UK ethnic minorities are set out in table 12. Our goal for the next two years is for each Service to increase the proportion of UK ethnic minority recruits by at least 0.5% each year.

88. As at 1 April 2004, women made up 8.9% (18,390) of Armed Forces' personnel, up from 8.7% (17,920) in April 2003. The Armed Forces recruited 2,710 women in 2003/04, a decrease of 530 over the previous year (3,240), representing 11.6% of the total intake (against 12.3% the previous year). Broken down by Service, the Royal Navy recruited 580 women (14.2% of total intake), the Army 1,260 (8.3% of total intake), and the Royal Air Force 870 (20.9% of total intake).

89. The Services recognise the importance of family life and there are already a number of options available to help personnel achieve a better balance between work and home commitments. Recent initiatives include:

- **Screening from Deployment for Childcare Reasons:** A Servicewoman who returns to work after a period of ordinary Maternity Leave will not be deployed on operations and exercises either overseas or in the UK for at least six months after the birth of her child, unless she volunteers otherwise. Single Service arrangements may permit further screening from deployment where this does not compromise operational capability;

- **Deployment of Serving Parents:** The Services will also endeavour not to deploy both serving parents of dependant children at the same time, where this does not affect operational capability;

Table 12: Recruitment of UK Ethnic Minorities			
	Naval Service	**Army**	**RAF**
Overall Target 03/04	2.5%	2.9%	2.6%
Overall Achievement	2.1%	2.8%	1.8%
Note: these figures are single Service estimates of UK ethnic minority intake.			

- **Flexible Working:** Regular Service personnel may request to vary their working patterns, such as starting and finishing the working day at different times from those considered to be the norm within a particular Service working environment, where this does not impinge on operational capability. Priority for flexible working requests is given to those who are the primary carers for young children or for disabled, sick or elderly relatives.

Civilian Equal Opportunities and Diversity

90.   The MoD is not yet meeting all of its civilian diversity targets. However, there are some encouraging indicators for the future: both the Fast Stream and MIDIT (the MoD's main internal development scheme) exceeded their targets for the intake of ethnic minority staff and there is a slow but steady increase in the percentage of women at Band B. These are all potential feeder grades for the SCS but will take time to feed through. A combination of low turnover and low baseline limits MoD's ability to increase the level of minority groups in the SCS.

91.   The Department is recognised for having good diversity and work-life balance policies, but their impact has been slow to materialise and a number of initiatives are in hand to facilitate improvement. A new post of Diversity Catalyst has been created to advise the Personnel Director on how to improve the Department's performance in its efforts to achieve a more diverse and representative workforce, and the coming year will see a renewed impetus to promote and embed diversity and work life balance across the Department and foster a more supportive culture for minority groups.

92.   The Department currently has three diversity focus groups representing civilian minority groups: the Ethnic Minority Steering Committee (EMSC); the Disability Steering Committee (DSC), and the Lesbian, Gay, Bisexual and Transgender (LGBT) group. The work of these groups continues to represent members' views and to raise issues relevant to promoting the equality and diversity agenda. The DSC hosted the Department's first disability conference in October 2003 for around 200 disabled personnel and

Table 13: Diversity Statistics and Targets of MoD Senior Civil Servants (Level 0)

	2001/02 Target	2001/02 Achievement	2002/03 Target	2002/03 Achievement	2003/04 Target	2003/04 Achievement	2005 Target
Women	9.0	8.9	11.0	8.3	13.0	8.8	15.0
Ethnic Minorities	2.7	1.6	2.9	3.1	3.0	2.2	3.2
Disabled	1.0	2.6	1.7	2.6	1.9	3.7	2.0

Table 14: Diversity Statistics and Targets of MoD Band B Civil Servants (Level 0)

	2001/02 Target	2001/02 Achievement	2002/03 Target	2002/03 Achievement	2003/04 Target	2003/04 Achievement	2005 Target
Women	13.0	13.6	14.0	15.1	15.0	16.6	16.0
Ethnic Minorities	2.2	2.4	2.4	2.3	2.7	2.5	3.0
Disabled	2.8	4.2	3.2	3.8	3.6	3.3	4.0

Table 15: Diversity Statistics and Targets of MoD Band D Civil Servants (Level 0)

	2001/02 Target	2001/02 Achievement	2002/03 Target	2002/03 Achievement	2003/04 Target	2003/04 Achievement	2005 Target
Women	34.0	34.0	36.0	35.1	38.0	36.7	40.0
Ethnic Minorities	2.5	2.7	3.0	2.9	3.5	2.9	4.0
Disabled	5.3	9.4	5.6	8.4	5.8	6.9	6.0

1. Percentages of Disabled and Ethnic Minority staff have been calculated as percentages of staff with known disability status or ethnicity.

2. All the tables above are based on the new definitions of the civilian workforce as proposed and agreed through a public consultation in line with the National Statistics Code of Practice Protocols. See www.dasa.mod.uk for more details.

line managers. The EMSC hosted their second ethnic minority conference in January 2004 for around 200 ethnic minority staff and line managers. Both events were declared a success by the attendees. The LGBT group intends to hold its first workshop event for members in June 2004, when the way forward and the group's objectives will be discussed.

Service Personnel Health

93. Keeping our soldiers, sailors and airmen fit for task remains a high priority. Improved data collection and analysis has shown that the main causes of medical downgrading are musculo-skeletal injuries and mental health. Locally-based provision of mental health services is being enhanced in line with developments in the NHS, with in-patient care being provided within the private sector. The Defence Medical Information Capability Programme (DMICP) remains on track with a planned phased in-service date starting in December 2005 and work is in hand to ensure it remains aligned with the NHS's National Programme for Information Technology (NPfIT).

94. Regional Rehabilitation Units (RRUs) have been enhanced to facilitate rapid access to diagnosis and treatment and have proved a great success. 65% of those who would have been referred for surgical opinion were found not to require surgery and therefore returned to work 6-18 months sooner than they would have previously. As at 1 January 2004, some 19,500 Service personnel (about 10% of the Armed Forces) had been reported medically downgraded (which mainly limits their deployability on operations). For the RN/RAF, some 20% were permanently downgraded and had been accepted as fit for alternative tasks; it is not currently possible to differentiate between temporary and permanent downgrading for the Army. Analysis suggests that a recent increase in the number medically downgraded is partly the result of improved application of the revised downgrading and reporting procedure. It is also linked to the current high operational tempo, which drives strict compliance with downgrading criteria to ensure unfit Service personnel do not deploy on operations. In order to provide a measure that is more reliable to commanders, work continues to develop a metric to measure "fitness for task" across all three Services.

Civilian Sick Absence

95. After an initial downward trend, the number of days lost through sickness of civilian non-industrial staff has now stabilised around 7.5 calendar days for the 2003 calendar year. The actual position as at 31 December was rounded at 7.6 days lost. As predicted in the 2002 report, the Department missed its PSA target of 7.0 days. This levelling out has been largely as a consequence of more accurate reporting of sick absence and has been replicated across other large Government Departments and the Private Sector. The MoD continues to compare favourably with the wider Public Sector – recent CBI and CIPD surveys suggest an average of 8.9 to 10.6 days lost per year in the Public Sector (including MoD) and 6.9 to 7.0 in the Private Sector. We continue to improve the quality of sick absence data available and have introduced a new absence reporting system following World Health Organisation guidelines.

Defence Estate

Objective

To have infrastructure of the right size and quality, effectively and efficiently managed.

Public Service Agreement Targets (SR2002 MoD Targets 4 and 7)

- Recruit, train, motivate and retain the personnel needed to meet the manning requirement of the Armed Forces:
  - Improve the condition of the housing in which our people live. There will be substantial new investment in family accommodation in the UK to improve the living conditions of Service personnel and their families to Standard 1 for condition by November 2005.

- Increase value for money by making improvements in the efficiency and effectiveness of the key processes for delivering military capability:
  - Achieve £500M receipts for disposal of surplus land and buildings, and identify for disposal land and buildings with a Net Book Value of over £300M (from 1 April 2003 to 31 March 2006).

Performance Measures and Assessment

Improve Single Living Accommodation to Grade 1 standard by delivering 1,000 Grade 1 bedspaces through Project SLAM and 1,500 Grade 1 bedspaces through other projects:

- *3,347 new-build bedspaces delivered in 2003/04 through Project SLAM and parallel projects by 31 March 2004.*

Improve Service Family Accommodation in the UK by upgrading 1,200 family houses to Standard 1 for condition:

- *1,402 Service family houses upgraded in 2003/04. 22,800 of 41,700 long-term core stock requirement now at Standard 1 for condition.*

Draw up Core Sites implementation plan by March 2004:

- *Core Sites implementation plan approved by Defence Estates Committee in February 2004;*
- *Proposals to Lyons Review for 3,900 posts to be relocated from London and the South East.*

Achieve gross estates disposal receipts of £187M and identify land and buildings for disposal with cumulative value of £134M by April 2004:

- *Accrued gross disposal receipts from surplus land and property of £207M in 2003/04 (in addition to £278M in 2002/03);*

- *Assets with Net Book Value of £95M transferred to Defence Estates in 2003/04 for disposal producing cumulative value of £230M.*

Demonstrate reduction of through-life costs and timeframes by using prime contracting methods, and by producing methodology to assess value for money efficiencies by 31 March 2004:

- *Regional Prime Contracting programme meeting strategic programme. Contract for Scotland live 1 October 2003. Contract for South West awarded 26 March 2004;*

- *Successful delivery of stand alone Prime Contracts and other PPP projects;*

- *Methodology for assessing efficiencies determined, trial model produced, and 80% of required baseline information established by 31 March 2004.*

Further Sources of Information:

- Quarterly PSA reports to HM Treasury;

- *Defence Estates Framework Document;*

- *Defence Estates Agency Annual Report & Accounts 2003/04* (HC661);

- *The Stewardship Report on the Defence Estate 2003;*

- *Defence Housing Executive Corporate Plan 2003;*

- *Defence Housing Executive Annual Report and Accounts 2003/04;*

- *Final Report of the Lyons Review: Well Placed to Deliver? – Shaping the Pattern of Government Service;*

- *Delivering Security in a Changing World* (Defence White Paper and supporting essays);

- *UK Defence Statistics 2004.*

Service Accommodation

Single Living Accommodation

96. The Secretary of State announced in 2001 the allocation of £1Bn ring-fenced funding for Single Living Accommodation (SLA) improvements over ten years. Project SLAM was set up to manage this and is now delivering new-build and refurbished Grade 1 Single Living Accommodation. Owing to changed programme requirements and minor delays in construction, Project SLAM only delivered 150 new-build bedspaces during 2003/04 (at RM Poole) against the original target of 1,000 for the year, with a further 2,371 bedspaces under construction at 14 other sites. However, this in-year shortfall was more than made up by the delivery of 3,197 bedspaces in 2003/04 through a number of legacy and parallel projects against the original target of 1,500. Overall, therefore, 3,347 Grade 1 bedspaces were delivered against the target of 2,500, and as at 31 March 2004, some 16,428 bedspaces out of a total of some 93,627 were at Grade 1.

Service Family Accommodation

97. The Defence Housing Executive (DHE) continued its housing modernisation programme, upgrading 1,402 Service family houses to Standard 1 for condition against an in-year target of 1,200 upgrades. Since gaining Agency status in 1999, the DHE consistently met or exceeded its annual upgrade targets. By 31 March 2004, some 22,800 properties were at Standard 1 for condition, (about 55% of the estimated long-term core stock requirement) and

95.5% of Service families were housed in properties at Standards 1 or 2. DHE was merged into Defence Estates from 1 April 2004.

Estates Management

Estate Rationalisation: Core Sites

98. 91% of MoD personnel are currently employed at identified Core sites. Following the endorsement of the Core Sites implementation plan by the Defence Estates Committee in February 2004, Defence Estates is taking forward work to scope and identify options for further rationalisation of our estate and to increase further the proportion of personnel employed on core sites. This should produce more efficiencies in the running costs of the estate.

Lyons Review

99. In April 2003, the Chancellor of the Exchequer and the Deputy Prime Minister asked Sir Michael Lyons, Director of the Institute of Local Government Studies at the University of Birmingham, to conduct an independent study into the scope for relocating a substantial number of public sector activities from London and the South East of England to other parts of the United Kingdom. Sir Michael published his report, *Well Placed to Deliver? – Shaping the Pattern of Government Service*, on 15 March 2004. The MoD has relocated a significant amount of Defence activity out of London and the South East in recent years, and indeed the Defence Procurement Agency's move to Bristol (involving some 7,200 posts) and the

Meteorological Office's move to Exeter (involving some 1,000 posts) were used as case studies by the Review. Building on this experience and the work already underway in the Department to rationalise the Defence Estate, the MoD put forward a strong set of proposals which will result in a further 3,900 posts moving out of London and the South East by 2010 and 340 posts being cut. These are:

- Rationalising Woolwich station in south-east London and relocating units as appropriate (1,020 posts relocated, 100 posts cut);

- Closure of the Army Technical Foundation College (ATFC) at Arborfield in Berkshire (1,230 posts relocated, 180 posts cut);

- Relocation of the Disposal Services Agency (DSA) from London (80 posts relocated);

- Relocation of the Defence Medical Service Training Centre (DMSTC) (1,070 posts relocated, 60 posts cut);

- Rationalisation of the Defence Science and Technology Laboratory (DSTL) (490 posts relocated).

100. Some of these are still subject to further work and will require consultation with the Trade Unions and Ministerial consideration before final decisions on whether to proceed.

Estate Disposals

101. Under the PSA target of achieving £500M Accrued Estates Disposals Receipts from 1 April 2003 to 31 March 2006, Defence Estates was set a target of £187M gross disposal receipts from surplus land and property in 2003/04, and achieved £207M. Major sites sold during the year included the RAF Staff College in Bracknell, Berkshire; Deyesbrook Barracks in Liverpool; Stiles Way, Antrim in Northern Ireland; Support Engineering Facility Exeter; RAF St Athan in South Wales; and the TA Centre at Gillingham, Kent. Assets with a net book value of £95M were transferred from user commands to Defence Estates for disposal.

Prime Contracting

102. The prime contracting initiative is delivering significant Estate management efficiencies. The roll out of the five Regional Prime Contracts (RPCs) continued to meet its strategic programme. The Core Services element of RPC (Scotland) went live on 1 October 2003 as planned, is delivering tangible results and has started to improve the level of service. The contract for RPC (South West) was awarded on 26 March 2004 and went live on 1 June 2004 with phased acceptance of core service provision leading to full operation by April 2005. The innovative approach taken by RPC (South West) in developing a through-life management plan and whole-life costing model, which is now being used as a model for the subsequent RPCs, earned the Integrated Project Team the Minister for Defence Procurement's Smart Acquisition award during the year. Planned contract awards for the three remaining RPCs are for the South East in November 2004, Central in May 2005, and East in October 2005. A number of stand-alone Prime Contracts have also been delivering improvements.

103. Regional Prime contracting is intended to deliver 30% value for money efficiencies in estate management by 2008/2009 (against a baseline for 2004/2005). Support to the programme has included development of a DE policy for the transition to Prime Contracting and a "lessons learned" database to disseminate best practice to the wider project management community. Work was also undertaken to ensure that through-life value for money efficiencies from the introduction of Prime Contracting could be identified and tracked. A methodology for assessing efficiencies was determined and a trial model produced by 31 March 2004, and 80% of required baseline information established. The full working version is expected to be agreed and delivered by the end of March 2005.

Other Procurement Initiatives

104. Project Aquatrine is a pan-departmental Public Private Partnership project split into three geographic regions across the estate, encompassing the MoD's sewage works, water processing plants and water mains, sewers and drains, removal of surface water and water supply for fire fighting use. The project is delivering better value for money, whilst mitigating risk water management through the transfer of responsibilities to the service provider. A 25-year contract covering the Midlands, Wales and South West England and delivering 30% savings against traditional procurement methods was awarded on 17 April 2003, only four months after announcing the preferred bidder, and the contract was awarded the Minister for Defence Procurement's excellence award for Smart Acquisition. Contract awards for the remaining two packages are expected during 2004, leading to in-service dates in 2005. Project Vanguard, for provision of non-core support services to the Army Training Estate (ATE), commenced on 1 April 2003, and became fully operational in February 2004. The contract covers around two-thirds of the Defence Estate in terms of land area, and provides range bookings, administration, information management and accommodation services, training area and range operations and management, catering and specialist rural services.

Reputation

Objective

To enhance our reputation with the UK public and internally within MoD and the Armed Forces.

Performance Measure and Assessment

5% increase in positive responses in aspects of Defence where the level of positive responses is less than 70%:

- *No change in overall average of 57% positive replies to external opinion survey;*

Further Sources of Information

- Detailed Opinion Surveys published on www.mod.uk;
- *Delivering Security in a Changing World* (Defence White Paper and supporting essays);
- Papers supplied to *The Hutton Inquiry.*

Communicating the Work of the Department to the Public

105. The work of the Ministry of Defence and the Armed Forces was never far from the public eye throughout the year, mainly as a result of operations in Iraq. Media reporting has been extensive. Despite concerns on some specific issues, our reputation research demonstrates that the Armed Forces continue to have the overwhelming support of the British public.

106. MoD Press Officers are responsible for day-to-day liaison with the media. They respond to questions from journalists as stories develop and provide the media with the factual background required. Our work is also explained via the workings of Parliament, in the form of answers to Parliamentary Questions, debates on defence issues and Ministerial statements (see Annex D). Beyond Parliament and the Press Office, the MoD uses a number of other means to explain its work and to get its messages across to the public. The news pages of the MoD website www.mod.uk received some 40,000 visits per day during the Iraq conflict and the online photo library www.photos.mod.uk received 3 million page requests in 2003. The Department also made a large quantity of material available to Lord Hutton's Inquiry into the circumstances surrounding the death of Dr David Kelly.

107. Each year, we conduct a wide array of activities, to which the public is invited. The Defence Tourer exhibition travels around the UK to locations as varied as county shows and shopping malls, attracting in the region of 120,000 visitors annually, while the Defence Schools Briefing Teams aim to visit 750 secondary schools each year, with an estimated 150,000 children taking part. All three Services also have Presentation Teams that undertake an annual UK tour to explain their roles and responsibilities to invited audiences. The Services also participate in many events that give the public the opportunity to view their skills and professionalism. Examples from the past year include HMS NORTHUMBERLAND's attendance at the London Boat Show, the Aldershot Army Show, which was attended by 60,000 people, and the RAF's involvement in the International Air Tattoo at Fairford, which was seen by 100,000 visitors each day.

MoD and Armed Forces Reputation

108. The successful achievement of many Defence objectives depends upon public support. The Department carries out regular public opinion surveys and surveys of staff, using an independent market opinion company, to test the reputation of the MoD and the Armed Forces, which help identify where action may be necessary. External opinion polls continue to demonstrate a high level of public support for the work and professionalism of the

Armed Forces (see Table 14 below). In a poll undertaken by MORI, 84% said that the UK needs strong Armed Forces and 77% said that they make the world a safer place. Less favourable responses were received on some issues, for example on whether the Armed Forces were well equipped (38%). Opinion among Service personnel and MoD Civil Servants was broadly consistent with public opinion but in some cases attitudes were more strongly marked than the equivalent general public perception.

Table 16: External Opinion Survey Results (Percentage of Positive Replies)		
(Survey in December 2003 of 2,094 adults aged 15+ across 200 sampling points in Great Britain)		
Statement		Change since 02/03
UK needs strong armed forces.	84%	-1%
Confidence in the ability of the UK Armed Forces to defend UK.	85%	+5%
UK Armed Forces make the world a safer place.	77%	+1%
Confidence in the ability of UK Armed Forces to defend overseas territories.	81%	+3%
UK Armed Forces have the highest professional standards.	70%	-4%
Confidence in the ability of UK Armed Forces to protect UK citizens overseas.	67%	+7%
The UK Armed Forces look after their people.	60%	+1%
Confidence in ability of UK Armed Forces to protect UK overseas economic interests.	60%	+5%
MoD is as open as it can be about its activities.	46%	-1%
UK Armed Forces are well equipped.	38%	-6%
MoD and UK Armed Forces promote their best people regardless of race, gender, religion or sexual orientation.	49%	-5%
UK Armed Forces make a positive contribution to wider communities.	42%	0%
MoD should support British industry's efforts to export military equipment.	38%	-1%
MoD and UK Armed Forces carry out their activities with due regard to environment	34%	-2%
MoD spends taxpayers' money wisely.	23%	-1%
Average	57%	0%

Enabling Processes

Training

Objective

To improve training and education to support changing operational and business needs.

Public Service Agreement Target (SR2002 MoD Target 7)

- Increase value for money by making improvements in the efficiency and effectiveness of the key processes for delivering military capability:
  - Reduce the per capita cost of successfully training a military recruit by an average of 6% by April 2006.

Performance Measures and Assessment

Complete 60% of Defence Training Review (DTR) recommendations by 31 March 2004:

- 73% of all DTR recommendations completed.

Efficient delivery of training by reduction in the per capita cost of successfully training a military recruit by an average of 4% from 2001/02 baseline by April 2004; reduction in personnel lost from the training pipeline (against Service targets by trade / specialisation); and reduction in average time overrun of time taken to train a military recruit to agreed standard:

- *4.2% average reduction in cost of successfully training a military recruit by April 2004;*

- *RN: rating wastage reduced to 25% in line with SR02 target profile of 30% for the year;*

- *Army: wastage reduced by 5.8% in line with SR02 target profile;*

- *RN: rating pipeline overrun reduced to 11% in 03/04, in line with SR02 target profile;*

- *Army: pipeline overrun reduced by 6 days in line with SR02 target profile.*

Quantifiable improvements in output of training and education through:

Basic Skills (RN / RAF): improvement of 50% of new entrants below National Level 2 basic skills by one level within one year of entry;

Basic Skills (Army): all new entrants below National Level 2 in basic skills to achieve National Level 1 within 3 years of entry:

- *RN – Meeting targets – Training Programmes ensure all recruits achieve the required standard;*

- *RAF – Meeting targets – Few RAF recruits are below the required standard on entry;*

- *Army – Plans in place to meet targets with an initial assessment of basic skills ability now undertaken at recruiting offices and a network of tutors in place.*

Information Communication Technology: all new entrants without competence level 1/2 in use of Information and Communication Technology to be in appropriate training scheme:

- *RN (including Royal Marines) – Greater than 95%;*

- *RAF – Greater than 95%;*

- *Army – Achieving approximately 30%;*

- *Award of Defence e-Learning Delivery and Management Capability contract in July 2004.*

Achievement of planned and agreed single-Service and Joint collective training and exercise programme:

- *Some 80% of major exercises completed, but exercise activity inevitably affected by operational activity and resource constraints.*

Further Sources of Information

- Quarterly PSA reports to HM Treasury;

- Evidence presented to House of Commons Defence Committee on *The Army Training and Recruiting Agency* (HC124-i);

- Evidence presented to House of Commons Defence Committee on *Duty of Care* (HC 620-i);

- *Modernising Defence Training:* Report of the Defence Training Review;

- Director of Operational Capability's *Appraisal of Initial Training* (February 2003), *Departmental Progress Report* (July 2003) and *Director of Operational Capability's Re-Appraisal of Initial Training* (July 2003);

- *Defence Academy Annual Report 2003/04* (to be published in October 04);

- Naval Recruiting and Training Agency *Annual Report and Accounts 2003/04;*

- Army Training and Recruiting Agency *Annual Report and Accounts 2003/04;*

- RAF Training Group Defence Agency *Annual Report and Accounts 2003/04;*

- Defence Medical Education and Training Agency *Annual Report and Accounts 2003/04;*

- Ministry of Defence Policy Paper no. 6: *Individual Training and Education in the Armed Forces;*

- *Delivering Security in a Changing World* (Defence White Paper and supporting essays).

Individual Training

109. The Defence White Paper and MoD Policy Paper no. 6 on *Individual Training and Education* highlighted the calibre of training and education delivered to our young soldiers, sailors and airmen, who enjoy a high reputation worldwide. Sustaining and building on our success in this area was at the heart of the Defence Training Review (DTR) 2001. By 1 April 2004, 73% of the Defence Training Review's recommendations had been completed against a target of 60%, up from about 45% in April 2003. This included a series of 20 recommendations designed to improve the way in which the Department prepares personnel to work in the acquisition field, improved arrangements for accreditation of Service and MoD civilian courses to nationally recognised awards, and improved arrangements for the delivery of e-learning.

Territorial Army soldiers on exercise in Cumbria.

110. All three Services have also continued to make progress towards the PSA target of reducing the per capita cost of successfully training a military recruit by 6% by April 2006 through savings in input costs and better management of the training pipeline, achieving an overall average reduction of 4.2% against a target of 4% by the end of March 2004. There are inevitably continuing tensions between achieving these efficiency targets and other initiatives, including the implementation of all the recommendations of the Director of Operational Capability's *Appraisal of Initial Training* (paragraph 116 below) in respect of supervisory ratios for Army training which may impact on future efficiency achievements. These are being kept under review.

Collective Training

111. In addition to personal training, it is essential that individuals, teams, units and the Services train together so that they are able to operate jointly when deployed on operations. Collective training activity continues to be constrained by the pressure of operational commitments and availability of Forces, including for joint Alliance and multinational collective training.

Basic Skills for our People

112. Beyond the specific training necessary to undertake the professional tasks of any serviceman, the MoD aims to ensure that all personnel achieve a minimum standard of literacy and numeracy. Around 7,500 new recruits per year require development in one or both of these areas. With DfES assistance, the MoD has now instigated mandatory screening and assessment of all new entrants to the Armed Forces, and the Services are working to facilitate learning opportunities for all personnel with a literacy or numeracy need. Similarly, all civilian employees are offered Basic Skills (literacy or numeracy training) as a development opportunity.

Training and Education for the Information Age

113. Operations in the networked battlespace will place new demands on our people and it is imperative that they are properly prepared. The Skills Framework for the Information Age (SFIA) programme is intended to equip the right people with the right IT skills across Defence. Currently, more than 95% of RN new recruits and RAF new recruit airmen, and approximately 30% of new recruit soldiers receive ICT Fundamental Skills Training. We need to keep pace with changes in technology, as increasing digitisation means that our people require up-to-the-minute IT skills to perform effectively. We must also develop our capacity to deliver training more flexibly, as operational pressures require minimising time spent on residential training. The Defence e-Learning Delivery and Management Capability (DELDMC) project is planned to provide a managed service, bringing coherence and efficiency to the distribution of e-learning across Defence, as the learning portal through which our people will access on-line learning, and a 10 year contract was signed with BT plc in July 2004.

The Rationalisation of Specialist Training

114. The programme to rationalise specialist training across Defence initiated in the DTR will provide modernised specialist training, responsive to current and future operational needs and to the increasing requirement for joint operations. Progress this year has been slower than originally planned, but the procurement strategy was approved in March 2004, and six Federated Defence Colleges stood up on schedule on 1 April 2004. The Federated Defence Colleges train against common objectives in the specialist trade areas of: Electrical Mechanical Engineering; Aeronautical Engineering; Communications and Information Systems; Security, Language Intelligence and Photography; Logistics; and Police and Personnel Administration. The Federated Colleges are an interim step in the progression to pan-Defence rationalised training delivered in partnership with industry.

Defence Academy: Education, Training and Research

115. The Defence Academy, which vested in April 2002, brings together 8 main colleges and schools. This has been a very busy and productive year for the Academy in terms of education and training of students across the Colleges, with 100,766 student place days delivered by the Joint Services Command and Staff Course and 226,180 student place days delivered by the Royal Military College of Science. Courses in all colleges have continued to develop to cover new concerns including terrorism, homeland security and peace support operations. The Royal College of Defence Studies has attracted an increasing number of students from other Government Departments and the private sector with a final term course on leadership in the strategic environment. The Defence Leadership Centre also ran a successful strategic leadership programme for senior officers and officials. The Royal Military College of Science has continued to develop as the Tri-Service and civilian focus for undergraduate technical training and to introduce new postgraduate courses in programme and project management. Initial Gate approval has been given for a Campus Integrator at Shrivenham to oversee all service support and building work, and for an Academic Provider when the current contract with Cranfield University comes to an end in 2006.

Monitoring and Evaluation of Training

116. In the latter part of 2002 and Summer 2003, the Director Operational Capability conducted two independent cross-cutting examinations of the Initial Basic and Specialisation Training of non-officer recruits of all 3 Services. Making good the recommendations arising from those appraisals has been a very high priority for each of the Services and a great deal has been achieved in improving the way in which the Department discharges its duty of care. In order to demonstrate our commitment to training, the Department has now invited the Adult Learning Inspectorate (ALI) to commence independent inspections of our training and education provision. These will focus in the first year on care and welfare issues. The open reporting of ALI inspection findings will drive continuous improvement activity and enable Defence training and education provision to be benchmarked against national standards.

Civilian Training

117. A new strategy for civilians in Defence introduced in 2002 emphasises (amongst other things) better skills planning and giving greater priority to development of employees. As part of this strategy, MoD has become much more pro-active in developing and sustaining individual potential to meet business needs. We are placing in sharper focus what the Department requires from its people and providing clearer structures around which to shape development discussion and activity. We are

reviewing our competence structures with a view to developing a skills framework which will enable every job in the department to be defined and explained in terms which will be understandable to all staff. Staff in turn will be able to judge their fitness for each job, drawing on their own skills profile which will also enable them to identify more accurately their personal training and development needs. To support this and provide better information about the options available at all levels, we are creating a single intranet portal for career and development advice.

118. In line with the Government skills strategy and to support the drive for greater professionalism across the Civil Service, we are looking to improve standards across all levels of the Department. At the basic level, we are developing a strategy for assessing and improving the literacy, numeracy and IT skills of the civilian workforce; we are promoting NVQs and apprenticeships where these qualifications meet the business need; and we are promoting a programme of Higher Education qualifications including a Foundation Degree specifically aimed at Government employees. We are working with our military colleagues to ensure that training and qualifications are accredited wherever appropriate to support our aim that MoD should be an employer of choice.

119. As part of wider public service reform we are engaged in a Cabinet Office initiative, Improving Professional Capacity, which aims to develop a more effective and efficient Civil Service through better defined professional skills paths. Allied to this, we are also involved in a Civil Service Management Board initiative to develop a Sector Skills Council for Central Government. It is envisaged this will help us to identify the skills and experience that we need and to match training and development opportunities to gaps identified in a more structured way.

120. We have a number of management development schemes in place, including a new band B development scheme, which will provide continuing development and tailored postings necessary to meet the requirements of leadership positions in the Senior Civil Service (SCS); the Acquisition Leadership Development Scheme which aims to develop current and future leaders for acquisition; the SCS Higher Potential Development Scheme; and MIDIT. We also have staff engaged in a number of personal development schemes including Public Sector Leadership and Druidstone. We have nearly 300 internal trainees currently studying for a professional accountancy qualification and 350 studying for qualifications below the professionally recognised level. More than 400 people in the HR function successfully achieved the MoD Certificate in HR Practice in its first year of operation and 2,147 Finance Licences had been issued up to July 2004. We encourage and support professional development and external accreditation of engineers and scientists, and in the last year, 67 engineers and scientists have completed their initial professional development through the Defence Engineering and Science Group Student and Graduate Training Scheme.

Procurement

Objective

To improve the procurement of equipment.

Public Service Agreement Targets (SR2002 MoD Targets 6 and 7)

- Develop and deliver to time and cost targets military capability for the future, including battle-winning technology, equipment and systems, matched to the changing strategic environment:
  - On average, in-year slippage of equipment in-service dates of fewer that 10 days for new major projects, to be attained during 2003/04;
  - On average, in-year slippage of equipment in-service dates of fewer than 4 weeks for existing major projects, to be attained during 2003/04;
  - 97% of customers' key requirements attained during 2003/04;
  - On average, no real terms increase in major project costs (measured against project approval levels as set out in the Major Projects Report), to be attained during 2003/04.

- Increase value for money by making improvements in the efficiency and effectiveness of the key processes for delivering military capability:
  - Achieve 0% average annual cost growth (or better) against the Major Equipment Procurement Projects (measured against estimated project costs at the beginning of the year).

Performance Measures and Assessment

Delivery of planned equipment with less than 15% variance between planned and actual asset delivery values in-year:

- *Equipment valued at over £3.6Bn delivered, with progress in key programmes to modernise our equipment capabilities;*

- *In-year variance of -3% between planned and actual asset delivery values.*

97% of customers' key requirements met:

- *98.8% of customers' key requirements met.*

Achieve customer satisfaction rating of 74%:

- *In-year customer satisfaction rating of 70%.*

In-year slippage of major equipment projects of 0.5 months, including fewer than 10 days for new projects and 4 weeks for existing projects:

- *2.4 months average slippage overall;*

- *2.2 months average slippage for new projects;*

- *2.8 months average slippage for existing projects.*

On average no increase in major project costs measured against approvals and against estimated project costs at the beginning of the year:

- *2.7% average increase in costs measured against approvals;*

- *3.1% average increase in costs measured against estimated cost at beginning of year.*

No excess against DPA resource control totals:

- *Outturn within resource control totals.*

Review implementation of Defence Industrial Policy:

- *Review published in November 2003.*

Further Sources of Information

- Quarterly PSA Reports to HM Treasury;

- Evidence given to the House of Commons Defence Committee on *Defence Procurement* (HC 694) and Government response (HC 1194);

- Evidence given to the House of Commons Defence Committee on *Defence Procurement* (HC 572-ii, iii);

- *Major Projects Report 2003;*

- Evidence given to the House of Commons Public Accounts Committee on *Major Projects Report 2003* (HC 383-i,ii);

- *Defence Procurement Agency Corporate Plan 2003;*

- *Defence Procurement Agency Business Plan 2003;*

- *Defence Procurement Agency Annual Report and Accounts 2003/04;*

- *Excellence in Defence Procurement 2004: Equipping the Armed Forces;*

- Ministry of Defence Policy Paper no.4: *Defence Acquisition;*

- Ministry of Defence Policy Paper no.5: *Defence Industrial Policy;*

- First Review of Defence Industrial Policy;

- *Delivering Security in a Changing World* (Defence White Paper and supporting essays);

- *UK Defence Statistics 2004.*

Procurement Performance

121. The Equipment Programme, which includes projects that harness new technologies and concepts, is rigorously reviewed each year. This ensures that the MoD makes the best possible use of available resources and provides the UK Armed Forces with the capabilities they need for operations today and in the future. Performance against the Equipment Programme is reported by capability areas. Significant equipment milestones in the year included contract award for the Skynet 5 PFI satellite communications service, selection of Hawk 128 as Advanced Jet Trainer for the Royal Air Force and Royal Navy, and contract activation on the multi-national A400M military transport programme. Taken together with the equipment delivered into service, these represent considerable progress in moving forward key programmes to modernise our equipment capabilities.

122. The tables at Annex E show the deliveries accepted in 2003/04 and/or planned as of 31 March 2004 for 2004/05, for major equipment projects. The Defence Procurement Agency (DPA) delivered equipment valued at over £3.6Bn during the year, including acceptance into service of two large Auxiliary Oilers (tankers) and one survey vessel, and achievement of the in-service date for Bowman battlefield communications equipment on schedule. This represented 97% of the asset value planned for delivery in-year and exceeded a Departmental target of less than 15% variance between planned and actual asset delivery value.

123. The table below summarises performance against project management and operating cost targets as set out in the MoD's PSA agreement and the *DPA Corporate Plan*. The DPA continued to do well in meeting 98.8% of customers' key requirements (Key Target 1), exceeding the PSA target of 97%, and in managing internal costs (Key Target 5). The average in-year forecast programme slippage for major projects (Key Target 2) was 2.4 months overall. This breaks down as an average slippage of 2.2 months for newer projects (reflecting revised forecasts from the Type 45 Destroyer, Typhoon Aircrew Synthetic Training Aids and Airborne Stand-Off Radar System projects) and 2.8 months for older projects (reflecting revised forecasts from the Brimstone anti-armour missile and Nimrod Maritime Reconnaissance Aircraft (MRA4) projects). The average in-year cost increase was 2.7% measured against approval levels (Key Target 3) and 3.1% compared to estimated project costs at the beginning of the year. This reflected revised forecasts for the A400M, Skynet 5, Beyond Visual Range Air-to-Air Missile, Joint Combat Aircraft, Nimrod MRA4, T45

Table 17: Defence Procurement Agency – Key Targets and Achievements

No.	Efficiency	2001/02	2002/03	2003/04
1[1]	Predicted achievement of projects' core requirements	97%	97%	**98%**
	Outturn	98.6%	99.5%	**98.8%**
2[1]	Average cumulative slippage of in-service dates not to exceed	11.4 months (11.9)[2]	12.1 months (12.3)[2]	**0.5[3] months**
	Outturn (of which in-year slippage)	12.5 (1.1)	19.0 (7.2)	**(2.4)**
3[1]	Average cumulative cost variation not to exceed	2.5% (2.8%)[2]	2.2% (2.7%)[2]	**0%[3]**
	Outturn (of which in-year)	2.4% (-0.3%)	8.1% (5.4%)	**(2.7%)**
5	Excess against Resource Control Totals (excludes nuclear RCT)[4]	[4]	0	**0**
	Outturn		0	**0**
6[5]	Asset Deliveries – variance between planned values and actual values not to exceed			
No.	Quality	2001/02	2002/03	2003/04
4	Customer satisfaction rating	70%	70%	**74%**
	Outturn	66.7%	72.5%	**70%**

Notes:

(1) Covers all equipment projects in the development and manufacture phase included in the Major Projects Report until 31/3/04. From 04/05 all projects over £20M that have passed their main investment decision point, but not yet achieved ISD, will be included.

(2) Following the National Audit Office review of the Major Projects Report data, the baseline in-service dates and costs were subsequently amended, leading to revised targets.

(3) For 2003/04 onwards only, the in-year, rather than cumulative, performance will be measured and reported. This is consistent with PSA targets.

(4) This measure applies to 2002/03 and 2003/04 only; the target is to have no excess against Resource Control Totals. From 04/05, a revised target has been introduced, comprising a basket of measures. Measure i) covers asset turnover, measure ii) measures the value of assets delivered as a multiple of operating cost, and measure iii) measures the value of assets added to the balance sheet as a multiple of operating cost. Actual target levels will be established at the beginning of each financial year based on the Agency opening position.

(5) A new Key Target introduced for 04/05 onwards.

Destroyer, Brimstone, Support Vehicles, CIP (Combat Battlefield Application Toolset, Digitisation of the Battlespace (Land) Infrastructure, Platform Battlefield Information System Application) and Light Forces Anti-Tank Guided Weapons System projects. PSA and DPA Key Targets for cost and time were therefore missed, as was DPA Key Target 4 on customer satisfaction. Further details on the DPA's performance can be found in the *Major Projects Report*, published annually by the National Audit Office and also in the DPA *Annual Report and Accounts.*

Smart Acquisition Programme

124. Smart Acquisition (SA) was initiated in 1998. Estimated reductions of some £2Bn were made to the MoD's planned equipment programme between 1998 and 2008. However, Smart Acquisition is now normal practice and data to support notional Smart Acquisition savings proved to be unreliable. The MoD is discussing with the NAO how to establish reliable performance metrics. Currently the most reliable metrics are from the National Audit Office *Major Projects Report 2003*, which indicate that Smart Acquisition programmes currently have less slippage and fewer cost overruns compared to legacy programmes. Examples of best practice in 2003/04 included:

- Skynet 5 applied partnership arrangements with industry, financial and legal advisers, for the delivery of an innovative contract in a highly complex technical area;

- The NITEworks team has broken down Intellectual Property Rights barriers with industry, and exploited Network Enabled Capability through innovation with high tempo and excellent stakeholder management;

- Project Aquatrine (see paragraph 104 above, under Defence Estates) demonstrated excellent management of key stakeholders, clear focus on environmental issues, effective risk transfer to industry and achieved contract signatures within 4 months of selection of preferred bidder.

125. Following the arrival of Sir Peter Spencer as Chief of Defence Procurement and DPA Chief Executive in May 2003, a review of Smart Acquisition in the DPA was launched to identify the way forward for improving Agency performance. A number of initiatives were set up to achieve this, including improved skills development, risk management, through-life management and joint working with industry, as well as business processes and organisational changes. This work is ongoing and may take some time to impact on performance results.

Acquisition Leadership Development Scheme (ALDS)

126. The ALDS aims to develop leadership in Smart Acquisition. Its membership is selected from Service personnel, MoD civil servants and industry. During 2003/04 it reached 462 current members, including an in-year intake of 123 new members and sabbatical returns.

Private Finance Initiative (PFI)

127. The Private Finance Initiative continues to play an important role in the provision of defence services and the MoD seeks to involve the private sector, where appropriate, in the delivery of efficient services for Defence. We remain committed to using PFI wherever this delivers best value and does not compromise operational effectiveness. This can include support close to the front line, as demonstrated in Op TELIC by the Heavy Equipment Transporter (HET) PFI. We signed five more PFI deals in 2003/04, with a capital value of £1.8Bn (see Table 18), bringing total capital investment through PFI to over £4.0Bn. Further details on our PFI programme are provided in note 22 to the Departmental Resource Accounts in Section 2, pages 149-151. We have a robust and diverse forward PFI programme (see Table 19) with an estimated capital value of approximately £4.0Bn.

Table 18: PFI Deals Signed in 2003/04

Project Name	Capital Value[1] (£M)
MoD-wide Water and Waste Water – Project Aquatrine Package A	154
Defence Sixth Form College	20
Pan-Government Records Management & Archive (Hayes PPP)	11
Skynet 5 (Provision of a range of satellite services)	1,079
Colchester Garrison	539

Note:
(1) Estimates based on private sector's capital investment where known (or otherwise the capital value of the Public Sector Comparator).

Table 19: Major PFI Projects In Procurement or Under Consideration, as at 31 March 2004

Project Name

Allenby/Connaught[1]
Aquatrine Packages B and C (MoD-wide Water and Waste Water)
Armada (Devonport Support Services and Fleet Accommodation Centre)[2]
Armoured Vehicle Training Service
C Vehicles (Earthmoving and Specialist Plant, Engineer Contractors and Materials Handling services)
Combined Aerial Target System
Corsham Development Project (rationalisation and development of the MoD Estate)
Defence Training Review
Future Provision of Marine Services
Future Strategic Tanker Aircraft
Northwood PPP (support services and associated infrastructure)
Portsmouth 2 (provision of fully serviced family housing)
RAF Brize Norton Service Families Association
Royal School of Military Engineering
UK Military Flying Training System

Note:
(1) Redevelopment of barracks in Aldershot and Salisbury Plain areas, and long-term provision of associated support services.
(2) Signed July 2004, estimated capital value £54M.

Defence Industrial Policy

128. The MoD is responsible for providing the Armed Forces with high quality equipment at best value for money for the taxpayer. We are also firmly committed to the UK manufacturing sector, and to promoting a strong and competitive UK defence industry that brings economic and technological benefits to the nation. Defence equipment decisions have to reconcile any tensions between these two objectives. The Government's Defence Industrial Policy, published jointly by the MoD and the Department of Trade and Industry in October 2002, set out the framework through which these issues should be considered, and we have continued to work closely with industry and other Government Departments on its implementation. As promised when it was launched, in November 2003 we published a review of progress over the first year of implementation of the policy. The conclusions are set out in *Defence Industrial Policy – One Year On*. The review highlighted that the policy had been a significant driver in bringing together government and industry and underlined the importance of engaging jointly in actions to deliver our objectives. We are grateful for the high level of support from industry. We plan to publish a further review this winter. We are also in the early stages of work to develop Defence Industrial Policy into an industrial strategy. This is being taken forward with DTI and HMT, keeping industry in touch through National Defence Industries Council arrangements.

Defence Exports

129. The MoD provides a high standard of support to legitimate defence exports. In 2003, the UK won defence orders of close to £5Bn, including the sale of EH 101 to Japan, Lynx to South Africa, Typhoon to Austria, and further orders to the United States related to the development of the Joint Strike Fighter. In a global market characterised by uncertainties about future threats, and with other nations' resource priorities competing against their defence budgets, this was a major achievement for our defence industry.

Logistic Support

Objective

To provide more responsive, integrated and efficient logistic support.

Public Service Agreement Target (SR2002 MoD Target 7)

- Increase value for money by making improvements in the efficiency and effectiveness of the key processes for delivering military capability: year-on-year output efficiency gains will be made each year from 2002/03 to 2005/06, including through a 20% output efficiency gain (relative to April 2000) in the Defence Logistics Organisation:
  - Reduce by 14% (relative to planned expenditure in 2002/03) the output costs of the Defence Logistics Organisation by April 2006, while maintaining support to the Front Line.

Performance Measures and Assessment

DLO delivery to TLBs of 98% of level of logistic support agreed in Customer Supplier Agreements (CSAs):

- *The DLO delivered 94.3% of the logistic support outputs called for by its Customer Supplier Agreements.*

Output costs of DLO cumulatively reduced by 6% by April 2004:

- *DLO output costs reduced by 3.7% in 2003/04, producing a cumulative reduction of 6.8% by 1 April 2004.*

Achieve total savings of at least £565M by April 2006 through Lean Support Continuous Improvement, Reliability Centred Maintenance, and Management of Material in Transit:

- *£297M of efficiencies in logistics support during 2003/2004 by taking end-to-end process perspective.*

Achieve £20M cash receipts from sale of surplus equipment:

- *The Disposal Services Agency achieved £22M in gross cash receipts.*

Further Sources of Information

- Quarterly PSA reports to HM Treasury;

- MoD Evidence to the House of Commons Public Accounts Committee on *Progress in Reducing Stocks* (HC 566);

- National Audit Office report on *Through Life Management* (HC 698);

- National Audit Office report on *Operation Telic – United Kingdom Military Operations in Iraq* (HC 60);

- MoD Evidence to the House Of Commons Public Accounts Committee on *Operation Telic – United Kingdom Military Operations in Iraq* (HC 273);

- MoD Evidence and Government Response to the House of Commons Defence Committee on *Lessons of Iraq* (HC 57-iii and HC 635);

- *Operations in Iraq: First Reflections;*

- *Lessons for the Future* (assessment of performance on Operation TELIC);

- *Review of Logistics to the Armed Forces, Hansard, Columns 26-27WS*

- *Delivering Security in a Changing World* (Defence White Paper and supporting essays);

- *UK Defence Statistics 2004;*

- *ABRO Annual Report and Accounts 2003/04;*

- Defence Aviation Repair Agency *Annual Report and Accounts 2003/04;*

- Warship Support Agency *Annual Report and Accounts 2003/04;*

- Defence Communication Services Agency *Annual Report and Accounts 2003/04;*

- Defence Storage and Distribution Agency *Annual Report and Accounts 2003/04;*

- Defence Transport and Movements Agency *Annual Report and Accounts 2003/04;*

- Medical Supplies Agency *Annual Report and Accounts 2003/04;*

- Disposal Services Agency *Annual Report and Accounts 2003/04.*

Logistic Support

130. Effective logistic support is a key enabler for ensuring forces are ready for operations. The DLO continued throughout the year successfully to meet the demanding operational logistic requirements of the front line while taking forward a wide ranging programme to improve further the ways in which the MoD and industry provide logistic support.

Soldiers of the Royal Gloucestershire, Berkshire and Wiltshire Regiment disembark from a C-17 transport in Kosovo.

In-year Delivery of Logistic Support

Performance Against Customer Supplier Agreements

131. The level of support provided by the Defence Logistics Organisation (DLO) to the Armed Forces is agreed and funded through Customer Supplier Agreements (CSAs) between the Chief of Defence Logistics and each of the other ten Top Level Budget holders. CSAs define, within the resources allocated, the logistic outputs to be provided by the Chief of Defence Logistics to support the Commanders-in-Chief and other Top Level Budget Holders in their delivery of military capability at the levels specified in

their own Service Delivery Agreements. In 2003/2004, the DLO achieved the agreed service levels for delivery of 94.3% of its logistic support outputs, against a target of 98% – marginally below last year's performance of 94.5%.

Supporting Operations in Iraq

132. The DLO Logistic Operations Centre (DLOC) continued to provide a more effective means of integrating the outputs of the Supply Chain and, to improve co-ordination of strategic movement and the delivery of logistic support from the home base to the operational theatres. Plans have been put in place to align the DLOC more closely with the Defence Transport and Movement Agency (DTMA).

133. The MoD has recognised the strategic requirement to track the location of individual components and consignments for some time. Op TELIC exposed the shortcomings in the current systems, the short-term rectification of which is being addressed as follows: an existing and proven system, Total Asset Visibility (TAV), was brought into service in early 2003 to enhance fielded UK systems; £17.5M was allocated to improve current consignment tracking systems; and a review of policy, procedures and training was carried out and acted upon.

134. In the longer term, the MoD is running two associated projects: Management of the Joint Deployed Inventory (MJDI); and Management of Materiel in Transit (MMiT). These will further improve the ability to track materiel to the front line and develop a 'picture' of the location of logistic materiel through the Supply Chain.

135. Within the DLO and Defence Communication Service Agency, the task of recuperating stocks and equipment to pre-TELIC funded level baseline has progressed well. The maritime and fixed wing areas progressed to plan. Recuperation of the land equipment was affected in part by the retention of certain equipments in Iraq to support ongoing operations.

Soldiers of 17 Port & Maritime Regiment unload supplies from the Royal Fleet Auxiliary Fort Rosalie using Mexe-Float lighters in the Gulf.

Improving Efficiency and Effectiveness

136. The Defence Logistics Organisation is working successfully to deliver very substantial efficiency gains. We aim to achieve total savings rising to at least £565M by April 2006 through initiatives such as Lean Support Continuous Improvement, Reliability Centred Maintenance, and Management of Materiel in Transit. By taking an 'end-to-end' process perspective, the Department has already achieved £297M of efficiencies in logistics support during 2003/04.

137. For example:
- The Tornado Nose Radar Bay at RAF Marham is now operating a lean maintenance regime with a 'demand pull' supply chain. With no additional personnel or equipment, this has enabled the Bay to meet the nose radar maintenance requirements for the entire Tornado GR4 Force. This has reduced the overall service manpower requirement by 17 posts and proves the single Depth Support concept;

- Review of the Base Overhaul regime for Warrior armoured vehicles enabled the Warrior repair cycle to be reduced by 38 vehicles during the year, and a further 7 by summer 2004, returning 45 vehicles to the Field Army. This represented a productivity improvement of around 20%;

- The Joint Supply Chain (JSC). The review of the expeditionary Supply Chain in Op TELIC has completed and many of the in-theatre recommendations have been implemented and are yielding improvements in the effectiveness and efficiency of the supply chain.

138. Our SR2002 PSA sets a target of a 20% output efficiency gain in the DLO relative to April 2000. As advised in the *Annual Report and Accounts 2002/2003*, this target was rebased to a 14% saving relative to April 2002, reflecting the change in the Government's cost of capital rate from 6% to 3.5% in April 2003, which made it harder for the DLO to achieve savings from asset reductions. Against that new baseline, the DLO achieved 3.7% savings in 2003/04, for a cumulative total of 6.8% savings, ahead of the target of 6% by April 2004. These savings are being delivered by over 300 separate measures monitored and tracked by a comprehensive benefits tracking system linked to the DLO Change Programme. Key elements are set out below.

Improving Support Solutions

139. The DLO has been working to improve the effectiveness and efficiency of its logistic support solutions.During the year this has included:

- Creating twelve Pathfinder Integrated Project Teams (IPTs) to lead a breakthrough in equipment support solutions. They are expected to challenge accepted practice and find ways to improve delivery of logistics capability to the front line while achieving the best value for money for Defence. The lessons and experience gained will be shared with the wider IPT community;

- Working with IPTs across the Sea, Land and Air environments, the Lean Support Continuous Improvement Team (LSCIT) successfully developed, piloted and implemented a new approach to forward repair and capital spares purchase planning – "Zero-Based Planning". This delivered benefits of £5M in 2003/04, with a further £30M expected over the next three years;

140. The Future Defence Supply Chain Initiative (FDSCi) was established in 2002, and received Ministerial approval to enter the Assessment Phase in October 2003. As part of the Defence Logistics Transformation Programme (DLTP), FDSCi considers a range of options for improving the efficiency and effectiveness of the Defence Supply Chain. FDSCi aims to reduce costs of ownership, by £34M per annum, whilst maintaining or improving service levels and enhancing operational capability. Alternative models of in-house provision are being developed and will be considered for comparison with a potential partnered solution, for which proposals have been sought from industry by competition. An announcement of the way ahead will be made around Spring 2005, with implementation of the preferred solution around six months later.

Working with the Defence Procurement Agency (DPA)

141. The DLO and DPA have set up a Procurement Reform Programme to exploit better their collective purchasing power by co-ordinating procurement activities. The Procurement Reform Implementation Office (PRIO) is now working to establish, test and refine the basic joint underpinning processes.

Working with Customers

142. The DLO is working with the Permanent Joint Headquarters (PJHQ) and the Front Line Commands to establish a standing Joint Force Logistic Component HQ within PJHQ. This will improve the planning and delivery of in-theatre logistic support at the tactical level, which was a lesson from both Exercise SAIF SAREEA and Op TELIC. We aim to achieve Initial Operating Capability by the end of 2004, and Full Operating Capability a year later.

143. We are also taking a new approach to the Defence land vehicle fleet by adopting industry best practice for the Services. So far, improved management has enabled a reduction of the land fleet by over 2,000 vehicles. During 10-month trials of vehicle storage in Controlled Humidity Environments, a reduction in maintenance and service has already saved over 1,500 labour days.

Working with Industry

144. We are always seeking to improve how we and industry can work together to mutual benefit. For example, introduction of an availability-based contract for support of RB199 engines fitted in Tornado reduced the number of modules being repaired at Rolls-Royce's Ansty facility by 40%, with the benefits shared between the MoD and Rolls-Royce, and saving a further £17M for Defence over the next three years.

Reducing Stockholdings

145. The DLO also continues to work to ensure that the Department holds only the minimum stock and capital spares needed to support the front line. In line with this, stockholdings continued to reduce in 2003/04, including a £377M reduction in the capital spares needed to support fixed and rotary wing aircraft. Reductions delivered by existing DLO review programmes were complemented by the findings and recommendations of the End-to-End Review Team. Further rationalisation is a key theme of logistics transformation.

Transforming Logistics Delivery

End-to-End (E2E) Logistics Review

146. In addition to the various initiatives set out above, in July 2003, a review of 'end-to-end' (E2E) Air and Land logistic support reported on how logistic support to Air and Land forces, including Naval Aviation and the Royal Marines, can be streamlined across organisational boundaries, from industry to the front line, and thereby generate improved logistic effectiveness and savings for investment in other Defence priorities. The Minister of State for the Armed Forces reported the findings to Parliament on 10 September 2003. The E2E Review Final Report proposed a future support strategy recognising that small and medium-scale operations outside Europe are now the norm, and that these will require logistic support that is joint, flexible, rapidly-deployable and robust. A more detailed Demonstration Phase validating the proposed scope and pace of change was completed in April 2004. It concluded that the original recommendations were sound and that the postulated benefits could be achieved.

147. One of the E2E recommendations resulted in the role of the Chief of Defence Logistics as Process Owner for logistics across Defence being reinforced and codified. As a consequence of this change, combined with the recognised need to bring together the various different strands of logistics reform into one programme, all logistic change projects were brought together under the Defence Logistics Transformation Programme (DLTP). The DLTP includes the End-to-End Review and the logistics elements of the DLO Change Programme and aims to form a single, coherent programme of logistics transformation, across organisational boundaries from industry to the front line.

DLO Restructuring

148. In parallel, the DLO carried out a review of its structure and internal processes to create a streamlined organisation that can deliver logistic support and sustainability with greater effectiveness and efficiency. This identified six critical success factors: a more robust and 'intelligent' relationship with the front line; an organisation focused on what it produces rather than what it uses; people with the skills needed to succeed in the new climate; a more strategic relationship with industry; better use of our purchasing power to get better value for money; and a DLO structure that meets requirements. Achieving this requires reorganising the DLO to develop a better relationship with the Defence Procurement Agency that will deliver effective through-life management options, to minimise conflicts between the DLO head office and its business units, and to address the fact that, compared to industry standards, too high a proportion of DLO staff are currently involved in support functions. The DLO is therefore creating senior posts responsible for ensuring coherence in the delivery by IPTs of the outputs agreed with their customers, and developing common enabling services, such as personnel and finance, across the DLO and working jointly with the DPA where appropriate. The new structure is being introduced progressively from 2005, but in due course should produce significant further financial benefits and a reduction of some 3,000 posts.

Equipment Disposals

149. The Disposal Services Agency (DSA) had a successful year in which it achieved £22M in gross cash receipts, exceeding its in-year target of £20M. Combined with estates disposals of £207M, this gives a total annual Departmental figure of £229M. Major capital disposals, including regeneration and modernisation work by UK industry, included: the completion of the sale of one Type 22 frigate to Chile (HMS Sheffield); the completion of the sale of five Offshore Patrol Vessels to Bangladesh; the completion of the sale of three C-130 aircraft to Austria; the final instalment of a ships and Seawolf missiles sale; the sale of HMS Scylla and several other smaller vessels; and the sale of Wessex and Gazelle aircraft.

Management

Objective

To improve management, accountability and efficiency across the Department.

Public Service Agreement Target (SR2002 MoD Target 7)

- Increase value for money by making improvements in the efficiency and effectiveness of the key processes for delivering military capability. Year-on-year output efficiency gains of 2.5% will be made each year from 2002/03 to 2005/06, including through a 20% output efficiency gain in the Defence Logistics Organisation:
  - Reduce the per capita cost of successfully training a military recruit by an average of 6% by April 2006;
  - Achieve 0% average annual cost growth (or better) against the Major Equipment Procurement Projects;
  - Reduce by 14% (relative to April 2002) the output costs of the Defence Logistics Organisation, while maintaining support to the Front Line;
  - Reduce MoD Head Office and other management costs by 13%;
  - Identify for disposal land and buildings with a Net Book Value of over £300M.

Performance Measures and Assessment

- Achieve 5% cumulative overall efficiency improvement compared to 2001/2002:
  - *2.9% overall improvement during 2003/04, and 5.2% cumulative overall improvement compared to 2001/2002;*
  - *4.2% cumulative reduction in training costs (target of 4.0%);*
  - *3.1% in-year cost growth on Major Equipment Projects (target of 0%);*
  - *6.8% cumulative reduction in Logistic costs (target of 6.0%);*
  - *10.6% cumulative reduction in Head Office costs (target of 9.0%);*
  - *Cumulative value of £230M land and buildings identified for disposal (target £134M).*
  - *Individual sub-targets are reported on in detail respectively under Training, Procurement, Logistic Support, Modernising Defence, and Defence Estate.*

Introduce a new Departmental Business Management System with identified Departmental Process Owners to improve management efficiency and coherence.

- *Business Management System approved in October 2003, but full implementation delayed by diversion of resources to deliver MoD input to Gershon Review;*

- *Continued development of risk identification and management arrangements.*

Continue to meet requirements for safety, health, the environment and fire:

- *Continued to meet all health and safety obligations;*

- *Active participation in development of Government policy on sustainable development;*

- *Concluded a best practice review of health and safety in the MoD in a joint project with the Health and Safety Executive.*

Further Sources of Information

- Quarterly PSA reports to HM Treasury;

- *Delivering Security in a Changing World* (Defence White Paper, and supporting essays);

- *Delivering Security in a Changing World (Future Capabilities).*

- *UK Defence Statistics 2004;*

- Evidence given to House of Commons Defence Committee on *Annual Report and Accounts 2002/03* (HC 589-i);

- *Releasing Resources to the Front Line: Independent Review of Public Sector Efficiency* http://www.hm-treasury.gov.uk;

- *The Stewardship Report on the Defence Estate 2003.*

- *MoD Sustainable Development Report 2003/04*

Efficiency

150. The Department is committed to increasing value for money by making improvements in the efficiency and effectiveness of the key processes for delivering military capability. Our overall PSA target is to achieve year-on-year output efficiency gains of 2.5% over the period from 2002/03 to 2005/06. It is measured by the weighted average of performance against a set of process-related supporting sub-targets, the weighting being determined by the relative resources covered by each sub-target. We made a 2.9% overall improvement in 2003/2004, and remain on track to achieve the overall target. Results are set out in table 20 below.

151. Additional information on the routine management of the Department in line with Government standards is set out in Annex D. Further detail on the five individual sub-targets can be found in the respective sections of this report on Training (paragraph 110), Procurement (paragraph 123), Logistic Support (paragraph 138), Modernising Defence (paragraph 184), and Defence Estate (paragraph 101). But in summary:

- the **Training** supporting target is on its planned trajectory;

- the **Procurement** supporting target has not been achieved;

- the **Logistics** supporting target is ahead of its planned trajectory;

- the supporting target to reduce Head Office and other **Management** costs is slightly above the planned trajectory; and

- the **Estates** supporting target is running well ahead of plan.

152. The good logistics performance, which counts for over two-thirds of the overall target, and of three of the other four sub-targets, means that despite so far missing the procurement sub-target (which counts for 6% of the overall target), the Department's overall performance is slightly ahead of the overall planned trajectory.

Efficiency Review

153. This has been the second year in which the MoD has tracked its efficiency performance using a system of process-related supporting targets. The experience gained proved invaluable in responding during the year to the cross-Government Efficiency Review led by Sir Peter Gershon. In response to the Efficiency Review, the Department is now developing a more comprehensive efficiency programme, with much more sophisticated tracking of benefits and enhanced governance arrangements, which will be set out in more detail in the associated Service Delivery Agreement and Technical Note for the Department's efficiency target in SR2004. Reporting against this will commence in 2005/06.

Table 20: Efficiency Improvements

Target	Weighting	Cumulative Trajectory			
		2002/03	2003/04	2004/05	2005/06
Reduce by an average of 6% the per capita cost of successfully training a military recruit to the agreed standard.	9	2%	4%	5%	6%
Achievement		**1.7%**	**4.2%**		
Achieve 0% average annual cost growth (or better) against the equipment procurement projects included in the Major Projects Report, while meeting customer requirements.	6	0%	0%	0%	0%
Actual in-year cost growth		**5.7%**	**3.1%**		
Reduce by 20% the output costs of the Defence Logistics Organisation, while maintaining support to the Front Line.	68	2%	6%	10%	14%
Achievement		**3.1%**	**6.8%**		
Reduce MoD Head Office and other management costs by 13%.	5	5%	9%	12%	13%
Achievement		**6.3%**	**10.6%**		
Identify for disposal land and buildings with a net book value of over £300M.	12	£84M	£134M	£258M	£300M
Achievement		**£135M**	**£230M**		
Overall Target	**100**	**2%**	**5%**	**8%**	**10%**
Overall Achievement		**2.3%**	**5.2%**		

Notes:

2003/04 figures subject to validation. The 2002/03 achievement against the Procurement and Logistics targets, and the overall achievement, have been amended from those reported in the *Annual Report and Accounts 2002/2003* to reflect subsequent checking and validation.

Business Management System

154. The Department has been developing a Business Management System (BMS) to improve the coordination of work across Top Level Budget boundaries and to ensure continuous improvement in the delivery of core defence outputs. The BMS is a management framework which defines the Department's high level business processes and their interconnections, and through single point accountability, enables Process Owners to identify where process improvements can be made and efficiencies delivered.

155. In October 2003, the Defence Management Board endorsed a paper which set out the principles of the BMS and provided direction for further development work. The Head Office Board has been acting as the BMS Steering Group. The Department aims to have a BMS Framework in place by April 2005.

Performance Management

156. 2003/04 saw further development of the MoD's performance management regime. At the heart of this regime remains the Defence Balanced Scorecard, which is used to communicate the Defence Management Board's priorities and forms the framework for planning across the Department (see accompanying essay). The year has seen greater vertical alignment of performance indicators throughout the management levels of the Department's tiered planning system, with departmental targets remaining tied to the external Public Service Agreement reporting internal outputs. During the year the NAO launched a preliminary study into PSA reporting systems across Government. A number of their findings are now being incorporated.

Corporate Governance and Risk Management

157. The MoD continued to develop its system of internal control to maintain compliance with developing Government requirements, drawing on the work being carried out as part of the Government-wide programme to improve the handling of risks to Government objectives. New initiatives being implemented include smarter approvals and management of acquisition risks; improved management of scientific and information risks; a revised approach to protective security; and embracing business continuity management planning as an integral part of good management. Active management of risk is now fundamental to the effective achievement of Defence objectives, and is central to the way business is conducted within the Department. It informs operational decision-making, contingency planning, investment decisions and the financial planning process, and risk forms an integral element of the Defence Management Board's performance reviews. Combined with other audit assurance work, this has ensured that the MoD was able to produce a fully compliant Statement on Internal Control for 2003/04 (to be found in Section 2 of this document) in accordance with revised Treasury instructions.

Safety, Health, Environment and Fire (SHEF)

158. The MoD is a very active participant in the development of Government policy and targets on sustainable development. The MoD has reported progress in the first *MoD Sustainable Development Report 2003/04*. The Department attaches great importance to ensuring the health and safety of Service and civilian personnel and others affected by our activities. A joint project with the Health and Safety Executive covering a best practice review of health and safety in the MoD was completed. The review consisted of a close analysis of the processes for auditing SHEF in the Department and concluded that the internal audit system was effective and robust. The Department produced a detailed, risk-based report on Safety (in its widest sense) in the MoD for consideration by the Defence Environment and Safety Board. More details on Safety, Health, Environment and Fire activities can be found at Annex D.

Essay: MoD Performance Reporting – The Defence Balanced Scorecard

The MoD has continued to use the balanced scorecard performance management approach to assess both current and forecast performance and to help set strategic planning resource priorities. The process has been firmly embedded across the whole Department for at least the past three years. Throughout this period the departmental scorecard objectives have continued to be refined by the Defence Management Board to ensure focus is maintained on the Department's PSA targets and other key areas of strategic priority, both at DMB level and across all levels of the MoD. Departmental performance metrics and reports are now designed and policed by identified "process owners", at 3★ level, one for each objective. This ensures that comparisons between the three Services, and all 11 TLBs, can be made more effectively, and that wherever possible, greater standardisation of measurement can be achieved. Scorecard data is regularly used, not only to facilitate DMB discussions and decisions, but also as the basis of reporting Departmental performance to Parliament, No 10, HM Treasury and the Cabinet Office.

The Department's internal auditors reviewed the scorecard process in 2002 and concluded at the end of the year that it provided substantial assurance of the robustness of the underlying data and analytical systems. Since then further external reviews of scorecard data have continued to take place. An examination of our PSA reporting arrangements by the National Audit Office during 2003/04 has helped to tighten further auditability. A second NAO review is currently underway into the performance reporting of front line unit readiness.

MoD performance management expertise has been used to help other Government Departments, local authorities and other nations' Defence forces, including the US Department of Defense, develop their own performance management regimes. A number have subsequently chosen to adapt the MoD scorecard system. We continue to develop the system further in house to meet our own needs better. We are also considering its potential for selling into wider markets as a commercially available performance management tool.

Building for the Future

Personnel Strategy

Objective

To invest in personnel and develop them for the future.

Public Service Agreement Target (SR2002 MoD Target 4)

- Recruit, train, motivate and retain the personnel needed to meet the manning requirement of the Armed Forces, so that by the end of 2004, the Royal Navy and RAF achieve, and thereafter maintain, manning balance, and that by the end of 2005, the Army achieves, and thereafter maintains, manning balance:
  - Achieve single Service guidelines for deployed Separated Service.

Performance Measures and Assessment

Achieve stable Premature Voluntary Release rates for each Service:

- Royal Navy 2% Officers, 5% Ratings:
  - *As at 1 April 2003: 2.5% Officers, 5.3% Ratings;*
  - *As at 1 April 2004: 2.4% Officers, 5.7% Ratings;*

- Army 4% Officers, 6% Soldiers:
  - *As at 1 April 2003: 3.4% Officers, 5.5% Soldiers;*
  - *As at 1 April 2004: 3.7% Officers, 5.3% Soldiers;*

- Royal Air Force 2.5% Officers, 4% Other Ranks:
  - *As at 1 April 2003: 2.1% Officers, 3.9% Other Ranks;*
  - *As at 1 April 2004: 2.1% Officers, 3.7% Other Ranks.*

Achieve separated Service targets:

- Royal Navy: no more than 660 days separated service over 3 years for Able Seaman within TOPMAST; no more than 60% of time away from base port over 2 years for non-TOPMAST personnel:
  - *At 1 April 2004 the average separated service for Able Ratings was 169 days over a 3 year period. (Data not yet available for other personnel.)*

- Army: 24 month average interval between unit tours:
  - *At 1 April 2004, average tour interval was 23.3 months, but with significant variation. The Royal Armoured Corps averaged 14 months, the Infantry and Royal Artillery 18 months.*

- Royal Air Force: no more than 6% of personnel with more than 140 days detached duty over 12 months; no more than 4% of personnel with more than 280 days detached duty over 24 months:
  - *5.4% of personnel more than 140 days detached duty over 12 months;*
  - *2.4% of personnel more than 280 days detached duty over 24 months.*

5% increase in positive responses to internal Service Attitude Surveys:

- *Continuous high levels of Service satisfaction;*

- *Aggregate increase of 2.9% (to 70.6%) in positive responses to Civilian attitude survey.*

Further Sources of Information

- Quarterly PSA reports to HM Treasury;

- *Delivering Security in a Changing World* (Defence White Paper and supporting essays);

- *UK Defence Statistics 2004;*

- *The Armed Forces Overarching Personnel Strategy;*

- Evidence given to House of Commons Defence Committee on *Armed Forces Pensions and Compensation* (HC 96-i/ii) and Government Response (Cm 6109);

- Defence White Paper 2003 Supporting Essay on People (Cm 6041-II);

- Evidence given to House of Commons Public Accounts Committee on *Improving service delivery: the Veterans Agency* (HC 551) and Government response (Cm 6271);

- Veterans Agency *Annual Report and Accounts 2003/04;*

- Naval Manning Agency *Annual Report and Accounts 2003/04;*

- Army Personnel Centre *Annual Report and Accounts 2003/04;*

- RAF Personnel Management Agency *Annual Report and Accounts 2003/04;*

- *Civilian Attitude Survey, Paperclips, September 2004;*

- *Strategy for Veterans* (www.veteransagency.mod.uk/vasec/strategy.pdf);

- Medical studies on Gulf Veterans:
    - *Psychiatric Disorder in Veterans of the Persian Gulf War of 1991*, Stimpson et al, British Journal of Psychiatry, 2003, 182, 391-403;
    - *Gulf War Illness – Better, Worse, or Just the Same?*, Hotopf et al, British Medical Journal, 2003, 327, p1370;
    - *Incidence of Cancer Among UK Gulf War Veterans*, Macfarlane et al, British Medical Journal, 2003, 327, p1373;
    - *Miscarriage, Stillbirth and Congenital Malformation in the Offspring of UK Veterans of the First Gulf War*, Doyle et al, International Journal of Epidemiology, 2004, 33, 74-86;

- *1990/1991 Gulf Conflict – UK Gulf Veterans Mortality Data: Cause of Death* (www.dasa.mod.uk);

- *Clinical Findings in 111 Ex-Porton Down Volunteers*, Lee et al, Journal of the Royal Army Medical Corps, 2004, 150, 14-19.

Service Personnel Developments

Premature Voluntary Release (PVR)

159. In order to gauge the success of Armed Forces' personnel retention, the MoD tracks the number of Servicemen requesting to leave the forces before the end of their agreed term, against the goal of stable long-term PVR rates of 2% and 5% for RN Officers and ratings respectively, 4% and 6% for Army Officers and soldiers, and 2.5% and 4% for RAF Officers and other ranks. Figures for April 2003 and April 2004 are set out below. Numbers have been broadly stable over the year.

Harmony and Separated Service

160. The purpose of Harmony is to allow Service personnel to have sufficient time away from operations for unit and formation training, personal training and development, and to spend time at home with their families. All three Services have agreed 'Harmony Guidelines'. At 1 April 2004, the average separated service for Able Ratings was 169 days over a three-year period. Further data for Navy personnel is not yet available. 2003/04 saw a continuously demanding operational tempo, and enduring high levels of commitment drove Army tour intervals for some units well below the guidance figure of 24 months, although the average was just under target at 23.3 months. The RAF achieved its guidelines with only 5.4% of RAF personnel serving more than 140 days detached duty over 12 months, and only 2.8% of personnel serving more than 280 days detached duty over 24 months. The Services have identified critical shortage groups that have borne the brunt of deployments. A tri-Service group was therefore set up to examine the management of those trades hardest hit by operations, while work continued to identify means of ameliorating the impact of operations on all of our personnel. Rollout of the Joint Personnel Administration System over the next few years will greatly enhance our ability to make meaningful comparisons across the three Services.

A soldier of the Royal Irish Regiment is welcomed home.

Operational Welfare Package (OWP)

161. The Operational Welfare Package policy and its implementation continued to be well received and was employed extensively during the year, specifically during Op TELIC. Considerable efforts and resources were directed towards delivering the OWP equitably and communication between those in-theatre and at home was significantly improved. In addition, we successfully trialled and deployed portable communications systems for early entry and manoeuvre forces, and developed early entry welfare equipment packs and more meaningful welfare policy provision for submariners.

Armed Forces Pay Award

162. The Government accepted in full the independent Armed Forces Pay Review Body (AFPRB) recommendation of an above inflation pay award of 2.8% (3.2% for the lowest paid privates and lance corporals). The award compared favourably with those of other public sector workers. Baroness Dean departed after 5 years as Chair of the AFPRB, and was replaced by Professor David Greenaway. There

Table 21: PVR Rates						
	RN Officers	RN Ratings	Army Officers	Army Soldiers	RAF Officers	RAF Other Ranks
April 2003	2.5%	5.3%	3.4%	5.5%	2.1%	3.9%
April 2004	2.4%	5.7%	3.7%	5.3%	2.1%	3.7%

are also two new Review Body members, Dr Peter Knight from the University of Central England and Mr Robert Burgin, a former Group Managing Director of Cambridge Water plc, Gas and Electricity Companies.

Housing

163. The Defence Housing Strategy is now in place to direct the future provision of housing through a 'mixed economy', comprising both high quality service family accommodation in the right locations to support mobility and choice for those individuals who choose greater stability. The Strategy will be delivered through a mix of private finance, rentals, hirings and capital expenditure, together with the provision of more help and advice for Service personnel on their housing options. As far as possible, basing and posting will also be focused to enable greater choice. As part of the Defence Housing Strategy, a Business Process Review of the Management and Delivery of Defence Housing has been completed. A number of recommendations were made to enable more effective and efficient management and delivery and to improve customer service, including the merger of DE and DHE, which took place on 1 April 2004. Performance against Service Family Accommodation upgrade targets is reported at paragraph 97.

Families

164. The Service Families Task Force continued to address issues affecting Service Families. A tri-Service relocation policy and aide memoire, to be given to all families when they are notified of a posting, was produced. The Tri-Service Schools Liaison Policy was issued, implemented and reviewed, resulting in a better and more co-ordinated liaison with schools and local authorities. The Tri-Service Families Working Group was re-vitalised to address policy issues affecting communications with families, housing, education, children, Foreign and Commonwealth families, and health. Consideration of family issues is firmly embedded within the personnel policy process and Ministers and officials across Government are fully aware of the unique position and challenges faced by the families of Service personnel.

Pension and Compensation Scheme

165. A bill to introduce the new Armed Forces Pension and Compensation Scheme is progressing through Parliament. Significant progress has been made on the Tri-Service Act, though the timetable remains demanding.

Resettlement

166. An Early Service Leavers policy was developed and agreed with the single Services to ensure all Service personnel, regardless of length of service, receive some form of resettlement. Guidance Notes for Early Service Leavers Resettlement Staff were issued in February 2004. Based on available data for the first five months of the year, 96.6% of Service leavers who make use of the Career Transition Partnership find employment within six months of discharge.

Service Personnel Strategy

167. The Armed Forces Overarching Personnel Strategy (AFOPS) provided a useful framework and was the driving force behind a number of important change initiatives. However, we have recognised that AFOPS does not focus sufficiently on the future and does not present information in a particularly manageable format. Consequently, the Service Personnel Plan and Balanced Scorecard were implemented, on 1 April 2004, to improve the analysis of how we are delivering sufficient, capable and motivated personnel today, and how we are preparing for the challenges of tomorrow.

Civilian Personnel Developments

168. The Civilian HR Transformation programme is implementing the new strategy for civilian personnel that was introduced in 2002. The six overall objectives are: an effective strategic HR capability leading the development of the civilian contribution to defence; better planning and preparation for the future; a sharper focus on performance; a line management culture of managing work through people; a better experience of working in MoD; and a more open, diverse and participative culture. Details on specific programme developments are tracked under the Defence Change Programme, and reported under the section below on Modernising Defence.

Personnel Attitude Survey Results

Royal Navy

169. The Personnel Attitude Surveys remained broadly the same as the previous year with the same top three issues for both satisfaction and dissatisfaction. RN personnel were most satisfied with security of employment (86%), medical and dental facilities (73%) and kit replacement (69%). They were least satisfied with the inability to plan own life long term (64%), degree of recognition and reward for long hours other than pay (58%), and separation from family and friends (53%). These reflect the benefits of employment in the Royal Navy and the nature of its role.

Army

170. A large number of officers and soldiers reported their satisfaction with Army life was high. Job security and job satisfaction topped the list. Satisfaction with combat clothing and equipment increased steadily between December 2002 and December 2003. The top two factors of dissatisfaction were operational commitments and the impact of Army lifestyle on personal and domestic life, with growing concern regarding accommodation, harmony, equipment and conditions of service. The level of officer satisfaction with the frequency and length of operational tours decreased between December 2002 and December 2003, while the level of soldier satisfaction remained steady.

RAF

171. The majority of officers and airmen reported they enjoyed serving in the Royal Air Force. Job satisfaction, quality of line management and the opportunity to gain qualifications and extend skills and knowledge topped the list. The main areas of concern were the effects of operational commitments, the effects of change programmes, civilianisation and contractorisation and the impact of Service life on family life.

Civilian

172. We have now concluded the second year of the continuous Civilian Attitude Survey, with improvement across the majority of areas covered, and an aggregate increase in positive responses of 2.9% to 70.6% overall. Over 90% of staff reported a good or better awareness of the how their job contributes to the Department's aims and objectives. 84% stated they were encouraged to develop their skills and knowledge at work and 86% that they had been spoken to, in the previous six months, about their performance, progress and development. In addition, there was an increase in the number of people who felt the MoD was an Equal Opportunities Employer as well as in those who felt fairly treated at work.

Investors in People (IiP)

173. At 31 March 2004, all MoD staff, military and civilian, apart from those in newly formed units, were working in organisations recognised as Investors in People. Six Top level Budget (TLB) areas had achieved recognition at that level and two further TLBs were working towards recognition at that level. A programme of recognition and post-recognition review is taking place, with a number of organisations making effective use of the internal review arrangements. We have played a leading role in the development of Investors in People across the Civil Service and in the development of a new national IiP Standard.

Veterans

174. The Department supports the Under Secretary of State in his role as Minister for Veterans with responsibility for drawing together policy and delivery across Government on issues affecting veterans. The work entails close cooperation with other Government Departments, the Devolved Administrations and the corporate and the voluntary sectors, particularly the ex-Service organisations.

Strategy for Veterans

175. The Strategy for Veterans published in March 2003 was developed to cover three areas of activity: improvements in the transition from service to civilian life; provision of support to veterans who need it; and enhancement of the recognition and status of veterans in society. During the year, projects involving a range of stakeholders have been continued or launched:

- The start of a new pilot study into the mentoring of vulnerable veterans, linked to the new Early Service Leavers policy;

- The start of work with the Department of Health and the Devolved Administrations to improve the understanding in the NHS of Service-related health problems affecting veterans;

- A range of initiatives with the public, voluntary and corporate sectors to prevent or tackle homelessness and joblessness among veterans;

- The start of work with the Home Office and HM Prison Service to ensure that every Prison Service Resettlement Team in the UK is aware of the support that the ex-Service organisations can provide for ex-Service prisoners and their families both during the period of imprisonment, when shortly to be released, and after release;

- Development with Citizens Advice Bureaus and others to improve veterans' advice arrangements, available to them across Government;

- Cooperation with the £27M Big Lottery Fund 'Veterans Reunited' programme to allow Second World War veterans to attend commemorative events linked to the 60th anniversaries of the Second World War in 2004/5;

- Cooperation with the Home Office and the UK Passport Service on the provision of concessionary passports for UK veterans and their carers attending Second World War commemorations in 2004/5;

- The launch of a major education project on veteran-related issues led by DfES and the Imperial War Museum, initially linked to and funded under the 'Veterans Reunited' programme;

- Preparation of a series of booklets on major campaigns, initially linked to the 60th anniversaries;

- Preparation for the introduction of a new 'UK Veteran' badge which will be issued in the first instance to First and Second World war veterans and those veterans involved in the 'Veterans Reunited' programme;

- The start of work with other Government Departments and the ex-Service organisations to develop a pilot 'Veterans Awareness Week' to be held for the first time in July 2005.

1990/91 Gulf Veterans

176. The £8.5M MoD sponsored research programme into the health of veterans of the 1990/91 Gulf Conflict has continued throughout the year. A number of medical/scientific papers have been published as a result including, in December 2003, a paper in the British Medical Journal reporting the incidence of cancer among veterans and, in March 2004, a paper in the International Journal of Epidemiology looking at the reproductive health of veterans. Mortality data for veterans of the 1990/91 Gulf Conflict is published every six months, with 2003/04 figures issued in July 2003 and January 2004: these showed there is no difference in the overall mortality of Gulf veterans compared to the control group.

Operation TELIC Veterans

177. A research programme into the health of Service personnel returning from recent and ongoing operations in Iraq was announced on 7 May 2003. Three main studies are underway; a study into the physical and psychological health, a study on relevant battlefield exposures, and a study to establish normal levels of uranium in the urine of a military population that did not deploy.

Depleted Uranium (DU)

178. A retrospective DU testing programme for concerned veterans of the 1990/91 Gulf Conflict and Balkans operations, developed by the independent Depleted Uranium Oversight Board, was prepared and a pilot testing exercise began in March 2004 at centres in London and Glasgow. The MoD's voluntary biological monitoring programme for DU for Op TELIC personnel has continued. As at 31 March 2004, some 250 personnel had had urine tests for DU. Contracts were issued for the first proposals in MoD's DU research programme. The first review workshop was held in October 2003. The research programme continues and a second workshop is planned for October 2004.

Porton Down Volunteers

179. In March 2004, a paper reporting the clinical findings in 111 ex-Porton Down Volunteers seen at the Medical Assessment Programme was published in the Journal of the Royal Army Medical Corps.

The study found no clinical evidence linking ill-health with participation in the volunteer programme, and found no unusual patterns of disease. The separate epidemiological survey of Porton Down Volunteers continues. The Crown Prosecution Service continues to consider a single potential case for prosecution, having ruled that in all other cases there was insufficient evidence to prosecute former scientists involved in the testing of chemical agents on human volunteers between 1939 and 1989.

Medical Assessment Programme

180. The Medical Assessment Programme, based at St Thomas' Hospital in London, was originally established to provide as full a diagnosis as possible to veterans of the 1990/1991 Gulf Conflict concerned about their health. The scope has since been extended to include former Porton Down Volunteers and, on 7 May 2003, it was announced that the Programme would also see veterans of Op TELIC. During 2003/04, the Programme saw 51 veterans of the 1990/91 Gulf Conflict, 5 Porton Down Volunteers and 16 veterans of Operation TELIC. Of those who responded to a patient questionnaire, 97% were satisfied with the Programme.

Essay: The Hutton Report – Learning the Lessons

Following the publication of the Hutton Report on 28 January 2004 into the death of Dr David Kelly, the PUS announced that the Department would be reviewing its procedures in light of Lord Hutton's findings. Lord Hutton's Report made two direct criticisms of the Department with regard to Dr Kelly: not telling him in advance that his name would be confirmed if it was put to the Department and not having a system in place to ensure he was informed the moment his name was made public. Both of these criticisms have been accepted and appropriate responses taken in terms of the way the Department communicates with and supports individuals in the media spotlight.

Learning the lessons of Hutton and providing the best personnel processes and support mechanisms for staff is a continuing project in MoD and across Government. We are always working to improve our procedures and we are taking account of the wider lessons of the Hutton Inquiry to build on work already underway before the Inquiry to streamline the guidance and training available to staff and line managers. The Department's rules on contact with the media have been closely examined in the light of the Inquiry. This review concluded that the current rules are broadly "sound" but we are taking the opportunity to issue updated rules in line with our drive to make all guidance as clear and straightforward as possible.

Contact with the Media

It remains vital for the coherent presentation of Defence that the Press Office is informed of communication with the media by anyone within the Department. Therefore our core rule remains – all contact with the media must be authorised in advance. The Department has conducted an audit of posts requiring media contact to identify post holders whose duties bring them into regular contact with the media. The aim of this has been to ensure that individuals who are required to communicate with the media in their posts have the appropriate training and support from the Press Office, and perform this duty within the boundaries of MoD and civil service rules. October 2004 will see the issue of a Defence Council Instruction containing the Department's reinforced rules on contact with the media, reflecting the lessons of Hutton and wider Departmental experience.

Issues of Conscience

The Civil Service and the MoD encourage people to speak up when they feel something is wrong. The Department is issuing comprehensive guidance on the appropriate ways to raise what are termed issues of conscience or professional concerns, both informally and formally in a Defence Council Instruction in October 2004. Generally, the best way to do this is through the normal management chain but there may be circumstances when an individual would find it difficult to raise the matter with his or her manager. To cater for this, MoD has nominated four senior officials who can be approached in confidence with any such concerns by civil servants working in any part of the Department. They are Richard Hatfield (Personnel Director), Carl Mantell (Director General Central Budget), Deborah Loudon (Director General Security and Safety) and Stan Porter (Commercial and Supplier Relations Director in the Defence Procurement Agency).

Parliamentary Committees

Comparatively few staff in the Department will ever experience appearing before Parliamentary Committees, but for those who do, part of the future preparation for these appearances will be a pre-assessment of any media implications likely to arise from it. A member of the Press Office will attend each evidence session, and a post appearance debrief will give individuals a chance to talk about their questioning by a Committee. Advice on media attention is available from the Press Office. These new measures are reflected in the Department's revised guidance for witnesses appearing before Select Committees which the Secretary of State approved in August 2004.

Training

Staff will, in the course of their work, sometimes find themselves operating under pressure. We are examining how we can improve the training given to line managers firstly to identify, and subsequently to support staff who may be in this position. The MoD's civil/military working structure is a unique environment, and this extension of training will therefore also be aimed at those military personnel who manage civilians.

Personnel Policy and the rules

More generally, the personnel rules and guidance that exist within each Top Level Budget (TLB) and Agency must follow the MoD core set of personnel rules and be easy to use and consistently applied throughout the Department. This will greatly facilitate movement throughout the Department and across TLB boundaries. The PUS has written to all TLB holders and Agency and Trading Fund Chief Executives reinforcing this point and the HR Transformation programme will build on this in updating and clarifying polices and rules wherever necessary.

Modernising Defence

Objective

To modernise Defence to meet future military requirements.

Public Service Agreement Target (SR2002 MoD Target 7)

- Increase value for money by making improvements in the efficiency and effectiveness of the key processes for delivering military capability:
  - Reduce MoD Head Office and other management costs by 13%.

Performance Measures and Assessment

Implementation of the Defence Information Strategy to provide Defence Information Infrastructure Initial Operating Capability by July 2005 and Full Operating Capability by December 2008, and ensure personnel are competent in the use of Information and Communication Technology:

- *Defence Information Infrastructure programme on course. Incremental improvements to MoD computing infrastructure underway. Head Office element of DII went live 24 May 2004.*

Smaller and more effective Head Office, reducing numbers by 600 to 3,000 for return to Main Building, and cumulative reduction of 9% in Head Office and other management costs by April 2004:

- *10% reduction in Head Office posts;*

- *4.3% further reduction in Head Office and other management costs in year, producing 10.6% cumulative reduction since April 2002.*

Implementation of baseline civilian Human Resources Management System (HRMS) with complete roll-out by April 2004:

- *Successful roll-out of HRMS across the Department.*

Achieve Initial Gate approval for establishment of civilian personnel Service Delivery Organisation by March 2004:

- *Initial Gate approved March 2004.*

Implementation of Joint Personnel Administration System (JPAS):

- *Implementation of JPAS on track. Harmonisation of pay and allowance policies endorsed and procurement strategy approved.*

Further Sources of Information

- Quarterly PSA reports to HM Treasury;

- *Delivering Security in a Changing World* (Defence White Paper and supporting essays);

- *Armed Forces Personnel Administration Agency Annual Report and Accounts 2003/04;*

- *Pay and Personnel Agency Annual Report and Accounts 2003/04;*

- *UK Defence Statistics 2004.*

Defence Change Programme

181. The Defence Change Programme joins up the major change initiatives across defence and introduces strong central direction and guidance to produce a single, coherent and prioritised modernisation programme that ensures key initiatives have robust governance and plans, with clearly identified benefits. The Programme aims to maximise investment in front-line operational capability by driving through improvements in departmental business processes. It is supported by the £580M Defence Modernisation Fund secured from HM Treasury in the 2002 Spending Review. Rigorous governance arrangements are key to the success of the Defence Change Programme. These include:

- **Top level ownership:** Senior Responsible Owners have been appointed for all major change initiatives and are personally accountable for maximising the delivery of benefits. Each programme is sponsored by one of the Department's Ministers;

- The **Defence Change Programme Board** leads, directs and manages the Defence Change Programme. The Board is responsible for cross-cutting issues such as common risks and interdependencies, together with loading and capacity issues; and

- Chaired by the Secretary of State, the **Change Delivery Group** challenges and supports major change initiatives across Defence and manages allocation of the Defence Modernisation Fund.

182. Key central enabling elements of the programme are set out in more detail below. Other important aspects of the overall change programme are covered separately in this report. These include modernisation of Estate delivery (paragraphs 102-104), Defence Training and Education (paragraphs 109-110) and Logistics Transformation (paragraphs 146-148).

Enabling Infrastructure

183. Following on from the Defence Information Strategy, good progress has been made in delivering the **Defence Information Infrastructure (DII) Programme**. The DII Programme will establish a single information infrastructure for Defence, replacing over 300 diverse information systems across 2000 locations worldwide. This programme will also enable many of the other benefits delivered by the Defence Change Programme, such as the modernisation of both military and civilian human resource management. It will also provide critical support to elements of the Equipment Programme and to the development of Networked Enabled Capability, which future military operations will demand. Placement of the main DII contract is expected in early 2005. Incremental improvements to the Department's computing infrastructure are already well underway, including the Head Office element of the DII, which went live as scheduled in May 2004, closely followed by Fleet HQ in July 2004.

The >home Programme

184. The **>home** (Head Office Modern Environment) Programme is a comprehensive modernisation programme embracing the redevelopment of Main Building, and the introduction of new technology and improved working practises. The Main Building Redevelopment (MBR) project remains on budget and several months ahead of contract completion. Approximately 3,100 staff began reoccupying Main Building over the summer of 2004, culminating in full building occupancy in September 2004. The increased capacity of Main Building allows the MoD to remain on target to dispose of five other buildings (Northumberland House, Metropole Building, St Giles Court, Great Scotland Yard and St Christopher House). Main Building redevelopment has been used as a catalyst for change at the corporate centre of the MoD, allowing activities to be concentrated as part of an overall reduction in staff in central London from 6,000 to 4,900 since 1999. St George's Court has been retained to accommodate some 900 non-Head Office personnel required to be in London, while the Old War Office continues to house the Defence Intelligence Staff. We reduced Head Office and other management costs by a further 4.3% during the year, reaching a cumulative reduction of 10.6% against an end year cumulative target of 9%. We are therefore slightly ahead of target to achieve the 13% reduction by April 2006 called for in our SR2002 PSA.

The Ministry of Defence's Main Building, Whitehall.

Managing People

185. We continued to introduce new information systems and harmonised and simplified personnel policies and processes designed to modernise service personnel management. The Joint Personnel Administration programme will be rolled out across the three Services towards the end of 2005 and through 2006, enabling considerable financial savings, chiefly through a leaner administrative function, as well as significant practical benefits, including management information to support evidence-based policy making, improved tracking of personnel deployed on operations and identification of reinforcements. The project continues to progress satisfactorily. Harmonised and simplified pay and allowances policies have been endorsed, the procurement strategy was agreed in early 2004 and we are now working with the contractor, EDS, to deliver the system. The Joint Personnel Administration Centre (JPAC) was opened in Glasgow in June 2004.

186. The Civilian Human Resources Transformation Programme has two pillars, to define the MoD's future requirements for personnel services and to develop the organisation to deliver those services. Good progress has been made with both pillars, and the project to deliver the Service Delivery Modernisation Programme passed its Initial Gate in March 2004. Additionally, the new Human Resource Management System (HRMS), covering all the Department's civilian staff, was successfully rolled out across the Department by the end of March 2004. This provides a core personnel management tool that will over time facilitate a more strategic approach to civilian skills and workforce planning.

Working with other Government Departments

187. In addition to the specialist military capabilities routinely provided by the Services to Home Departments, such as search and rescue, fisheries protection and explosive ordnance disposal (see Output and Deliverables), the MoD continued to expand its work with other Government Departments, Devolved Administrations and agencies. This both maximises the most efficient delivery of defence objectives, and also ensures that the significant contribution we can make to wider Government objectives is understood and taken into account by the Departments concerned.

188. Good progress was made to expand joint working with the **Department of Health** under the NHS/MoD Partnership Board. A surgical team from the University Hospital Birmingham NHS Trust deployed to Bosnia in 2003 to provide clinical care to deployed troops. When not deployed, military doctors and nurses worked within the NHS, providing health services for both military and civilian patients. The NHS has been actively engaged in ensuring that reception arrangements for military patients returning from Op TELIC worked effectively. Since June 2001, University Hospital Birmingham Trust has been the main receiving hospital for routine aeromedical evacuations back to the UK. We remain committed to developing further the military medical centre of excellence already up and running at the Royal Centre for Defence Medicine (RCDM) in Birmingham. The University of Central England and the Defence School of Health Studies deliver nurse training in Birmingham. We continued to work closely with the Southampton University Hospitals NHS Trust to provide a paediatric aeromedical evacuation capability for Service dependants stationed overseas. There are also good working relations between the MoD's Defence Leadership Centre, the NHS Leadership Centre, and the Centre of Health Leadership Wales.

189. Working with the **Department for Education and Skills,** our youth initiative in schools, Skill Force, was successfully established as a public interest company supported by grant in aid. It continues to use former Service personnel to deliver key skills training to disaffected young people with outstanding impact on their attendance, employment and education outcomes. With an almost 80% reduction in those not entering employment, education or training on leaving school, Skill Force represents excellent value for money. Each team produces outcomes which save £0.5M annually to the public purse. As set out in Training, in Enabling Processes, we also provide a wide range of training and education to Defence personnel, ranging from basic literacy and numeracy skills to complex technical and professional training, and we work to ensure that this training is recognised by appropriate national qualifications.

190. In taking forwards issues affecting **Service Veterans**, we have coordinated our work closely both with other Government Departments and a wide range of corporate and voluntary sector stakeholders. Key Government partners during the year included the Department of Health and the Devolved Administrations on health initiatives affecting veterans; the Office of the Deputy Prime Minister and the Department of Work and Pensions on initiatives to tackle aspects of social exclusion among some veterans; the Department of Culture, Media and Sport and the New Opportunities Fund (now the Big Lottery Fund) on the 'Veterans Reunited' initiative; the Department for Education and Skills on education projects linked to veterans issues; the Department for Constitutional Affairs on public information strategies of potential benefit to veterans; and the Home Office and UK Passport Service on passport concessions for Second World War veterans attending commemorative events in 2004/05.

Science, Technology and Equipment

Objective

To invest in technology and develop equipment capability for the future.

Performance Measures and Assessment

Access to the technology the MoD needs to support defence capability requirements:

- *Establishment of Research Acquisition Organisation on schedule;*

- *Placing of research contracts for over £440M;*

- *Establishment of three Defence Technology Centres;*

- *Establishment of a Tower of Excellence for Underwater Sensors.*

Assessment of Future Capability Requirements:

- *Future capability requirements and gaps assessed and identified.*

Coherence, Integration and Affordability of the Equipment Plan:

- *The 2004 Equipment Plan made provision for continued investment in areas identified as key to the UK's future military capability.*

Further Sources of Information

- Quarterly PSA reports to HM Treasury;

- *Defence Science and Innovation Strategy*
  www.mod.uk/issues/science_innovation;

- *Delivering Security in a Changing World* (Defence White Paper and supporting essays);

- *Delivering Security in a Changing World: Future Capabilities;*

- NAO report on *The Management of Defence Research and Technology* (HC 360);

- Defence Science and Technology Laboratory (Dstl) *Annual Report and Accounts 2003/04;*

- *UK Defence Statistics 2004.*

Technology in Support of Capability Requirements

191. In addition to driving forward the Departmental Science and Technology research programme (placing contracts for over £440M), the MoD science staffs made a significant contribution to the planning and conduct of operations in Iraq, and also to the post-conflict "lessons identified" process. Science and technology research has led to notable advances in the protection and treatment of personnel, and has identified scope for significant savings in both near-term and long-term equipment acquisition.

192. The main benefits that MoD obtains from its investment in Science and Technology are provision of war winning capability, from support to front-line operations to far-reaching novel technology solutions; underpinning operational, procurement and capability analysis which leads to enhanced performance, new capabilities, cost reduction and risk reduction in the Equipment Programme; identification of emerging threats and the potential solutions to them; enabling the UK to be a significant player in the international arena as a valued partner for research and project collaboration; major enabling support to the battle against terror and the gathering of information to combat it; and through technology transfer, helping to underpin the competitiveness of our national Defence industry.

193. We have cooperated closely with the National Audit Office in its review of *The Management of Defence Research and Technology* during the year. The NAO review was a positive document and stated that progress was being made through greater alignment with MoD high level policy and strategy, a move to managing research by outputs for greater focus of research on what we wish to achieve, good progress on competition of the work and partnership initiatives, such as Defence Technology Centres (see below). We accept the NAO report's view that a good start had been made but further work was required. We are looking to draw on their suggestions to build on our progress.

Management of research by output

194. The MoD is moving towards management by output rather than management by input. Within this, the Science and Technology community has developed a set of seven outputs for the direction and management of the Science and Technology research programme; each strategy sets out what it is trying to achieve and how success will be measured. We have also established a new Research Acquisition Organisation, which is located at the Defence Academy in Shrivenham.

Initiatives for partnership

195. Three Defence Technology Centres (DTCs) were established last year, for Data and Information Fusion, Human Factors Integration, and Electromagnetic Remote Sensing. We are looking to establish an additional DTC, and subject areas are being considered. The DTCs are a key element in achieving improved collaboration with industry and academia. They represent a new approach to delivering the Department's research needs: MoD concentrates on defining the outcomes it requires, allowing the DTC industrial and academic partners the freedom to use their combined expertise and experience to propose innovative and cost-effective solutions. We also established a further Tower of Excellence, for Underwater Sensors, in addition to those for Guided Weapons and Radar established last year (Towers of Excellence are focused towards the system-level application of research).

Defence Science & Technology Laboratory (Dstl)

196. Dstl provides the Government's core expertise on defence and security-related science and engineering. This year there have been many defence and security-related problems where science and technology have provided the solution or supported key decisions, not least in Iraq where we have continued to make a significant contribution to military operations. Dstl published an initial technical strategy and will now work with MoD to identify those areas where Dstl involvement in the programme should be a priority and where most impact can be made. At the end of year, Ministers endorsed Dstl's proposals to concentrate its activities on three core sites at Porton Down, Portsdown West and Fort Halstead. It will now focus on how it intends to move to a more integrated laboratory, not only with regard to the physical environment, but also in terms of business processes, culture and technical capability.

Future Capability Requirements

197. Early visibility of potential future capability gaps is important to deliver a balanced defence capability that will continue to allow the Armed Forces to meet the Government's requirements over time. Potential shortfalls in the Armed Forces' future operational effectiveness are assessed by a variety of means including scenario modelling taking account of anticipated concurrency demands. The results, together with the outcome of the annual Equipment Capability Audit, provide a rounded picture of where capability gaps might arise. This work informs the Defence Strategic Guidance and the Equipment Plan, and the results are routinely reported to the Defence Management Board. Our future requirements were set out in the July 2004 White Paper *Delivering Security in a Changing World: Future Capabilities*.

Coherence, Integration and Affordability of the Equipment Plan

198. The 2004 Equipment Plan, building on the additional resources made available in the 2002 Spending Review, has made provision for continued investment in those areas identified as key to the UK's future military capability. This includes investing in areas such as Network Enabled Capability, deployability and precision effects. The Department's ability to identify, prioritise and appropriately fund key capabilities such as these has been improved by the effective use of the Decision Conferencing process, which draws together stakeholders from across the Department, and the utilisation of Whole Life Cost data.

Section 2

Consolidated Departmental
Resource Accounts 2003-04

Annual Report

History and Background

The present Ministry of Defence (MoD), the Department, was formed by the amalgamation in 1964 of the Ministry of Defence, the Admiralty, the War Office and the Air Ministry, and the inclusion in 1971 of the Ministry of Aviation Supply. In 1973, the operations of the Atomic Weapons Establishment (AWE) were transferred from the UK Atomic Energy Authority to the MoD.

Principal Activity

The principal activity of the Department is to deliver security for the people of the United Kingdom and the Overseas Territories by defending them, including against terrorism; and to act as a force for good by strengthening international peace and stability.

Further definition of the Departmental Objectives in terms of output is given in Schedule 5, Resources by Departmental Aims and Objectives.

Departmental Boundary

At 31 March 2004 the Department consisted of the 11 (2002-03:11) Top Level Budget (TLB) Holders detailed in Note 27 to the financial statements, responsible for providing forces and support services required for a modern defence force. Within these TLBs there were 72 (2002-03: 81) reporting entities known as management groupings. There are 30 (2002-03: 31) on-vote Defence agencies listed in Note 31. All on-vote agencies are also management groupings, except for the Defence Procurement Agency (a TLB) and the Disposal Services Agency (part of a management grouping). Also included within the Departmental Boundary are Advisory Non-Departmental Public Bodies (NDPB) sponsored by the Department listed in Note 31. Defence Agencies also publish their own financial statements.

The five (2002-03: five) Defence Executive Agencies established as Trading Funds and owned by the Department at 31 March 2004 fall outside the Departmental Boundary and are detailed in Note 10. The seven Executive NDPBs listed in Note 11 are sponsored by the Department and fall outside the Departmental Boundary. The accounts of these bodies are published separately.

QinetiQ Holdings Limited (hereafter referred to as "QinetiQ") is a Self-Financing Public Corporation which falls outside the Departmental Boundary. The Navy, Army and Air Force Institutes (NAAFI) is also outside the Departmental Boundary.

The transactions and balances of the Armed Forces Pension Scheme (AFPS) are not consolidated within these financial statements. The report and accounts of the AFPS are prepared separately.

Future Developments

The Defence White Paper, published in December 2003, set out the Department's analysis of the future security environment, the implications for defence, strategic priorities and how it intends to adapt its planning and force structures to meet potential threats. Using the policy baseline established in the White Paper and following a rigorous examination of force structure, specific equipment requirements and supporting infrastructure, manpower and organisational structure, the Secretary of State set out, in July 2004, the changes the Department should make to the force structure and its key capacity requirements for the future.

From 1 April 2004 a new Top Level Budget was created called the Corporate Science Technology TLB. Headed up by the Chief Scientific Advisor this TLB brings together functions formerly managed in different areas of the department relating to science and technology. As at that date the Department also merged the Defence Housing Executive Agency and Defence Estates Agency with the aim of making efficiencies and improvements to the delivery of service housing. In addition, the three service manning agencies, the Naval Manning Agency, the Army Personnel Centre and the RAF Personnel Management Agency were disestablished. These changes arose as a result of one of the recommendations of a major end to end review of the Service Personnel Process and will contribute towards the rationalisation of the Armed Forces manpower, planning and career management functions as well as giving stronger emphasis to the needs of individual Service personnel.

Fixed Assets

Changes in fixed assets during the year are summarised in Notes 8, 9 and 10 to the financial statements.

Research and Development

Research and development expenditure is incurred mainly for the future benefit of the Department. Such expenditure is primarily incurred on the development of new fighting equipment and on the improvement of the effectiveness and capability of existing fighting equipment.

Amounts spent on research are not capitalised, and certain development expenditure is expensed, in accordance with SSAP13 "Accounting for Research and Development", and are included in Other Operating Costs detailed in Note 3.

Development expenditure is included in Intangible Assets, where appropriate, and shown in Note 8.

Net Expenditure

The Operating Cost Statement shows net expenditure of £34,530,547,000 which has been charged to the General Fund. Cash voted by Parliament and drawn down for the provision of Defence Capability (RfR 1), Conflict Prevention (RfR 2) and War Pensions and Allowances (RfR 3) amounting to £29,257,550,000 has been credited to the General Fund (Note 18).

Operating and Financial Review

The Operating and Financial Review is included on pages 97 to 98.

Management

Ministers who had responsibility for the Department during the year were:

Secretary of State for Defence
>The Right Honourable Geoffrey Hoon, MP

Minister of State for the Armed Forces
>The Right Honourable Adam Ingram, MP

Parliamentary Under Secretary of State for Defence and Minister for Defence Procurement
>The Lord Bach of Lutterworth

Parliamentary Under Secretary of State for Defence and Minister for Veterans
>Dr Lewis Moonie, MP (to 13 June 2003)
>Ivor Caplin, MP (appointed 13 June 2003)

Composition of Defence Management Board (DMB), during the year ended 31 March 2004:

Permanent Under Secretary of State
>Sir Kevin Tebbit KCB CMG

Chief of the Defence Staff
>Admiral the Lord Boyce GCB OBE DL (to 1 May 2003)
>General Sir Michael Walker GCB CMG CBE ADC Gen (appointed 2 May 2003)

First Sea Lord and Chief of the Naval Staff
>Admiral Sir Alan West GCB DSC ADC

Chief of the General Staff
>General Sir Mike Jackson KCB CBE DSO ADC Gen

Chief of the Air Staff
>Air Chief Marshal Sir Peter Squire GCB DFC AFC DSc ADC FRAeS RAF (to 31 July 2003)
>Air Chief Marshal Sir Jock Stirrup KCB AFC ADC FRAeS FCMI RAF (appointed 1 August 2003)

Vice Chief of the Defence Staff
>Air Chief Marshal Sir Anthony Bagnall GBE KCB FRAeS RAF

Second Permanent Under Secretary of State
>Ian Andrews CBE TD

Chief of Defence Procurement
>Sir Robert Walmsley KCB FEng FIEE (to 30 April 2003)
>Sir Peter Spencer KCB (appointed 1 May 2003)

Chief of Defence Logistics
>Air Chief Marshal Sir Malcolm Pledger KCB OBE AFC BSc FRAeS RAF

Chief Scientific Adviser
>Professor Sir Keith O'Nions FRS

Non-Executive members
>Charles Miller Smith, Chairman of Scottish Power
>Philippa Foster Back, Director of the Institute of Business Ethics

Since the end of the financial year the following changes in appointment have arisen:

Lieutenant General Kevin O'Donoghue CBE to be appointed Chief of Defence Logistics on 1 January 2005 in succession to Air Chief Marshal Sir Malcolm Pledger KCB OBE AFC BSc FRAeS RAF.

Professor Roy Anderson FRS to be appointed Chief Scientific Advisor on 4 October 2004 in succession to Professor Sir Keith O'Nions FRS.

Trevor Woolley, Finance Director, was appointed to the Board on 24 June 2004.

Remuneration of Ministers, and details of salary and pension entitlements of the members of the DMB, are shown in Note 2.3.

The Methodology of Senior Appointments

The Senior Civil Service was formed in April 1996 through an Order in Council. The recruitment principles, and their application, under which senior appointments, including those of the Permanent Under Secretary of State and Second Permanent Under Secretary of State, are made are specified in the "Commissioners' Recruitment Code", responsibility for which lies with the Civil Service Commissioners.

The Chief of Defence Procurement and the Chief Scientific Adviser are recruited on three year fixed-term appointments. The conditions covering the termination of their employment are set out in their contract documents.

The Chief of the Defence Staff, Vice Chief of the Defence Staff, Single-Service Chiefs of Staff and Chief of Defence Logistics are appointed on the recommendation of the Secretary of State for Defence to the Prime Minister. The final approval of the appointee lies with Her Majesty The Queen.

Pension Liabilities

Pension liabilities for the majority of civilian personnel and Service personnel are provided by the Civil Service Pension Scheme (CSP) arrangements and the Armed Forces Pension Scheme (AFPS) respectively. The Department makes regular payments of Accruing Superannuation Liability Charge (ASLC) into the relevant pension schemes at rates determined by the Government Actuary.

On 1 October 2002 the new CSP arrangements came into effect. Since that date all new entrants to the Department have had the option to join either the defined benefits (DB) scheme, known as "Premium", or to join the defined contributions (DC) scheme which is known as "Partnership". The previous scheme, now known as "classic", was closed to new members when the new CSP arrangements came into effect. Member contributions to Premium are 3.5% and are considered to be a general contribution to the scheme. Members in Classic continue to contribute 1.5% in respect of the Widows Pension Scheme (WPS) benefits. The Department's contributions to Partnership vary depending on the age of the individual and the amount that they contribute.

Both the Premium and Classic schemes are accounted for as Defined Contribution schemes in accordance with Treasury requirements. The pension liabilities are not included in the Department's Balance Sheet. The financial statements of these schemes are published separately.

Elements of Remuneration

Senior Civil Service and Ministers' emoluments are reviewed annually by the Review Body on Senior Salaries (SSRB). For civil servants outside the Senior Civil Service, emoluments are set on the basis of annual negotiations between the Department and the Trades Unions.

Emoluments for Service personnel are paid in accordance with rank and conditions of service and are reviewed annually by the Armed Forces Pay Review Body (AFPRB) or, for senior officers at two-star rank and above, the SSRB.

Performance and Reward

Civilian members of the DMB do not participate in any incentive/performance schemes. Their basic salary and annual increases, which could include a bonus payment, are performance related and are set by the Permanent Under Secretaries Remuneration Committee.

Pay and management arrangements for members of the SCS (one-star to three-star) reward individuals for delivery and personal achievement. These arrangements include:

a.   An objective-setting regime complementary to the Department's developing performance management system embodied in the Defence Balanced Scorecard.

b.   A performance-related incremental pay system.

Employees

The Department is committed to recruiting and retaining the best people for the job from all walks of life irrespective of race, gender or background.

Payments to Suppliers

The Department's bills, with the exception of some payments to suppliers by units locally and outside Great Britain, are paid through the Defence Bills Agency (DBA). In 2003-04, the DBA met its target of paying 99.9% of all correctly submitted bills within eleven calendar days, ensuring that the Department is in compliance with its statutory obligation under the Late Payment of Commercial Debts (Interest) Act 1998. Commercial debt interest paid by units locally during the year amounted to £336 (2002-03: £1,196).

Environmental Protection Policy

The Ministry of Defence acts as a force for good in the world, by enabling a climate that supports the pursuit of sustainable development objectives. The MoD is an operational government department and is required to manage its sustainable development aspects and impacts alongside Defence imperatives. Ensuring a better quality of life for everyone now and for future generations to come lies at the heart of the Government's Sustainable Development Strategy. The MoD is committed to these objectives in pursuit of core business.

It is the Department's intention to comply with the Government's strategy for sustainable development and to take into consideration environmental and socio-economic factors in the development of policies, projects, acquisition programmes and training activities. A Sustainable Development Steering Group has been set up to oversee the development and implementation of a Departmental Sustainable Development Strategy. A report on the Department's performance against core sustainable development indicators will be published annually.

The Department will comply with the Environmental Protection Act 1990 and Environment Act 1995 and other relevant statutory provisions and any additional requirements arising from international treaties and protocols to which the UK is a signatory. Where the Department has been granted specific exemptions, disapplications or derogations from legislation, international treaties and protocols, Departmental Standards and arrangements will be introduced which are, as far as reasonably practical, at least as good as those required by the legislation. Any powers not to apply legislation on the grounds of national security will be invoked only when such action is absolutely essential for the maintenance of operational capability.

Departmental Report

The MoD's Departmental Report which is presented to Parliament each year comprises the "Ministry of Defence Performance Report 2003-04" and "The Government's Expenditure Plans 2004-05: Ministry of Defence". The Departmental Report sets out the performance of the MoD against the objectives stated in Schedule 5 and also includes developments since the year-end, where appropriate. The Departmental Performance Report forms the first Section of the Annual Report and Accounts.

Financial Instruments

The Department does not trade or enter into any speculative transactions in foreign currencies. Forward contract commitments entered into to cover future expenditure in foreign currencies are stated in Note 28.

Provision of Information and Consultation with Employees

The MoD has a strong Whitley committee structure through which employees' representatives, in the form of recognised industrial and non industrial trades unions (TUs), are consulted on and informed of all matters likely to affect our civilian personnel. This structure is supported by formal policy and procedures for consulting and informing TUs. We also advocate the development of informal relationships with the TUs to discuss ideas together. Our policy makes clear that consulting the TUs is not a substitute for dealing with personnel direct, and vice versa. Managers and project leaders for example are encouraged to use all media available, including cascade briefings, newsletters and intranet websites/email. In respect of service personnel, the process operates through the chain of command, with no formal representation through the Trade Unions.

Auditor

The financial statements for the Department are audited by the Comptroller and Auditor General under the Government Resources and Accounts Act 2000. The Certificate and Report of the Comptroller and Auditor General on the financial statements are set out on pages 104 to 110.

Kevin Tebbit
Accounting Officer
21 September 2004

Operating and Financial Review

Last year was the first year that the Department presented the Departmental Performance Report and the Departmental Resource Accounts as a combined document, the "Annual Report and Accounts". The combined report was well received, as it brought together the non-financial performance and operational activities carried out during the year and related them to the financial outcome and the resources utilised in the year.

The operational activity during the year was again dominated by events in Iraq (Operation TELIC). The military operation that had started in March 2003 came to an end in May 2004. Since then the armed forces have been mainly engaged in various stabilisation operations and in providing much needed humanitarian assistance. The operational activities in Afghanistan and the Balkans are continuing although on a smaller scale than in the previous year. Further details of these operations are given in Section 1 of the Annual Report and Accounts.

Financial Review

The Department, for the first time since the implementation of Resource Accounting, has received a clean audit opinion on its Accounts. This is a significant achievement considering the size and complexity of the Department. One of the challenges was adapting the supply systems to provide resource based financial data; under the legacy systems only the minimum amount of financial data was held. The Department has over the last few years made significant efforts in improving these systems and the one remaining supply system issue brought forward from last year has now been resolved. The Department is for the first time able to obtain more accurate information on its stock levels and consumption. Through sound planning and control, the Department has stayed within the resources allocated to it under each of the three "Request for Resources", agreed in the Supplementary Estimates.

Net Resource Outturn

The total Net Resource Outturn was £1,002 million below the Estimate. Schedule 1 provides a summary explaining the reasons for the underspend, which is mainly due to lower than forecast non-cash costs of £674 million; the remaining £328 million is due to other costs. Of the total underspend, the Provision for Defence Capability (Request for Resources 1) accounted for £780 million, Conflict Prevention (Request for Resources 2) £180 million, and War Pensions and Allowances (Request for Resources 3) £42 million.

The Net Resource Outturn of £34,651 million was £7,362 million below last year. However, 2002-03 was an exceptional year when, some £4,000 million in the value of fixed assets was written down as a direct impact of the Quinquennial Valuation of fixed assets. The impact of the substantial write down also had the effect of reducing the depreciation charge in 2003-04 by some £1,200 million. A further £1,700 million in exceptional charges were also made in last year's accounts in respect of nuclear decommissioning provisions following a strategic review, changes in methodology carried out by BNFL, and the Quinquennial review of AWE. The balance of the reduction is accounted for by various costs, as listed in Note 3.

The Treasury standard rate for the cost of capital charge calculation was reduced from 6% to 3.5% with effect from 1 April 2003. This resulted in a reduced cost of capital charge of £2,770 million. However, there was a corresponding increase in the unwinding of interest charge relating to the discounted provisions, mainly in respect of decommissioning, which crystallised as at 1 April 2003.

Net Cash Requirement

The net cash utilised in the year was £29,338 million and was £750 million below the Estimate. The underspend is mainly due to lower cash expenditure on operations, lower than forecast capital expenditure and lower working capital expenditure.

Financial Position

The net asset value at 31 March 2004 of £81,147 million declined against last year by £291 million.

The reduction in the net asset value is largely due to the increase in the amount of provisions for liabilities and charges, as a result of recalculating the discounted provisions using a discount rate of 3.5% instead of 6% at 31 March 2003. The net impact was an increase in liabilities by some £2,400 million. This was offset by increases in fixed assets of £1,033 million and working capital of £1,073 million. The increase in working capital includes a reclassification of some £750 million, in respect of items which had been previously designated as fixed assets and now reclassified as stock.

Cash Flow

The amount drawn from the Consolidated Fund was £29,258 million. This amount was mainly utilised in financing operating activities (£23,110 million) and net capital expenditure (£5,986 million). Closing cash and bank balances were £313 million (2002-03: £416 million).

Future Developments

In July 2004, the Department announced that significant changes would be required to the force structure to meet the needs of the future, including the potential threats from terrorism. Change would also involve the level of resource capability required in the civilian work force. The changes are presently being evaluated and, when implemented, will have a significant impact on the results in future years.

Statement of Accounting Officer's Responsibilities

Under the Government Resources and Accounts Act 2000, the Department is required to prepare resource accounts for each financial year, in conformity with a Treasury direction, detailing the resources acquired, held, or disposed of during the year and the use of resources by the Department during the year.

The resource accounts are prepared on an accruals basis and must give a true and fair view of the state of affairs of the Department, the net resource Outturn, resources applied to objectives, recognised gains and losses, and cash flows for the financial year.

HM Treasury has appointed the Permanent Head of the Department as Accounting Officer of the Department, with responsibility for preparing the Department's accounts and for transmitting them to the Comptroller and Auditor General.

In preparing the accounts the Accounting Officer is required to comply with the *Resource Accounting Manual* (RAM) prepared by HM Treasury, and in particular to:

- Observe the relevant accounting and disclosure requirements, and apply suitable accounting policies on a consistent basis;

- Make judgements and estimates on a reasonable basis;

- State whether applicable accounting standards, as set out in the RAM, have been followed, and disclose and explain any material departures in the accounts; and

- Prepare the accounts on a going concern basis.

The responsibilities of an Accounting Officer, including responsibility for the propriety and regularity of the public finances for which an Accounting Officer is answerable, for keeping proper records and for safeguarding the Department's assets, are set out in the Accounting Officers' Memorandum issued by HM Treasury and published in *Government Accounting*.

Statement on Internal Control

1. Scope of responsibility

As Accounting Officer, I have responsibility for maintaining a sound system of internal control that supports the achievement of Departmental policies, aims and objectives, set by the Department's Ministers, whilst safeguarding the public funds and Departmental assets for which I am personally responsible, in accordance with the responsibilities assigned to me in Government Accounting.

During the Financial Year 2003/04, the Department's outputs were delivered through 11 Top Level Budget areas, each managed by a military or civilian Top Level Budget (TLB) Holder, together with 5 Trading Fund Agencies and 7 Non-Departmental Public Bodies (NDPB) with delegated responsibilities. Included within the TLBs are 30 (2002-03: 31[1]) on-vote Defence Agencies whose Chief Executives are responsible for producing annual accounts which are laid before Parliament but which also form part of the Departmental Resource Accounts. TLB Holders operate within a framework of responsibilities delegated by me and to assist me in assessing the adequacy of control arrangements across the Department, TLB Holders provide their own Statements of Internal Control to me on an annual basis including the Agencies for which they are responsible. The MoD Trading Funds fall outside the Departmental Accounting Boundary and their Chief Executives are Accounting Officers in their own right. They therefore publish their own SICs together with their Annual Accounts. Although sponsored by the Department, the 7 NDPBs also fall outside the Departmental Boundary and their accounts are published separately. With the exception of the Oil and Pipelines Agency (OPA), the NDPBs operate within a strategic control framework contained in a financial memorandum agreed between their respective Boards of Trustees and the Department. The OPA has a Board of Directors on which the Department is represented.

Ministers are involved in the delivery of outputs, including the management of risks to delivery, through the Defence Council which is chaired by the Secretary of State for Defence and includes all the senior executive members of the Defence Management Board. Ministers also chair a variety of internal Boards which review the performance of the Trading Funds, the primary on-vote Agencies and other elements of MoD business such as Environment and Safety, and Estates. In particular, 4 Trading Funds (the Defence Aviation Repair Agency, the Army Base Repair Organisation, the Defence Science and Technology Laboratory (Dstl), and the UK Hydrographic Office) together with the Defence Procurement Agency (DPA) report to Advisory Boards chaired by MoD Ministers. The Met Office, which is also a Trading Fund, reported to the UK Met Board chaired by the 2nd PUS[2]. Ministers are also consulted on all key decisions affecting defence, including major investment decisions and on operational matters. The Chief of Defence Staff is the Secretary of State's principal advisor on military operations and is responsible for the maintenance of military operational capability and for the preparation and conduct of military operations, including risks to successful outcomes.

2. The purpose of the system of internal control

The system of internal control is designed to manage risk to a reasonable level rather than to eliminate all risk of failure to achieve policies, aims and objectives; it can therefore only provide reasonable and not absolute assurance of effectiveness. The system of internal control is based on an ongoing process designed to identify

---

[1] On 1 April 2003 the Defence Medical Education & Training Agency was formed, subsuming the responsibilities of the Defence Medical Training Organisation and the Defence Secondary Care Agency.

[2] From 27 July 2004 the UK Met Board became the Met Office Owner's Council, chaired by the Under Secretary of State.

and prioritise the risks to the achievement of Departmental policies, aims and objectives, to evaluate the likelihood of those risks being realised and the impact should they be realised, and to manage them efficiently, effectively and economically. The system of internal control has been in place in the Department for the year ended 31 March 2004 and up to the date of approval of the annual report and accounts, and accords with Treasury guidance.

3. Capacity to handle risk

Active management of risk is fundamental to the effective achievement of Defence objectives, and is central to the way business is conducted within the Department. It informs operational decision making, contingency planning, investment decisions and the financial planning process. Risk forms an integral element of the Defence Management Board's performance reviews. Guidance on the Department's approach to risk is detailed in a Joint Service Publication[3], which is periodically reviewed and updated. This sets out the Department's corporate governance and risk management policy statement and strategy to be cascaded down through TLB Holders, and provides extensive guidance to staff on definitions, criteria and methods available for risk assessment and management. It is made available to all personnel in either hard copy or via the Department's intranet. Individual training, at both awareness and practitioner level, is available to all staff via the Department's in-house training provider.

Across the Department a network of Risk Improvement Managers (RIMs) has been established. The aim of the network is to share good practice, helping those involved in improving risk management in their area to learn from others across the Department, and also drawing from the work being carried out as part of the Government-wide programme to improve the handling of risks to Government objectives.

4. The risk and control framework

The Department's Performance Management System provides the strategic framework for the consideration of risks within the Defence Balanced Scorecard and lower level scorecards, offering a starting point for the identification, evaluation, control and reporting of risk against a balanced assessment of Departmental objectives. Key Departmental objectives, performance indicators and targets are defined annually by the Defence Management Board (DMB) and cascaded to TLB Holders through Service Delivery Agreements. Performance is monitored and discussed quarterly at DMB and lower level management board meetings, including explicit consideration of key risks.

The Department's risk appetite is determined through the advice on operations given to Ministers, through decisions taken as part of the Department's annual planning round including assessing any gaps against Planning Assumptions as set out in the Defence White Paper, and through the limits and controls placed on individual investment projects as part of the Department's Investment Approval process.

5. Review of effectiveness

As Accounting Officer, I have responsibility for reviewing the effectiveness of the system of internal control. My review of the effectiveness of the system of internal control is informed by the work of the internal auditors and the executive managers within the Department who have responsibility for the development and maintenance of the internal control framework, and comments made by the external auditors in their management letter and other reports. I have been advised on the implications of the result of my review of the effectiveness of the system of internal control by the Defence Management Board and the Defence Audit Committee and a plan to address weaknesses and ensure continuous improvement of the system is in place.

---

[3] JSP 525 *Corporate Governance and Risk Management 2nd Edition May 2004.*

The following processes are in operation in order to maintain and review the effectiveness of the system of internal control:

- A Defence Management Board (DMB), which meets monthly to manage the plans, performance and strategic direction of the Department, which comprises the senior members of the Department and has two external independent members.

- A Defence Audit Committee (DAC), chaired by an external independent member of the DMB, which has adopted a risk-based approach to internal control and is placed at the heart of the assurance process, co-ordinating the activities of internal audit, and drawing on reports from specialist assurance bodies, including:
  - Defence Environment and Safety Board
  - Departmental Security Officer
  - Defence Internal Audit
  - Director General Financial Management
  - Director of Operational Capability
  - Defence Fraud Analysis Unit
  - Scientific & Technical Director
  - National Audit Office

- A Departmental risk register, supported by operational-level risk registers, which complements the Defence Balanced Scorecard. The Departmental risk register has been reviewed and endorsed by both the DAC and the DMB.

- Through TLB Holders, a cascaded system for ensuring compliance with legal and statutory regulations. Each TLB holder is supported by an Audit Committee, which includes non-executive directors and at which representatives from the internal and external auditors are present. Like the DAC these committees have refocused their activities to provide advice on wider-business risk and assurance processes.

- A developing Business Management System through which responsibility for the effective and efficient operation of the key pan-Departmental processes, such as Planning, Human Resources and Procurement, including the identification of risks within these processes and the maintenance of effective controls to manage them, is assigned to functional heads or process owners. Process Owners report directly to the Defence Management Board.

- Through TLB Holders, a cascaded system for ensuring that business continuity plans are in place, and that these plans are tested on a regular basis. Following a revamp of the Department's business continuity management policy[4], an in-year review by the Directorate General of Safety and Security was undertaken to ascertain how the policy is being adopted across the Department, what improvements are planned and to identify specific areas of risk and the measures being taken to mitigate those risks. The review revealed that all business continuity plans currently in place had been at minimum desktop tested and that there are no significant internal control problems.

---

[4] Revised policy and guidance issued in Joint Service Policy 503 Business Continuity Management, 2nd Edition, published May 2003, and Defence Council Instruction (General) 160/03 dated 20 June 2003.

- An annual risk-based programme of internal audit provided by Defence Internal Audit (DIA), who are the primary source of independent assurance, which is complemented by the activity of the Directorate of Operational Capability (DOC), which provides independent operational audit and assurance to the Secretary of State and the Chief of Defence Staff. On the basis of the audit work conducted during the year, DIA offered Substantial Assurance that the systems of internal control, risk management and governance reviewed are operating effectively.

- Annual and Quarterly Reports providing measurable performance indicators and more subjective assessments on the Health of Financial Systems from all TLB Holders and key functional specialists. Improvements have continued to be made to our financial control during the year. The Department has delivered its outputs within the resources voted by Parliament and the Treasury's expenditure limits despite the additional workload generated by Operation TELIC and the migration to a new accounting system. The remaining NAO concern on Supply Systems has now been satisfactorily resolved with the result that the Department has for the first time achieved a true and fair audit opinion.

- Centres of Excellence for project and programme management in key areas - including Change, Equipment and Estates, integrating Office of Government Commerce (OGC) processes, tools and structures into existing Departmental management and control processes - to ensure that high-risk mission-critical projects and programmes carried out by the Department do not suffer from any of the common causes of failure identified by the OGC and the National Audit Office.

- Senior Responsible Owners across the Department who are personally responsible for delivering major programmes and their benefits to cost and time in line with best Office of Government Commerce practice.

- A dedicated team to co-ordinate, and appropriate mechanisms to strengthen, the management of scientific risks, particularly to Service personnel health, and in health, safety and environmental matters.

- Association of the Department's Directorate of Management Consultancy Services with the broader assurance community with their tasking flowing from the identification of business risk.

- A change programme to address the key risks that the introduction of the general right of access under FOI from January 2005 presents to the organisation. Stakeholders from across the department have been involved and an effective governance structure put in place. A maturity model has been used to highlight how the constituent parts of the department are progressing and as a diagnostic tool for the department to feed into performance management systems.

Kevin Tebbit
Accounting Officer
21 September 2004

The Certificate of the Comptroller and Auditor General to the House of Commons

I certify that I have audited the financial statements on pages 111 to 168 under the Government Resources and Accounts Act 2000. These financial statements have been prepared under the historical cost convention as modified by the revaluation of certain fixed assets and stocks and the accounting policies set out on pages 119 to 125.

Respective responsibilities of the Accounting Officer and Auditor

As described on page 99, the Accounting Officer is responsible for the preparation of the financial statements in accordance with the Government Resources and Accounts Act 2000 and Treasury directions made thereunder and for ensuring the regularity of financial transactions. The Accounting Officer is also responsible for the preparation of the other contents of the Annual Report and Accounts. My responsibilities, as independent auditor, are established by statute and guided by the Auditing Practices Board and the auditing profession's ethical guidance.

I report my opinion as to whether the financial statements give a true and fair view and are properly prepared in accordance with the Government Resources and Accounts Act 2000 and Treasury directions made thereunder, and whether in all material respects the expenditure and income have been applied to the purposes intended by Parliament and the financial transactions conform to the authorities which govern them. I also report if, in my opinion, the Annual Report including the annual performance report is not consistent with the financial statements, if the Department has not kept proper accounting records, or if I have not received all the information and explanations I require for my audit.

I read the other information contained in the Annual Report and Accounts, and consider whether it is consistent with the audited financial statements. I consider the implications for my certificate if I become aware of any apparent misstatements or material inconsistencies with the financial statements.

I review whether the statement on pages 100 to 103 reflects the Department's compliance with Treasury's guidance on the Statement on Internal Control. I report if it does not meet the requirements specified by Treasury, or if the statement is misleading or inconsistent with other information I am aware of from my audit of the financial statements. I am not required to consider, nor have I considered whether the Accounting Officer's Statement on Internal Control covers all the risks and controls. I am also not required to form an opinion on the effectiveness of the Agency's corporate governance procedures or its risk and control procedures.

Basis of audit opinion

I conducted my audit in accordance with United Kingdom Auditing Standards issued by the Auditing Practices Board except that the scope of my work was limited as explained below. An audit includes examination, on a test basis, of evidence relevant to the amounts, disclosures and regularity of financial transactions included in the financial statements. It also includes an assessment of the significant estimates and judgements made by the Department in the preparation of the financial statements, and of whether the accounting policies are appropriate to the Department's circumstances, consistently applied and adequately disclosed.

I planned and performed my audit so as to obtain all the information and explanations which I considered necessary in order to provide me with sufficient evidence to give reasonable assurance that the financial statements are free from material misstatement, whether caused by error, or by fraud or other irregularity and that, in all material respects, the expenditure and income have been applied to the purposes intended by Parliament and the financial transactions conform to the authorities which govern them.

In forming my opinion I have also evaluated the overall adequacy of the presentation of information in the financial statements.

Opinion

In my opinion:

- the financial statements give a true and fair view of the state of affairs of the Ministry of Defence at 31 March 2004 and of the net resource outturn, resources applied to objectives, recognised gains and losses and cash flows for the year then ended, and have been properly prepared in accordance with the Government Resources and Accounts Act 2000 and directions made thereunder by Treasury; and

- in all material respects the expenditure and income have been applied to the purposes intended by Parliament and the financial transactions conform to the authorities which govern them.

My Report on these financial statements is at page 106.

John Bourn
Comptroller and Auditor General
29 September 2004

National Audit Office
157-197 Buckingham Palace Road
Victoria
London SW1W 9SP

The Report of the Comptroller and Auditor General to the House of Commons

Section 1: Summary

1 The Ministry of Defence (the Department) is required by Directions issued by the Treasury to prepare annual Resource Accounts. The Resource Accounts, drawn up on an accruals basis, should be prepared in accordance with the Treasury's *Resource Accounting Manual* and should give a true and fair view of the state of affairs of the Department and of its net resource outturn, recognised gains and losses and cashflows for the year.

2 In producing its Resource Accounts the Department faces a number of challenges. It undertakes a wide range of complex functions and holds a vast range of assets. Some of these assets are held by contractors for manufacture and repair purposes. It has many old information systems which although adequate for the purposes they were designed for, are not suited in all respects to the production of accurate and timely accruals based information, particularly during the escalation of military operations. The Department has therefore had to invest considerable efforts in implementing resource accounting and budgeting, both in IT and staffing.

3 The Department has made significant efforts to improve the standard of its financial accounting information over the last five years. I qualified my audit opinion on the 2002-2003 resource accounts because I was unable to confirm some figures in the operating cost statement in respect of consumption charges for certain stock and fixed assets generated by the Defence Logistics Organisation's Air environment. The Department has continued over this last year to make strenuous efforts to secure further improvements. In Section 2 of my Report I describe these efforts in more detail and explain why as a result I have concluded that this year for the first time the Department's resource accounts are robust enough to support a true and fair opinion.

4 The Treasury's *Resource Accounting Manual* requires that losses and special payments be reported in Departments' Resource Accounts. The Ministry of Defence has faced significant changes in its expenditure programmes over recent years because of a variety of factors, including changes in threat and advances in weapons technology and the scale of change in organisational structures. These factors have led to many of the losses and special payments recorded in Note 29 to the 2003-2004 Resource Accounts. In Section 3 of my Report I consider some of the more significant losses.

5 In Section 4 of my Report I confirm that according to Departmental records the maximum numbers of military personnel maintained during 2003-2004 for the Naval, Army and Air Force Services in all active and reserve categories were within the numbers voted by Parliament.

6   The Department continues to demonstrate a strong and effective grip on the accounts production process. For 2003-2004, it has again submitted Resource Accounts for audit in line with the timetable agreed with my staff and the Treasury and it has accelerated their finalisation and publication. When compared with the quality of the Department's first Resource Accounts for 1999-2000, on which I placed a disclaimer covering a range of accounting deficiencies, the Department has consistently made good progress during the last four years in improving the quality of its accounts. As a result this year the Department has successfully cleared the one remaining substantive issue which was the basis for the qualification of my audit opinion last year. This is a significant achievement but the Department recognises that it has more to do to get the maximum benefit from the Resource Accounting and Budgeting regime. The Department assures me it is fully aware of what remains to be done and is committed to securing further improvements. My staff will continue to work closely with the Department in this task.

Section 2: Is the Department still making good progress to implement Resource Accounting effectively?

7   In my Report on the 2002-2003 Accounts[1] I explained my reasons for qualifying my audit opinion. I was unable to confirm whether stock and fixed asset accounting transactions generated by the Defence Logistics Organisation's Air environment were complete or correctly recorded. The Department has now made sufficient progress on this issue such that I am able to remove my qualification in this regard.

Stock and fixed asset accounting transactions generated by the Defence Logistics Organisation's Air environment are more robust

8   In my Report on the 2002-2003 accounts I noted the continuing problems the Department had with stock inventory systems which were not designed to provide stock accounting data for accruals based financial accounts. In particular, the supply system for the Defence Logistics Organisation's Air environment generated data that could not be wholly supported. Then, as now, the stock accounting system compares each month the opening and closing values with the movements generated by the stock inventory system. Where there is a difference a reconciling balance is automatically created. This 'autobalance' entry ensures that the accounts reflect the stock inventory system but in previous years there had been no audit trail to support it.

9   Throughout 2003-04, the Defence Logistics Organisation continued to investigate the causes of autobalance. Some of the causes identified arose from technical deficiencies within the software programming. For example, spurious transactions generated when both the definition of quantity and the unit price changed simultaneously in the stock management system. The Defence Logistics Organisation has improved the mapping of transactions from the inventory system through to the accounting system, thus reducing the need for the intervention of autobalance. There has also been an educational programme for supply system users to reduce the level of incomplete and incorrect data input, which was another major cause of autobalance transactions.

10   As a result of these actions, the Defence Logistics Organisation has reduced the net credit to the operating cost statement arising from autobalance to £181 million in 2003-04 (in 2002-2003 it was some £1,128 million). More significantly, the Defence Logistics Organisation has for the first time established an audit trail for all autobalance transactions that provides sufficient evidence to support the validity and accuracy of these transactions. Audit testing has shown that the autobalance mechanism functions as an effective and valid accounting tool. It is in this regard that I have been able to remove my qualification.

---

[1] MoD: Departmental Resource Accounts 2002-2003 HC 1125 Session 2002-2003: 30 October 2003

11 In order to further improve the effectiveness of its business decisions, which in a high degree depend upon the quality of its accounting data, the Defence Logistics Organisation is continuing with its programme of reducing the technical and procedural causes of autobalance.

Other developments in Resource Accounting and the disclosure of financial information

The Department has reported some £1 billion net additional resource costs were incurred on operations in Iraq during 2003-04

12 Note 27 to the Resource Account summarises the financial impact of operation TELIC during 2003-2004. TELIC is the UK name for military operations in Iraq. The total costs to date of the operation are summarised below.

£m	2002-03	2003-04	Total
Resource costs	629	1,051	**1,680**
Capital expenditure	218	260	**478**
Total	**847**	**1,311**	**2,158**

13 In accordance with the accounting principles agreed with HM Treasury, the Department has identified these costs on the basis of net additional costs. Expenditure such as normal wages and salaries of armed forces and civilian personnel are excluded as these would have been incurred anyway and the costs of training and exercises which have been cancelled because of the operational commitment are deducted.

14 The Department's chart of accounts is not designed to record automatically the cost of individual operations. The Department therefore undertook a specific review to determine the additional resource costs of operation TELIC attributable to the 2003-2004 account. My staff have reviewed the Department's estimates of the cost of operation TELIC up to 31 March 2004 and concluded that they are robust.

15 Some of the remaining stock and fixed assets sent to Iraq are still in use there for peacekeeping purposes. Until all unused stock and fixed assets are returned to the United Kingdom the Department will be unable to make a comprehensive assessment of stock consumption and the level of asset impairment in order to determine the full cost of operation TELIC.

16 I reported last year[2] that TELIC is the first major conflict where the Department has accounted for a military operation on a resource basis and that this had generated a number of accounting issues not encountered in previous operations managed under a cash accounting regime. These issues have continued to have an impact in 2003-04 and include the following:

- calculating the correct level of stock consumption to report in the resource accounts;

- the loss or impairment of fighting and other equipments which have to be recognised in the correct accounting period on an accruals basis;

- assets acquired quickly to support operations (Urgent Operational Requirements) need to be brought to account correctly.

17 The Department is committed to working in consultation with my staff to further refine its accounting policies and systems in these areas.

---

[2] MoD: Departmental Resource Accounts 2002-2003 HC 1125 Session 2002-2003: 30 October 2003

Section 3: The Department has reported significant losses and special payments

18   The Department's expenditure programmes are subject to many changes in requirements because of advances in weapons technology; changes in threat and the pace and scale of changes in organisational structures. These changes can result in the Department having to abandon procurement or development projects before the equipments are introduced into service or write off the value of assets no longer required.

19   The Treasury gives departments delegated authority to write off such expenditure as a loss or special payment after careful appraisal of all the facts, but requires departments to bring them to Parliament's attention at the earliest opportunity. Nevertheless, investigation of the circumstances can take some time. Where final details cannot be reported this may be noted as an advisory loss in departmental resource accounts.

20   The table below summarises the value of the resulting losses and special payments reported by the Department in the last four years and shows that reported losses have increased significantly in 2003-04. Note 29 of the Department's Resource Accounts for 2003-2004 discloses details of the losses, special payments and gifts.

£000	Losses	Special Payments
2000-01	78,950	180,820
2001-02	42,072	74,262
2002-03	131,084	129,118
2003-04	460,945	98,124

21   The Department has also identified some £442 million of losses incurred in previous years and not previously reported. I highlight below some of the more significant cases recorded in the Note.

The Department has incurred significant constructive losses

22   HM Treasury's *Government Accounting* defines a constructive loss as one where, for example, services are correctly ordered, delivered or provided, and are paid for as being in conformity with the order, but which owing to a change of policy or similar reason prove not to be needed or to be less useful than when the order was placed.

Nuclear submarine facilities at Devonport

23   In my Report on the 2002-2003 Accounts[3], I noted that the Department had given advance notification of a constructive loss of £287 million relating to nuclear submarine facilities at Devonport and explained the reasons for the loss. This amount has been confirmed and formally reported as a constructive loss in the 2003-04 accounts.

Multi Role Armoured Vehicle (MRAV) Programme

24   The Department withdrew from the MRAV Programme, a collaborative project with Germany and the Netherlands, during 2003 and has reported a constructive loss of £48 million. This was due to changing capability requirements, with increased emphasis placed on the ability of the armed forces to meet the requirements of rapid deployment and expeditionary operations. The MRAV programme did not meet these requirements, leading to the Department's decision to withdraw from it.

---

[3] MoD: Departmental Resource Accounts 2002-2003 HC 1125 Session 2002-2003: 30 October 2003

25   A new national programme, the Future Rapid Effect System (FRES) will meet the requirement for lighter more easily deployable armoured vehicles. These vehicles will also be integrated with the new framework of network centric capability.

The Department has given advance notification of significant losses

26   HM Treasury's *Government Accounting* requires that losses and special payments should be brought to the attention of Parliament at the earliest opportunity. Notification is separate from the accounting treatment, which will depend on the nature of the loss or special payment. A loss should be noted in the accounts even if it may be reduced by subsequent recoveries. The Department has provided advance notification for the following significant loss.

Chinook MK3 Helicopters Impairment

27   A loss of £205m arose due to the impairment of eight Chinook MK3 Helicopters. The impairment arose as it was established that, although the terms of the contract had been met, these helicopters did not meet operational requirements and could not acquire Military Aircraft Release.

28   Significant modifications to the avionics software are required to enable the helicopters to be of use operationally and it is not now anticipated that the helicopters will enter service until mid 2007. I examined these issues in more detail in my report earlier this year[4].

Section 4: Ministry of Defence – Votes A

29   The Ministry of Defence's Votes A is presented annually to Parliament to seek statutory authority for the maximum numbers of personnel to be maintained for service with the armed forces. Note 33 to the Accounts shows that the maximum numbers maintained during 2003-04 for the Naval, Army and Air Force Services in all active and reserve categories were within the numbers voted by Parliament. My staff have been provided with strength returns to support this Note to the financial statements.

John Bourn
Comptroller and Auditor General
29 September 2004

National Audit Office
157-197 Buckingham Palace Road
Victoria
London SW1W 9SP

[4]   Battlefield Helicopters HC486 Session 2003-04: 1 April 2004

Schedule 1

Summary of Resource Outturn
for the year ended 31 March 2004

	Estimate			Outturn			Net Total compared to Estimate Savings/(Excess)
	Gross Expenditure 1	A-in-A* 2	Net Total 3	Gross Expenditure 4	A-in-A* (note 4) 5	Net Total 6	7
	£000	£000	£000	£000	£000	£000	£000
Request for resources 1	34,459,419	1,377,823	33,081,596	33,679,847	1,377,823	32,302,024	779,572
Request for resources 2	1,413,610	–	1,413,610	1,233,155	–	1,233,155	180,455
Request for resources 3	1,158,005	–	1,158,005	1,116,047	–	1,116,047	41,958
Total resources	37,031,034	1,377,823	35,653,211	36,029,049	1,377,823	34,651,226	1,001,985
Non operating cost A-in-A			367,798			367,798	0
Net cash requirement			30,087,210			29,337,645	749,565

Outturn in Respect of Prior Year
The corresponding figures for 2002-03 outturn were as follows:

Total Resources	42, 013, 684
Non operating cost A-in-A	373, 756
Net cash requirement	26, 991, 365
*Appropriations-in-Aid (A-in-A)	

Summary of Income payable to the Consolidated Fund

	Note	Forecast 2003-04 Income £000	Receipts £000		Outturn 2003-04 Income £000	Receipts £000
Total	4	–	–		258,004	258,004

Reconciliation of resources to cash requirement

	Note	Estimate £000		Outturn £000	Savings/(Excess) £000
Net total resources	Sch 2	35,653,211		34,651,226	1,001,985
Capital:					
*Purchase of fixed assets:					
– RfR 1	8/9	6,435,770		6,321,438	114,332
– RfR 2	8/9	334,000		260,275	73,725
– RfR 1 Capitalised provisions	8/9	–		(99,276)	99,276
New loans to the Trading Funds	10	–		19,200	(19,200)

The notes on pages 119 to 168 form part of these financial statements.

	Note	Estimate £000		Outturn £000	Savings/ (Excess) £000
Non operating cost A-in-A:					
Proceeds on sale of fixed assets	8/9/3	(355,371)		(481,298)	125,927
Excess non-operating costs Appropriation-in-Aid payable to the Consolidated Fund		–		137,325	(137,325)
Repayment of loans made to the Trading Funds and QinetiQ after deducting loan repayments treated as CFERs amounting to £4,213,977 shown against Outturn	10	(12,427)		(23,825)	11,398
*Repayment of Loans from the National Loans Fund	Sch 4	–		1,375	(1,375)
Accruals adjustments:					
Non-cash transactions-					
Included in operating costs	Sch 4	(7,934,719)		(7,124,595)	(810,124)
Included in net interest payable	6	(2,467,307)		(2,609,205)	141,898
Capitalised provisions shown above		–		99,276	(99,276)
		(10,402,026)		(9,634,524)	(767,502)
Cost of capital charge	18	(2,676,403)		(2,769,726)	93,323
		(13,078,429)		(12,404,250)	(674,179)
*Changes in working capital other than cash	Sch 4	621,756		422,188	199,568
*Use of provisions for liabilities and charges	17	488,700		539,167	(50,467)
Adjustment for movements on cash balances in respect of collaborative projects	14	–		(5,900)	5,900
Net cash requirement	Sch 4	**30,087,210**		**29,337,645**	**749,565**

* Stated in accordance with Schedule 1 requirement to include accruals within the movements in the year

The notes on pages 119 to 168 form part of these financial statements.

Explanation of the variation between estimate and outturn (net total resources)

The Department's underspend against total net resources was caused by lower than expected conflict prevention costs under RfR2, a small underspend on war pensions under RfR3 and lower than forecast non-cash depreciation and cost of capital charges following management action across the Department to dispose of surplus assets and the impact of the Quinquennial Review (QQR) of Fixed Assets carried out towards the end of Financial year 2002-03. In the QQR there were fewer downward valuations of assets than expected, resulting in smaller accelerated depreciation charges, and the lives of many assets were extended thereby reducing associated annual depreciation costs. As part of the normal course of business resources need to be reallocated and redistributed between TLB holders as and when required in order to optimise the use of those resources in the generation of military capability and its effective use on operations. This process contributed to the in-year shortfalls and excesses shown against some of the TLB Holders. These offset each other, with no material impact on the Department's Total Resources.

Analysis of the costs of operations conducted during the year is shown in Note 27.

Explanation of the variation between estimate and outturn (net cash requirement)

Creditor and accrual balances are difficult to estimate due to uncertainties over the timing of supplier invoicing and therefore the timing of cash payments cannot be accurately predicted. In the event more goods and services were accrued due to later than anticipated presentation of bills by creditors. This had the effect of less cash being paid out than forecast when the Spring Supplementary Estimates were prepared.

The notes on pages 119 to 168 form part of these financial statements.

Schedule 2

Operating Cost Statement
for the year ended 31 March 2004

	Note	2003-04 £000	2002-03 £000
Staff costs	2	10,435,157	9,969,242
Other operating costs	3	20,126,927	27,840,791
Gross operating costs		**30,562,084**	37,810,033
Operating income	5	(1,412,306)	(1,357,700)
Net operating cost before interest		**29,149,778**	36,452,333
Net interest payable	6	2,611,043	266,532
Cost of capital charge	18	2,769,726	5,074,726
Net operating cost		**34,530,547**	41,793,591
Net resource Outturn	7	**34,651,226**	42,013,684

Statement of Recognised Gains and Losses
for the year ended 31 March 2004

	Note	2003-04 £000	2002-03 £000
Net gain on revaluation of fixed assets and stocks	19	(2,473,614)	(4,463,447)
Receipts of donated assets and (gain) on revaluation	19	32,702	(521,653)
Prior year adjustments		–	152,917
Recognised gains during the year		**(2,440,912)**	(4,832,183)

The results shown above are in respect of continuing activity.

The notes on pages 119 to 168 form part of these financial statements.

Schedule 3

Balance Sheet
as at 31 March 2004

	Note	31 March 2004		31 March 2003	
		£000	£000	£000	£000
Fixed Assets					
Intangible assets	8	20,186,743		19,437,608	
Tangible fixed assets	9	66,737,257		66,444,536	
Investments	10	420,838		429,678	
			87,344,838		86,311,822
Current Assets					
Stocks and work-in-progress	12	6,318,224		5,337,125	
Debtors	13	2,675,419		2,201,652	
Cash at bank and in hand	14	312,564		415,928	
		9,306,207		7,954,705	
Creditors: amounts falling due within one year	15	5,662,598		5,383,850	
Net current assets			3,643,609		2,570,855
Total assets less current liabilities			90,988,447		88,882,677
Creditors: amounts falling due after more than one year	16	451,649		450,333	
Provisions for liabilities and charges	17	9,389,690		6,994,227	
			9,841,339		7,444,560
Net assets			**81,147,108**		81,438,117
Taxpayers' equity					
General fund	18		64,028,508		65,445,156
Revaluation reserve	19		15,396,444		14,181,634
Donated assets reserve	19		1,722,156		1,811,327
			81,147,108		81,438,117

Kevin Tebbit
Accounting Officer
21 September 2004

The notes on pages 119 to 168 form part of these financial statements.

Schedule 4

Cash Flow Statement
For the year ended 31 March 2004

	Note	2003-04 £000	2002-03 £000
Net cash outflow from operating activities before interest	A	**23,110,005**	21,165,066
Returns on investments and servicing of finance	B	**(7,225)**	4,363
Net capital expenditure and financial investment	C	**5,977,172**	5,647,360
Payments to the Consolidated Fund		**279,587**	533,726
Financing from the Consolidated Fund	14	**(29,257,550)**	(27,136,321)
Repayment of loans from the National Loans Fund		**1,375**	1,559
Decrease in cash at bank and in hand	14	**103,364**	215,753
Notes to the cash flow statement:			
A. Net cash outflow from operating activities before interest			
Net operating cost before interest	Sch 2	29,149,778	36,452,333
Non-cash transactions:			
– Depreciation and amortisation charges	3	(5,719,358)	(6,981,455)
– Impairment in value of fixed assets	3	(299,009)	(5,388,224)
– Provisions to reduce value of stock to its net realisable value	3	72,345	(111,125)
– Stocks written-off – net	3	(528,120)	(321,811)
– Auditors' remuneration	3	(3,150)	(3,405)
– Surplus/(deficit) arising on disposal of tangible fixed assets	3	71,725	45,260
– Surplus/(deficit) arising on disposal of investments	3	–	(8,397)
– Fixed Assets written off – net	3	(26,017)	(101,604)
– Fixed Asset investment written off	3	–	(219,886)
– Capital project expenditure written off	3	(268,310)	(584,928)
– Movement in provisions for liabilities and charges (excluding capitalised provisions)	17	(424,701)	(2,039,490)
		(7,124,595)	(15,715,065)
Dividends received from Trading Fund	5	8,902	8,587
Adjustments for movements in working capital other than cash			
– Increase/(decrease) in stocks/WIP		757,323	(26,645)
– Increase/(decrease) in debtors		83,431	540,276
– (Increase)/decrease in creditors		(206,831)	(507,279)
		633,923	6,352
Paid against provisions for liabilities and charges		441,997	412,859
		23,110,005	21,165,066
B. Returns on investments and servicing of finance			
Dividends received from Trading Fund	5	(8,902)	(8,587)
Interest received		(28,125)	(21,704)
Interest paid		2,639,007	282,357
Deduct: Unwinding of discount on provisions for liabilities and charges	6	(2,609,205)	(247,703)
		29,802	34,654
		(7,225)	4,363

The notes on pages 119 to 168 form part of these financial statements.

	Note	2003-04 £000	2002-03 £000
C. Analysis of capital expenditure and financial investment			
Acquisition of fixed assets		6,467,310	6,116,938
Proceeds on disposal of tangible fixed assets		(481,298)	(404,774)
Proceeds on disposal of investments		–	(39,427)
		5,986,012	5,672,737
Repayment of loans made to the Trading Funds and QinetiQ	10	(28,040)	(59,577)
Loans made to Trading Funds	10	19,200	34,200
		5,977,172	5,647,360
Analysis of Financing			
Parliamentary Funding from the Consolidated Fund (Supply)	14	29,257,550	27,136,321
(Increase)/decrease in cash at bank and in hand during the year	14	103,364	215,753
Consolidated Fund Extra Receipts (CFERs) received and not paid over		222,659	90,437
Consolidated Fund Extra Receipts (CFERs) received in prior year paid over		(134,737)	(69,430)
Part proceeds of certain fixed assets payable to Consolidated Fund		–	44,300
Grant drawn in the previous year and not spent, repaid to the Consolidated Fund during the year		(105,291)	(420,321)
Adjustment for movements on cash balances in respect of collaborative projects		(5,900)	(6,000)
Adjustment for Machinery of Government change during the year		–	305
Net cash requirement	Sch 1	**29,337,645**	26,991,365

Amount of grant actually issued to support the net cash requirement = £29,257,550,000.00

The notes on pages 119 to 168 form part of these financial statements.

Schedule 5

Resources By Departmental Aim And Objectives

for the year ended 31 March 2004.

Aim

The principal activity of the Department is to deliver security for the people of the United Kingdom and the Overseas Territories by defending them, including against terrorism; and to act as a force for good by strengthening international peace and stability.

In pursuance of this aim, the Department has the following objectives:

	2003-04			2002-03		
	Gross £000	Income £000	Net £000	Gross £000	Income £000	Net £000
Objective 1: Achieving success in the tasks we undertake	3,818,272	(336,995)	3,481,277	3,752,347	(277,683)	3,474,664
Objective 2: Being ready to respond to the tasks that might arise	27,796,553	(1,019,105)	26,777,448	34,711,064	(1,016,998)	33,694,066
Objective 3: Building for the future	3,211,981	(56,206)	3,155,775	3,487,027	(60,547)	3,426,480
	34,826,806	(1,412,306)	33,414,500	41,950,438	(1,355,228)	40,595,210
Paying war pensions and allowances	1,116,047	–	1,116,047	1,200,853	(2,472)	1,198,381
Total	35,942,853	(1,412,306)	34,530,547	43,151,291	(1,357,700)	41,793,591

See additional details in Note 26.

The notes on pages 119 to 168 form part of these financial statements.

Notes to the Accounts

1. Statement of Accounting Policies

Introduction

1.1 These financial statements have been prepared in accordance with the generic Accounts Direction issued by HM Treasury under reference DAO(GEN)2/04 on 30 January 2004 and comply with the requirements of HM Treasury's Resource Accounting Manual (RAM). In order to reflect the particular circumstances of the Department, the following exceptions to the RAM have been made:

The Operating Cost Statement is not segmented into programme and non-programme expenditure, as agreed with HM Treasury.

The Department's fixed assets are not analysed using the categories set out in the RAM. The different categorisation of the fixed assets became effective from the year 2002-03, but dispensation from this new requirement has been granted by HM Treasury until 2004-05.The Department is on schedule to implement these changes for the 2004-05 Accounts.

Accounting Convention

1.2 These financial statements are prepared on an accruals basis under the historical cost convention, modified to include the revaluation of certain fixed assets and stocks.

Basis of preparation of Departmental Resource Accounts

1.3 These financial statements comprise the consolidation of the Department, its Defence Supply Financed Agencies and those Advisory NDPBs sponsored by the Department which are not self-accounting. The Defence Agencies and the Advisory NDPBs sponsored by the Department are listed in Note 31.

1.4 Five of the Department's agencies are established as Trading Funds. They therefore fall outside Voted Supply and are subject to a different control framework. Consequently, the Department's interests in the Trading Funds are included in the financial statements as fixed asset investments. Executive NDPBs operate on a self-accounting basis and are not included in the consolidated accounts. They receive grant-in-aid funding from the Department which is treated as an expense in the Operating Cost Statement.

1.5 The Department's interest in QinetiQ, a Self-Financing Public Corporation, is included in the financial statements as a fixed asset investment.

1.6 The Armed Forces Pension Scheme (AFPS) is not consolidated within these financial statements. Separate accounts are prepared by the AFPS.

1.7 Machinery of Government changes which involve the merger of two or more Departments into one new Department, or the transfer of functions or responsibility of one part of the public service sector to another, are accounted for using merger accounting in accordance with the Financial Reporting Standard (FRS) 6.

Net Operating Costs

1.8 Costs are charged to the Operating Cost Statement in the period in which they are incurred and matched to any related income. Costs of VAT recoverable from Contracted-Out Services are included net of related VAT. Other costs are VAT inclusive, although a proportion of this VAT is recovered via a formula agreed with HM Customs and Excise. Surpluses and deficits on disposal of fixed assets and stock are included within Other Operating Costs (Note 3).

1.9 Income from services provided to third parties is included in operating income, net of related VAT. Dividends are included in the operating income in the year in which the cash is received.

Fixed Assets

1.10 Through the application of the Modified Historical Cost Accounting Convention (MHCA), the Department's fixed assets are expressed at their value to the Department on an inflation-adjusted basis, i.e. at actual or estimated current values. The Department achieves this through the application of prospective indices that are applied in April of each financial year and look ahead to the subsequent balance sheet date. A suite of indices is determined by the Department's Senior Economic Advisor, in conjunction with the Defence Analytical Services Agency. Different indices are used for the following asset categories and are "self correcting" in the subsequent financial year i.e. they are adjusted to account for the actual change in prices as compared to the earlier prediction:

- Land (by region and type);

- Buildings (UK and specific overseas indices);

- Fighting Equipment (one index for each of the three Sea, Air and Land systems);

- Plant, Machinery and Vehicles – Motor Vehicles and Trailers;

- Plant, Machinery and Vehicles – Other Transport Equipment;

- Plant, Machinery and Vehicles – Machinery and Equipment;

- IT and Communications Equipment – Office Machinery and Computers; and

- IT and Communications Equipment – Communications Equipment.

1.11 Additionally all fixed assets are subject to a quinquennial revaluation by external professional valuers in accordance with FRS15.

1.12 Assets under construction are valued at cost and are subject to indexation. On completion they are released from the project account into the appropriate asset category.

1.13 The Department's policy on the capitalisation of subsequent expenditure under FRS15 is to separately account for material major refits and overhauls when their value is consumed by the Department over a different period to the life of the corresponding core asset and where this is deemed to have a material effect on the carrying values of a fixed asset and the depreciation charge. Subsequent expenditure is also capitalised where it is deemed to enhance significantly the operational capability of the equipment, including extension of life and when it is incurred to replace or restore a component of an asset that has been treated separately for depreciation purposes.

Intangible Assets

1.14 Pure and applied research costs are charged to the Operating Cost Statement in the period in which they are incurred.

1.15 Development costs are capitalised where they contribute towards defining the specification of an asset that will enter production. Development costs not capitalised are charged to Other Operating Costs. The development costs are amortised over the planned operational life of that asset type, e.g. class of ship or aircraft, on a straight-line basis. Amortisation commences when the asset type first enters operational service within the Department. If it is decided to withdraw the whole or a significant part of an asset type early, then a corresponding proportion of any remaining unamortised development costs are written off to the Operating Cost Statement along with the underlying tangible fixed assets. For the purposes of development costs, a significant withdrawal of assets is deemed to be 20% or greater of the total of the asset class.

Tangible Fixed Assets

1.16 The useful economic lives of tangible fixed assets are reviewed annually and adjusted where necessary. The capitalisation threshold is £10,000.

1.17 In these financial statements, guided weapons, missiles and bombs (GWMB) and capital spares are categorised as fixed assets and subject to depreciation. The depreciation charge in the Operating Cost Statement also includes the cost of GWMB fired to destruction. The principal asset categories and their useful economic lives, depreciated on a straight line basis, are:

	Category	Years
Land and Buildings	Land Buildings, permanent Buildings, temporary Leasehold	Indefinite, not depreciated Useful economic life 5 – 20 Shorter of expected life and lease period
Fighting Equipment (including GWMB)		Useful economic life (on a pooled basis for GWMB)
Plant, Machinery and Vehicles	Plant and Machinery Specialised Vehicles (includes non-fighting vessels and aircraft) Other standard vehicles	5 – 15 Useful economic life 3 – 5
IT and Communications Equipment	Computers Satellites Communications Equipment	3 – 7 Useful economic life Useful economic life
Operational Heritage Assets*		As other tangible fixed assets
Capital Spares	Items of repairable material retained for the purpose of replacing parts of an asset undergoing repair, refurbishment, maintenance, servicing, modification, enhancement or conversion.	Useful economic life (on a pooled basis, consistent within the life of the prime equipment supported)
*Operational Heritage Assets are included within the principal asset category to which they relate.		

Donated Assets

1.18 Donated assets (i.e. those assets that have been donated to the Department or assets for which the Department has continuing and exclusive use but does not own legal title and for which it has not given consideration in return) are capitalised at their current valuation on receipt and are revalued/depreciated on the same basis as purchased assets.

1.19 A donated assets reserve represents the value of the original donation, additions, any subsequent professional revaluation and indexation (MHCA) or a professional valuation. Amounts equal to the donated asset depreciation charge, impairment costs and deficit/surplus on disposal arising during the year, are released from this reserve to the Operating Cost Statement.

Impairment

1.20 The charge to the Operating Cost Statement in respect of impairment arises on the decision to sell a fixed asset and take it out of service; on transfer of a fixed asset into stock; on reduction in service potential and where the application of MHCA indices causes a downward revaluation below the historical cost and which is deemed to be permanent in nature. Impairment also includes the cost of capital spares that are embodied into a fixed asset, as part of a major refit and overhaul, but which cannot be capitalised in accordance with FRS 15. Any reversal of an impairment cost is recognised in the operating cost statement to the extent that the original charge was recognised in the Operating Cost Statement. The remaining amount is recognised in the revaluation reserve.

Disposal of Tangible Fixed Assets

1.21 Disposal of assets is principally handled by two specialist agencies: Defence Estates for property assets and the Disposal Services Agency for non-property assets.

1.22 Property assets identified for disposal are included at the open market value with any resulting changes in the net book value charged to the Operating Cost Statement under Impairment or credited to the revaluation reserve as appropriate. On subsequent sale the surplus or deficit is included in the Operating Cost Statement under surplus/deficit on disposal of fixed assets.

1.23 Non-property assets are subject to regular impairment reviews. An impairment review is also carried out when a decision is made to dispose of an asset and take it out of service. Any write down in value to the net recoverable amount (NRA) is charged to the Operating Cost Statement under Impairment. The surplus or deficit at the point of disposal is included in the Operating Cost Statement under surplus/deficit on disposal of fixed assets. Non-property assets, where the receipts on sale are anticipated not to be separately identifiable, are transferred to stock at their NRA and shown under assets declared for disposal. Any write down on transfer is included in the Operating Cost Statement under Impairment.

1.24 Disposals exclude fixed assets written off and written on. These items are included within Other Movements in Notes 8 and 9.

Leased Assets

1.25 Assets held under finance leases are capitalised as tangible fixed assets and depreciated over the shorter of the lease term or their estimated useful economic lives. Rentals paid are apportioned between reductions in the capital obligations included in creditors, and finance charges charged to the Operating Cost Statement. Expenditure under operating leases is charged to the Operating Cost Statement in the period in which it is incurred. In circumstances where the Department is the lessor of a finance lease, amounts due under a finance lease are treated as amounts receivable and reported in Debtors.

Private Finance Initiative (PFI) Transactions

1.26 Where the substance of the transaction is that the risks and rewards of ownership remain with the Department, the assets and liabilities remain on the Department's Balance Sheet. Service charges in respect of on-balance sheet PFI deals are apportioned between reduction in the capital obligation and charges to the Operating Cost Statement for service performance and finance cost. Where the risks and rewards are transferred to the private sector the transaction is accounted for in the Operating Cost Statement through service charges in accordance with FRS 5 and Treasury Guidance.

Investments

1.27 Investments represent holdings that the Department intends to retain for the foreseeable future. Fixed asset investments are stated at market value where available, otherwise they are stated at cost. They include the Public Dividend Capital of those Executive Agencies owned by the Department and established as Trading Funds. Investments may either be equity investments, held in the name of the Secretary of State for Defence, or medium or long-term loans made with the intention of providing working capital or commercial support.

1.28 Joint Ventures are accounted for using the Gross Equity method of accounting. Under this method the Department's share of the aggregate gross assets and liabilities underlying the net equity investments are shown on the face of the Balance Sheet. The Operating Cost Statement includes the Department's share of the investee's turnover.

Stocks and Work-in-Progress

1.29 Stock is valued at current replacement cost, or historical cost if not materially different. Provision is made to reduce cost to net realisable value (NRV) where there is no expectation of consumption or sale in the ordinary course of the business. Stock provision is released to the operating costs on consumption, disposal and write-off.

1.30 Internal Work-in-Progress represents ongoing work on the manufacture, modification, enhancement or conversion of stock items. This is valued on the same basis as stocks. External Work-in-Progress represents ongoing work on production or repair contracts for external customers. This is valued at the lower of current replacement cost and NRV.

1.31 Assets declared for disposal include stock held for disposal and those non-property fixed assets identified for disposal where receipts are not anticipated to be separately identifiable.

1.32 Stocks written-off, included within other operating costs, represents the book value of stock which has been scrapped, destroyed or lost during the year, and adjustments to agree the book values with the figures shown on the supply systems.

Provisions for Liabilities and Charges

1.33 Provisions for liabilities and charges have been established under the criteria of FRS 12 and are based on realistic and prudent estimates of the expenditure required to settle future legal or constructive obligations that exist at the Balance Sheet date.

1.34 Provisions are charged to the Operating Cost Statement unless they have been capitalised as part of the cost of the underlying facility where the expenditure provides access to current and future economic benefits. In such cases the capitalised provision will be depreciated as a charge to the Operating Cost Statement over the remaining estimated useful economic life of the underlying asset. All long-term provisions are discounted to current prices by use of HM Treasury's Test Discount Rate (TDR) which was 3.5% (2002-03: 6%) for the financial year 2003-04. The discount is unwound over the remaining life of the provision and shown as an interest charge in the Operating Cost Statement.

Reserves

1.35 The Revaluation Reserve reflects the unrealised element of the cumulative balance of revaluation and indexation adjustments on fixed assets and stocks (excluding donated assets and those financed by Government grants). The Donated Asset Reserve reflects the net book value of assets that have been donated to the Department.

1.36 The General Fund represents the balance of the taxpayers' equity.

Pensions

1.37 Present and past employees are mainly covered by the CSP arrangements for civilian personnel and the AFPS for Service personnel. There are separate scheme statements for the AFPS and CSP as a whole.

1.38 Both pension schemes are contracted out, unfunded, defined benefit pay as you go occupational pension schemes, although they are being accounted for as if they were defined contribution schemes in accordance with the HM Treasury RAM. The employer's charge is met by payment of an ASLC, which is calculated based on a percentage of pensionable pay. The ASLC represents an estimate of the cost of providing future superannuation protection for all personnel currently in pensionable employment. In addition, civilian personnel contribute 1.5% of salary to fund a widow/widower's pension if they are members of Classic and 3.5% if they are members of Premium. The Department's Balance Sheet will only include a creditor in respect of pensions to the extent that the contributions paid to the pension funds in the year fall short of the ASLC and widow/widower's pension charges due.

1.39 The pension schemes undergo a reassessment of the ASLC contribution rates by the Government Actuary at three-yearly intervals. Provisions are made for costs of early retirement programmes and redundancies up to the normal retirement age and charged to the Operating Cost Statement.

1.40 The Department operates a number of small pension schemes for civilians engaged at overseas locations. These schemes have been accounted for in accordance with the application of SSAP 24 – Accounting for Pension Costs, as set out in the HM Treasury RAM. With effect from 1 April 2003 they are accounted for in accordance with FRS 17 – Retirement Benefits. Prior year's figures have not been restated as any adjustments would not be material.

1.41 The disclosures required under FRS 17 are included in Note 2.4

Early Departure Costs

1.42 The Department provides in full for the cost of meeting pensions up to normal retirement age in respect of civilian personnel early retirement programmes and redundancies announced in the current and previous years. Pensions payable after normal retirement age are met by the CSP arrangements for civilian personnel.

1.43 There is no comparable early retirement or redundancy scheme for Service personnel but an immediate entitlement to draw pension under the AFPS accrues after 22 years' service for other ranks and 16 years' service for officers, or earlier in circumstances where exceptional approval is given.

Cost of Capital Charge

1.44 A charge, reflecting the cost of capital utilised by the Department, is included in the Operating Cost Statement and credited to the General Fund. The charge is calculated using the HM Treasury standard rate for financial year 2003-04 of 3.5% (2002-03: 6%) in real terms on all assets less liabilities except for:

- Donated assets and cash balances with the Office of HM Paymaster General (OPG) where the charge is nil.

- Liabilities for the amounts to be surrendered to the Consolidated Fund and for amounts due from the Consolidated Fund where the charge is nil.

- Assets financed by grants, where the charge is nil.

- Additions to heritage collections where the existing collection has not been capitalised, where the charge is nil.

1.45 The cost of capital charge on the fixed asset investments in the Trading Funds and in the Self Financing Public Corporation is calculated at a specific rate applicable to those entities, and is based on their underlying net assets.

Foreign Exchange

1.46 Transactions that are denominated in a foreign currency are translated into Sterling using the General Accounting Rate (GAR) ruling at the date of each transaction. US$ and Euros are purchased forward from the Bank of England. Monetary assets and liabilities are translated at the spot rate applicable at the Balance Sheet date and the exchange differences are reported in the Operating Cost Statement.

1.47 Overseas non-monetary assets and liabilities are subject to annual revaluation and are translated at the spot rate applicable at the Balance Sheet date and the exchange differences are taken to the revaluation reserve for owned assets, or the donated asset reserve for donated assets.

2. Staff Numbers and Costs

2.1 The average number of whole-time equivalent persons employed during the year was: Service 213,600 (2002-03: 211,453) and Civilian 92,720 (2002-03: 92,358). [Source: Defence Analytical Services Agency]

2.2 The aggregate staff costs, including grants and allowances paid were as follows:

	2003-04 £000	2002-03 £000
Salaries and Wages	8,332,356	7,819,361
Social Security costs	609,865	506,837
Pension costs (see Note 2.4)	1,442,696	1,357,703
Redundancy and severance payments	50,240	285,341
	10,435,157	9,969,242
Made up of:		
Service	7,973,835	7,385,185
Civilian	2,461,322	2,584,057
	10,435,157	9,969,242

2.3 For the year ended 31 March 2004 the salary, pension entitlements and the value of any taxable benefits-in-kind for Ministers in respect of their services to the Department is detailed below and should be read in conjunction with the following notes.

Ministerial Salaries and Allowances

† The presentation below is based on payments made by the Department and thus recorded in these Accounts. In respect of Ministers in the House of Commons, Departments bear only the cost of the additional ministerial remuneration. The salary for their services as an MP £56,358 pa with effect from 1 April 2003 (2002-03 £55,118 pa with effect from 1 April 2002), and various allowances to which they are entitled are borne centrally by the House of Commons. However, the arrangements for Ministers in the House of Lords is different in that they do not receive a salary but rather an additional remuneration which cannot be quantified separately from their Ministerial salaries. This total remuneration, as well as the allowances to which they are entitled, is paid by the Department and is therefore shown in full in the figures below.

** Lords Ministers' Night Subsistence paid to The Lord Bach of Lutterworth was £27,866 in 2003-04 (2002-03: £27,133). These figures are included in the salary figures disclosed. No Minister received payment of the London Supplement allowance this year.

Ministers who have not attained the age of 65, and who are not re-appointed to a relevant Ministerial or other paid office within three weeks, are eligible for a severance payment. One such payment was made in 2003-04 (2002-03: Nil).

Ministerial Pensions

Pension benefits for Ministers are provided by the Parliamentary Contributory Pension Fund (PCPF). The scheme is statutory based (made under Statutory Instrument SI 1993 No 3253, as amended).

Those Ministers who are Members of Parliament are also entitled to an MP's pension under the PCPF. The arrangements for Ministers provide benefits on an 'average salary' basis with either a 1/50th or 1/40th accrual rate, taking account of all service as a Minister. (The accrual rate has been 1/40th since 15 July 2002 but Ministers, in common with all other members of the PCPF, can opt to increase their accrual rate from 5 July 2001, or retain the former 1/50th accrual rate and the lower rate of employee contribution.)

Benefits for Ministers are payable at the same time as MPs' benefits become payable under the PCPF or, for those who are not MPs, on retirement from ministerial office on or after age 65. Pensions are increased annually in line with changes in the Retail Prices Index. Members pay contributions of 6% of their Ministerial salary if they have opted for the 1/50th accrual rate, and 9% if they have opted for the 1/40th accrual rate. There is also an employer contribution paid by the Exchequer representing the balance of cost. This is currently 24% of the Ministerial salary.

The Cash Equivalent Transfer Value (CETV)

This is the actuarially assessed capitalised value of the pension scheme benefits accrued by a member at a particular point in time. The benefits valued are the member's accrued benefits and any contingent spouse's pension payable from the scheme. It is a payment made by a pension scheme or arrangement to secure pension benefits in another pension scheme or arrangement when the member leaves a scheme and chooses to transfer the pension benefits they have accrued in their former scheme. The pension figures shown relate to the benefits that the individual has accrued as a consequence of their total ministerial service, not just their current appointment as a Minister. CETVs are calculated within the guidelines and framework prescribed by the Institute and Faculty of Actuaries.

The real increase in the value of the CETV

This takes account of the increase in accrued pension to owing inflation and contributions paid by the Minister and is calculated using common market valuation factors for the start and end of the period.

Benefits-in-kind for Ministers

Minister's private use of Official cars is exempt under the rules governing the definition of taxable benefits-in-kind. Mr Hoon was provided with living accommodation. The value of the benefit is calculated in accordance with the Inland Revenue regulations. No tax is charged on the living accommodation itself; a charge is made on the value of associated services, limited to 10% of taxable Ministerial salary.

Ministers:

Figures for 2003-04 in bold, 2002-03 in italics

	Salary (as defined below) £000	Taxable Benefits-in-kind (to nearest) £000	Total Accrued Pension at retirement as at 31 March 2004 £000	CETV at 31March 2003 £000	CETV at 31 March 2004 £000	Real increase in CETV as funded by employer £000
Secretary of State for Defence: The Right Honourable Geoffrey Hoon, MP †	**70-75** *65-70*	**7,100** *3,500*	**5-10** *0-5*	54	72	8
Minister of State for the Armed Forces: The Right Honourable Adam Ingram MP †	**35-40** *35-40*	**Nil** *Nil*	**5-10** *0-5*	54	66	7
Parliamentary Under Secretary of State and Minister for Defence Procurement: The Lord Bach of Lutterworth † **	**90-95** *90-95*	**Nil** *Nil*	**5-10** *0-5*	58	78	12
Parliamentary Under Secretary of State for Defence and Minister for Veterans: Dr Lewis Moonie, MP † *(Until 13 Jun 2003)*	**10-15** *25-30*	**Nil** *Nil*	**0-5** *0-5*	25	27	1
Ivor Caplin MP † *(From 13 June 2003)*	**20-25**	**Nil**	**0-5**	9	14	3
Salary includes gross salary, performance pay and allowances paid.						

Defence Management Board:

The salary, pension entitlements and the value of taxable benefits-in-kind for the Department's senior management board, the DMB, were as below.

Figures for 2003-04 in bold, 2002-03 in italics

	Salary (as defined below) £000	Taxable Benefits-in-kind (to nearest £100)	Total Accrued Pension at retirement as at 31 March 2004 £000	CETV at 31 March 2003 £000	CETV at 31 March 2004 £000	Real increase in CETV as funded by employer (Note) £000
Permanent Under Secretary of State Sir Kevin Tebbit KCB CMG	**165-170** *150-155*	**33,000** *29,200*	**Pension 65-70 Lump sum 205-210**	1,075	1,223	101
Chief of the Defence Staff Admiral the Lord Boyce GCB OBE DL *(Until 1 May 2003)*	*175-180*	*25,400*	*CONSENT*	*TO DISCLOSE*	*WITHELD*	
General Sir Michael Walker GCB CMG CBE ADC Gen *(From 2 May 2003)*	**165-170** *(see below)*	**27,900** *(see below)*	**Pension 85-90 Lump sum 265-270**	1,207	1,604	
First Sea Lord and Chief of the Naval Staff Admiral Sir Alan West KCB DSC ADC	**125-130** *65-70*	**21,300** *12,100*	**Pension 60-65 Lump sum 185-190**	1,241	1,292	
Chief of the General Staff General Sir Mike Jackson KCB CBE DSO ADC Gen *(From 3 Feb 2003)*	**135-140** *20-25*	**22,200** *3,300*	**Pension 65-70 Lump sum 200-205**	1,162	1,185	
General Sir Michael Walker GCB CMG CBE ADC Gen *(Until 2 Feb 2003)*	*105-110*	*17,900*				
Chief of the Air Staff Air Chief Marshal Sir Peter Squire GCB DFC AFC ADC FRAeS RAF *(Until 31 Jul 2003)*	**40-45** *125-130*	**7,600** *22,500*	**Pension 65-70 Lump sum 195-200**	1,245	1,263	
Air Chief Marshal Sir Jock Stirrup KCB AFC ADC FRAeS FCMI RAF *(From 1 Aug 2003)*	**85-90** *Nil*	**14,800** *Nil*	**Pension 55-60 Lump sum 175-180**	1,069	1,260	
Vice Chief of the Defence Staff Air Chief Marshal Sir Anthony Bagnall KCB OBE ADC FRAeS RAF	**130-135** *125-130*	**22,900** *20,500*	**Pension 65-70 Lump sum 200-205**	1,243	1,262	
Second Permanent Under Secretary of State Ian Andrews CBE TD	**125-130** *115-120*	**28,300** *29,500*	**Pension 40-45 Lump sum 115-120**	569	641	55
Chief of Defence Procurement Sir Robert Walmsley KCB FEng FIEE *(Until 30 Apr 2003)*	**10-15** *130-135*	**2,600** *43,200*	**Pension 5-10 Lump sum 25-30**	151	152	1

Note:

Figures for the real increase in Cash Equivalent Transfer Values (CETV) are not yet available for Service members of the Defence Management Board.

	Salary (as defined below) £000	Taxable Benefits-in-kind (to nearest £100)	Total Accrued Pension at retirement as at 31 March 2004 £000	CETV at 31 March 2003 £000	CETV at 31 March 2004 £000	Real increase in CETV as funded by employer £000
Sir Peter Spencer KCB (From 1 May 2003)	105-110 *Nil*	29,000 *Nil*	Pension 0-5	0	18	15
Chief of Defence Logistics Air Chief Marshal Sir Malcolm Pledger KCB OBE AFC BSc FRAeS RAF *(From 2 Sep 2002)*	125-130 *65-70*	Nil *Nil*	Pension 60-65 Lump sum 115-120	1,204	1,284	
Chief Scientific Adviser Professor Sir Keith O'Nions FRS	145-150 *135-140*	25,700 *27,700*	Pension 35-40 Lump sum 115-120	676	720	15
Non-executive member of the DMB Charles Miller Smith (Chairman of Scottish Power) (From 29 May 2002)	25-30 *15-20* *Fees*					
Non-executive member of the DMB Philippa Foster Back † (Director of the Institute of Business Ethics) (From 10 Jul 2002)	35-40 *10-15* *Fees*					
† Mrs Foster Back's fees are £25,000 per annum. Fees for 2003–04 include an increase payable from July 2002.						
Salary includes gross salary, performance pay and allowances paid.						

Benefits-in-kind figures for civilian members of the DMB represent the value obtained from the private use of official cars, and for Service members of the DMB represents the value obtained from use of Official Service Residences. The Department has an arrangement with the Inland Revenue where MoD pays the tax liability that would ordinarily be paid by the individual. The tax liability consists of income tax, and where applicable, employees NIC. This tax liability is therefore included in the figures disclosed to arrive at the full 'value' of the benefit to the individual.

Details of Chief Executives and other senior staff of agencies are given in the agency accounts.

Pensions

2.3   The Principal Civil Service Pension Scheme (PCSPS) is an unfunded multi-employer defined benefit scheme but the Ministry of Defence is unable to identify its share of the underlying assets and liabilities. A full actuarial valuation was carried out at 31 March 1999 for the PCSPS. Details can be found in the resource accounts of the scheme which are published and laid before the House of Commons. The PCSPS accounts are also available on the web at www.civilservice-pensions.gov.uk.

For 2003-04, employers' contributions of £218,459,000 in respect of civilian staff were payable to the OPG (2002-03: £211,677,000) at one of the four rates in the range of 12 to 18.5 per cent of pensionable pay, based on salary bands. Rates will remain the same for next year, subject to revalorisation of the salary bands. Employer contributions to the PCSPS are to be reviewed every four years following a full scheme valuation by the Government Actuary.

For Service personnel, employers' contributions of £1,224,237,000 (2002-03: £1,146,025,000) were also made to the Armed Forces Pension Scheme (AFPS) based on rates determined by the Government Actuary. The applicable rates were 33.8% of pensionable pay for Officers and 18.2% for other ranks.

The contribution rates reflect benefits as they are accrued, not when costs are actually incurred, and reflect past experience of the scheme.

2.4   Certain other employees are covered by other schemes such as the NHS Superannuation Scheme and the Teachers' Superannuation Scheme. Contributions to these schemes in 2003-04 are included within the amount of £218,459,000 shown in Note 2.4 above.

Cash Equivalent Transfer Values

2.5   A Cash Equivalent Transfer Value (CETV) is the actuarially assessed capitalised value of the pension scheme benefits accrued by a member at a particular point in time. The benefits valued are the member's accrued benefits and any contingent spouse's pension payable from the scheme. A CETV is a payment made by a pension scheme or arrangement to secure pension benefits in another pension scheme or arrangement when the member leaves a scheme and chooses to transfer the benefits accrued in their former scheme. The pension figures shown relate to the benefits that the individual has accrued as a consequence of their total membership of the pension scheme, not just their service in a senior capacity to which disclosure applies. The CETV figures, and from 2003-04 the other pension details, include the value of any pension benefit in another scheme or arrangement which the individual has transferred to the CSP arrangements and for which the CS Vote has received a transfer payment commensurate to the additional pension liabilities being assumed. They also include any additional pension benefit accrued to the member as a result of their purchasing additional years of pension service in the scheme at their own cost. CETVs are calculated within the guidelines and framework prescribed by the Institute and Faculty of Actuaries.

Real increase in CETV

2.6   This reflects the increase in CETV effectively funded by the employer. It takes account of the increase in accrued pension to owing inflation, contributions paid by the employee (including the value of any benefits transferred from another pension scheme or arrangement) and uses common market valuation factors for the start and end of the period.

3. Other Operating Costs

	2003-04 £000	2002-03 £000
Operating expenditure:		
– Fuel	161,329	184,665
– Stock consumption	1,059,775	1,222,151
– Surplus arising on disposal of stock (net)	(29,456)	(14,388)
– Provisions to reduce stocks to net realisable value	(72,345)	111,125
– Stocks written off (net)	528,120	321,811
– Movements: includes personnel travelling, subsistence/relocation costs and movement of stores and equipment	491,226	505,272
– Utilities	220,327	223,048
– Property management	1,393,283	1,453,041
– Hospitality and entertainment	7,991	7,320
– Accommodation charges	422,888	320,557
– Equipment support costs	3,804,132	3,135,174
– Increase in nuclear and other decommissioning provisions (Note 17)	154,509	1,635,223
– IT and telecommunications	737,717	628,447
– Professional fees	549,048	468,201
– Other expenditure	2,032,368	1,870,940
– Research expenditure and expensed development expenditure	1,011,213	977,707
Depreciation and amortisation:		
– Intangible assets (Note 8)	902,707	1,256,067
– Tangible owned fixed assets (Note 9)	4,838,283	5,766,924
– Donated assets depreciation - release of reserve	(46,625)	(48,845)
– Tangible fixed assets held under finance leases (Note 9)	24,993	7,309
Impairment on fixed assets (Notes 8 & 9):		
– Quinquennial valuation	–	3,855,123
– Other	299,010	1,534,601
Impairment – donated assets release of reserve	(1)	(1,500)
(Surplus)/ Deficit arising on disposal of tangible and intangible fixed assets		
– Tangible and Intangible fixed assets	(68,676)	(44,219)
– Donated assets – release of reserve	(3,049)	(1,041)
– Loss on sale of shares in QinetiQ	–	8,397
Fixed assets written off/(written on) - net	26,017	101,604
Write down of the value of investment in QinetiQ	–	219,886
Capital project expenditure written off	268,310	584,928
Bad debts written off	27,491	14,709
Decrease in bad debts provision	(2,939)	(5,523)
Rentals paid under operating leases	214,328	311,003
Auditors' remuneration – audit work only	3,150	3,405
Grants-in-Aid	54,790	49,128
Exchange differences on foreign currencies: net deficit/(surplus)	(622)	12,276
War Pensions and Allowances	1,117,635	1,166,265
Total Other Operating Costs	**20,126,927**	27,840,791

4. Analysis of income payable to the Consolidated Fund

In addition to Appropriations-in-Aid the following income relates to the Department and is payable to the Consolidated Fund. (Cash receipts are shown in italics).

| | 2003-04 Forecast | | 2003-04 Outturn | |
	Income £000	Receipts £000	Income £000	Receipts £000
Operating income and receipts – excess A-in-A	–	–	85,315	*85,315*
Non operating income and receipts – excess A-in-A	–	–	137,325	*137,325*
Subtotal	–	–	222,640	*222,640*
Other operating income and receipts not classified as A-in-A	–	–	35,364	*35,364*
Other non-operating income and receipts not classified as A-in-A	–	–	–	–
Other amounts collectable on behalf of the Consolidated Fund	–	–	–	–
	–	–	258,004	*258,004*

The table above does not include loans repaid by QinetiQ and paid to the Consolidated Fund amounting to £4,213,977.

5. Operating Income

	2003-04 £000	2002-03 £000
External customers		
Rental Income – property	54,717	54,020
Other	1,171,897	1,115,777
Other Government Departments and Trading Funds and QinetiQ		
Rental income – property	4,974	2,058
Dividends received from Trading Funds (Note 10)	8,902	8,587
Other	171,816	177,258
	1,412,306	**1,357,700**
Of which:		
Appropriations-in-Aid	1,378,937	1,334,286
CFER – Payable to the Consolidated Fund	33,369	23,414
	1,412,306	**1,357,700**
Appropriations-in-Aid shown on Schedule 1 is the lower of the amounts shown in the Estimate and the Outturn:		
Outturn:		
– Operating Income (see above)	1,378,937	1,334,286
Included in other operating costs:		
– Refunds of formula based VAT recovery	46,766	44,112
– Profit on disposal of stock (net) (Note 3)	–	14,388
– Profit on disposal of tangible and intangible fixed assets (net) (Note 3)	–	45,260
– Foreign exchange gains	37,435	11,721
	1,463,138	**1,449,767**
Estimate:		
Appropriations-in-Aid as shown in the Spring Supplementary Estimate	1,377,823	1,695,949
Excess Appropriations-in-Aid payable to the Consolidated Fund as CFERs	**85,315**	–

6. Net Interest Payable

	2003-04 £000	2002-03 £000
Interest receivable:		
– Bank interest	(20,006)	(3,643)
– Loans to Trading Funds	(6,637)	(7,119)
– Loans to a Self Financing Public Corporation – QinetiQ	(1,346)	(5,054)
– Other interest receivable	(137)	–
	(28,126)	**(15,816)**
Interest payable:		
– Bank interest	164	6
– Loan interest	3,536	3,612
– Unwinding of discount on provision for liabilities and charges (Note 17)	2,609,205	247,703
– Finance leases and PFI contracts	26,264	31,026
– Commercial debt	–	1
	2,639,169	282,348
Net interest payable	**2,611,043**	266,532

7. Reconciliation of Net Operating Cost to Control Total and Net Resource Outturn

	2003-04 £000	2002-03 £000
Net operating cost (Schedule 2)	34,530,547	41,793,591
– Add income scored as Consolidated Fund Extra Receipts and included in operating income and interest (inc. excess Appropriation-in-Aid) (Note 4)	120,679	39,197
– Proceeds on part disposal of QinetiQ included in operating costs	–	39,427
– Prior year adjustment	–	141,469
Net resource outturn	**34,651,226**	42,013,684

Net operating cost is the total of expenditure and income appearing in the Operating Cost Statement. Net Resource Outturn is the total of those elements of expenditure and income that are subject to parliamentary approval and included in the Department's Supply Estimate. The Outturn against the Estimate is shown in the Summary of Resource Outturn (Schedule 1).

8. Intangible Assets

	£000
Cost or Valuation	
At 1 April 2003	23,753,098
Additions	1,665,395
Disposals	(31,372)
Impairment	(46,867)
Revaluations	97,738
Other movements	(513,174)
At 31 March 2004	24,924,818
Amortisation	
At 1 April 2003	(4,315,490)
Charged in Year	(902,707)
Impairment	(10,916)
Disposals	31,372
Revaluations	334,143
Other movements	125,523
At 31 March 2004	(4,738,075)
Net Book Value:	
At 31 March 2004	**20,186,743**
At 1 April 2003	19,437,608

Note:

i)   Intangible asset valuations are based on the actual costs incurred over time, where available, or derived by applying a ratio to the tangible fixed asset valuations based on the historical relationship between development and production costs. The intangible asset valuations were indexed using the appropriate Gross Domestic Product (GDP) deflator to determine the opening balance sheet valuation;

ii) Intangible assets include development expenditure in respect of fixed assets in use and assets under construction where the first delivery into operational use of the asset type has taken place;

iii) Additions on intangible and tangible fixed assets (Note 9) include accruals amounting in total to £2,204,303,000 (2002-03: £2,066,322,000); and

iv) Other movements comprise reclassifications to tangible fixed assets and transfers to operating costs.

9. Tangible Fixed Assets

	Land and Buildings £000	Fighting Equipment £000	Plant, Machinery and Vehicles £000	IT and Comms Equipment £000	Capital Spares £000	Assets Under Construction £000	Total £000
Cost or Valuation							
At 1 April 2003	16,080,431	42,050,778	6,840,039	1,226,425	18,947,812	12,511,081	97,656,566
Additions	53,721	90,004	77,998	183,309	580,583	3,930,703	4,916,318
Capitalised provisions	(20,633)	(78,643)	–	–	–	–	(99,276)
Donations	911	–	2,819	3	–	–	3,733
Impairment	(34,374)	(116,496)	(35,009)	(41,699)	(57,612)	(7,862)	(293,052)
Disposals	(406,764)	(7,672)	(82,071)	(13,623)	(1,097,824)	(436)	(1,608,390)
Revaluations	836,551	554,643	958,436	(46,354)	393,616	200,800	2,897,692
Other movements	(2,879)	1,661,208	(562,841)	(78,724)	42,801	(3,457,076)	(2,397,511)
At 31 March 2004	16,506,964	44,153,822	7,199,371	1,229,337	18,809,376	13,177,210	101,076,080
Depreciation							
At 1 April 2003	(738,095)	(15,523,883)	(2,544,096)	(412,646)	(11,993,310)	–	(31,212,030)
Charged in year	(617,950)	(2,583,599)	(454,778)	(181,101)	(1,025,848)	–	(4,863,276)
Impairment	45,199	193,104	(14,702)	11,146	(182,922)	–	51,825
Disposals	2,487	7,622	79,625	12,411	1,093,623	–	1,195,768
Revaluations	(29,154)	(158,489)	(920,115)	48,311	(231,756)	–	(1,291,203)
Other movements	130,307	1,068,418	107,755	188,488	285,125	–	1,780,093
At 31 March 2004	(1,207,206)	(16,996,827)	(3,746,311)	(333,391)	(12,055,088)	–	(34,338,823)
Net Book Value:							
At 31 March 2004	**15,299,758**	**27,156,995**	**3,453,060**	**895,946**	**6,754,288**	**13,177,210**	**66,737,257**
At 1 April 2003	15,342,336	26,526,895	4,295,943	813,779	6,954,502	12,511,081	66,444,536

Note:

i)   Additions on intangible assets (Note 8) and tangible fixed assets include accruals amounting in total to £2,204,303,000 (2002-03: £2,066,322,000);

ii) Other movements comprise reclassifications between tangible fixed asset categories, intangible assets, assets under construction, stock and transfers to operating costs;

iii) Fixed Assets as at 31 March 2004 include capitalised provisions at cost of £222,519,000 (2002-03: £321,000,000); and

iv) The figure impairments above includes the following amounts in respect of reversals of impairments: Land and Buildings £32.296 million, Fighting Equipment £122.305 million, Plant, Machinery and Vehicles £0.495 million and IT and Comms Equipment £0.581 million.

9.1 The net book value of tangible fixed assets by each major class of asset includes an amount of £329,852,000 (2002-03 £115,389,000) in respect of assets held under finance leases and PFI contracts. Detail by asset category is as follows:

	Land and Buildings £000	Fighting Equipment £000	Plant, Machinery and Vehicles £000	IT and Comms Equipment £000	Capital Spares £000	Assets Under Construction £000	Total £000
Gross Cost:							
At 31 March 2004	**102,604**	**130,804**	**87,263**	**64,797**	–	–	**385,468**
At 1 April 2003	41,708	42,305	77,560	5,437	–	–	167,010
Accumulated Depreciation:							
At 31 March 2004	**8,046**	**42,553**	**4,794**	**223**	–	–	**55,616**
At 1 April 2003	1,719	20,511	27,429	1,962	–	–	51,621

9.2 Analysis of Land and Buildings:

	Freehold £000	Long Lease £000	Short Lease £000	Beneficial Use* £000	Total £000
Net Book Value:					
At 31 March 2004	**13,726,472**	**268,518**	**71,471**	**1,877,832**	**15,944,293**
At 1 April 2003	13,967,993	215,304	54,147	1,767,858	16,005,302

The net book values at 31 March 2004 and 1 April 2003 include assets under construction of £644,535,000 and £662,966,000 respectively.

*Relates to properties that are being used by the Department where no legal title is held. Such properties have been valued on the same basis as all other properties used by the Department.

9.3 Professional valuation of Land and Buildings was carried out by external valuers, as follows:

Year last valued	Valuation £000
Before 1 April 2001	535,207
2001-2002	696,405
2002-2003	13,847,177*
2003-2004	618,959

*2002-03 Quinquennial Revaluation

9.4 All categories of fixed assets, except Intangibles, Assets under Construction and Capital Spares, were subject to a quinquennial revaluation with an effective valuation date of 1 April 2002.

9.5 Operational land and buildings were valued by two firms of external professional valuers: the Valuation Office Agency valued the UK estate and the Overseas estate was valued by ATIS REAL Weatheralls, whose valuers are members of the Royal Institution of Chartered Surveyors (RICS). These valuations were undertaken in accordance with the RICS Appraisal and Valuation Manual and were on the basis of the existing use value to the Department and did not take account of alternative use value. Because of the specialised nature of the Departmental estate, the great majority of assets were thus valued on the Depreciated Replacement Cost basis.

9.6 Surplus land and buildings were valued by qualified internal Defence Estates staff, on the basis of Open Market Value.

9.7 Plant, Machinery & Vehicles and IT & Communications were both valued on a Depreciated Replacement Cost basis by the Valuation Office Agency, whose valuers are members of the Royal Institution of Chartered Surveyors.

10. Investments

	Trading Funds Public Dividend Capital £000	Trading Funds Loans £000	Other Investments £000	QinetiQ £000	Total £000
At 1 April 2003	184,254	117,203	1	128,220	429,678
Movements during year:					
DARA – new loan		19,200			19,200
Repayment of Loans					
–QinetiQ				(4,214)	(4,214)
–DARA		(7,240)			(7,240)
–UK Hydro Office		(303)			(303)
–DSTL		(2,128)			(2,128)
–ABRO		(14,155)			(14,155)
At 31 March 2004	184,254	112,577	1	124,006	420,838

Public Dividend Capital and Loans at 31 March 2004 were held in the following Trading Funds:

	Public Dividend Capital £000	Loans £000	Interest Rate % p.a.	
DSTL	50,412	1,064	8.375	
Met Office	58,867	–	–	
The UK Hydrographic Office	13,267	11,679	8.375	
DARA	42,303	71,830	4.882	
ABRO	19,405	28,004	5.375 - 5.625	
	184,254	112,577		

Analysis of loans repayable by instalments:

	Due within one year £000	Due after one year £000	Total £000
DSTL	1,064	–	1,064
The UK Hydrographic Office	303	11,376	11,679
DARA	7,240	64,590	71,830
ABRO	2,154	25,850	28,004
	10,761	101,816	112,577

At 31 March 2004, the loan made to QinetiQ Group Limited, a subsidiary undertaking of QinetiQ, amounted to £45,886,000 (31 March 2003: £50,100,000) and the book value of investment in QinetiQ amounted to £78,120,000. The loan note is repayable from the net proceeds of disposals of certain identified assets. The loan note was interest free until 30 June 2003 and thereafter interest has been charged at rates relating to LIBOR.

As at 31 March 2004, the loans repaid by QinetiQ and subsidiary undertakings, representing the partial original asset value of the business since its formation on 1 July 2001, amounted in total to £104,114,000 (2002-03: £99,900,000). Cash received on part disposal of the shares to The Carlyle Group during 2002-03 amounted to £39,427,000.

10.1 Other Investments:

Investments, including "Golden" shares, were held in the following at 31 March 2004 and 31 March 2003:

		7.5% Non-cumulative irredeemable preference shares at £1 each
Chamber of Shipping Limited		688 Shares
British Shipping Federation Limited		55,040 Shares
		Preferential 'Golden' Shares at £1 each
Devonport Royal Dockyard Limited		1 Share
Rosyth Royal Dockyard Limited		1 Share
Atomic Weapons Establishment plc		1 Share
Atomic Weapons Establishment Pension Trustees Limited		1 Share
QinetiQ Group plc		1 Share
QinetiQ Limited		1 Share
BAE Systems Marine (Holdings) Ltd (formerly VSEL Limited)		1 Share
		Non Preferential Shares of £1 each
International Military Services Limited		19,999,999 Shares

Shareholding in QinetiQ

The Department holds 5 classes of shares in QinetiQ. A brief summary of the financial and voting rights of each class are detailed below in order of their ranking in accordance with the Articles of Association of QinetiQ.

Convertible "A" ordinary (3,773,481 shares of 1p each – 49% of class)

Voting rights – holders of these shares are entitled to receive notice of, attend, speak and vote at general meetings of the company.
Dividends – none to be paid until Preference Shares have been redeemed in full along with any accrued Preference Dividend.

Convertible "B" ordinary (285,833 shares of 1p each – 49% of class)

Dividend and Voting rights as per "A" Ordinary shares.

Convertible Preferred (3,752,686 shares of 1p each – 100% of class)

Voting rights – this class of shareholder is not entitled to receive notice of, nor attend, speak or vote at general meetings of the company.

Dividends – until conversion each Convertible Preferred share in issue will be entitled to the same dividend as paid on each "A" Ordinary Share.

Redeemable Cumulative Preference (70,308,000 shares of £1 each – 62.5% of class)

Voting rights – preference shareholders are not entitled to receive notice of, nor attend, speak or vote at general meetings of the company.

Dividend – to be paid at the rate of 9% per annum on the nominal value of the preference shares held.

Dividends will not be paid, but will accrue until the preference shares are redeemed at the Sale, Listing or the Winding up of the company. The dividend accrued on these shares will be recognised in the Operating Cost Statement in the year in which it is received, in accordance with accounting policy in Note 1.9.

In June 2004, the Department received £48,542,475 on the partial redemption of some of these shares and an amount of £5,759,382 in respect of the dividend accrued on these shares up to the date of redemption.

Special Rights Redeemable of £1 each - the one "Special Share", which is held by MoD

The Special Shareholder has the right to require the Company to implement and maintain a regime which protects the defence and security interests of the nation. Voting rights – the Special Shareholder must receive notice of, and may attend and speak at general company and share class meetings, but carries no voting rights, except to enforce certain aspects of the compliance regime.

Preferential "Golden" Shares at £1 each (1 share QinetiQ Group plc, 1 share QinetiQ Limited)

The Preferential "Golden" Shareholder has the right to require the Company to implement and maintain a regime which protects the defence and security interests of the nation. Voting rights – the Special Shareholder must receive notice of, and may attend and speak at general company and share class meetings, but carries no voting rights, except to enforce certain aspects of the compliance regime.
Dividends – the Special Shareholder has no right to share in the capital or profits of the company other than – in the event of a liquidation – to be repaid the capital paid up in respect of the special share before other shareholders receive any payment.

QinetiQ also issued other classes of shares on its formation, which are not shown above. These shares were issued to the employees of the company.

10.2 Net assets

The reported net assets, after deducting loans due to MoD, of the investments held at 31 March 2004 and 31 March 2003 were:

	31 March 2004 £Million	31 March 2003 £Million
The UK Hydrographic Office	48.7	40.9
Met Office	167.8	159.5
Defence Aviation Repair Agency (DARA)	67.2	59.1
Defence Science and Technology Laboratory (DSTL)	176.5	140.5
QinetiQ	225.2	140.0
Army Base Repair Organisation (ABRO)	57.3	43.7
Total	742.7	583.7

During the year, a dividend of £6,000,000 (2002-03: £6,000,000) was received from DSTL and a dividend of £2,902,359 (2002-03: £2,587,166) was received from The UK Hydrographic Office in respect of the financial year ended 31 March 2003. These are included within operating income. No dividend was received from Met Office, Defence Aviation Repair Agency, QinetiQ and ABRO.

10.3 The Department has a 100% interest in the non-preferential shares of International Military Services Limited, a company registered in England. International Military Services Limited ceased trading on 31 July 1991. Following settlement of outstanding contracts, the company will be liquidated. The Department has written down the value of the investment to nil.

10.4 All the shares held are unlisted and are valued at historical cost. The 7.5% Non-cumulative irredeemable preference shares in Chamber of Shipping Limited and British Shipping Federation Limited are valued at 1p each reflecting the value at which shares would be recovered by the two companies should membership by the Department be ceded, as laid down in the articles of association of the respective companies.

10.5 "Golden" shares confer on the Secretary of State for Defence special rights regarding ownership, influence and control, including voting rights in certain circumstances, under the individual articles of association of the relevant companies in which the shares are held. Further detailed information can be obtained from the companies' individual annual reports and accounts which can be obtained from:

Company	Registration Number
Devonport Royal Dockyard Limited, Devonport Royal Dockyard, Devonport, Plymouth PL1 4SG	02077752
Rosyth Royal Dockyard Limited, Rosyth Royal Dockyard, Rosyth, Fife KY11 2YD	SC101959
Atomic Weapons Establishment plc, AWE Aldermaston, Reading, Berkshire RG7 4PR	02763902
Atomic Weapons Establishment Pension Trustees Limited, AWE Aldermaston, Reading, Berkshire RG7 4PR	02784144
QinetiQ Group plc, 85 Buckingham Gate, London SW1E 6PD	4154556
QinetiQ Limited, 85 Buckingham Gate, London SW1E 6PD	3796233
BAe Systems Marine (Holdings) Limited, Warwick House, PO Box 87, Farnborough Aerospace Centre, Farnborough, Hants, EU14 6YU	1470151

11. Related Party Transactions

11.1 The Defence Science and Technology Laboratory, The UK Hydrographic Office, the Met Office, the Defence Aviation Repair Agency and the Army Base Repair Organisation (ABRO) operate as Executive Defence Agencies financed by Trading Fund. QinetiQ is a Self Financing Public Corporation. These fall within the ambit of the Department and are regarded as related parties outside the Departmental Boundary with which the Department has had material transactions. All transactions are carried out on terms which are contracted on an arms length basis, and are subject to internal and external audit. The NAAFI is outside the Departmental Boundary and is also regarded as a related party.

The following bodies are Executive NDPBs of the MoD. They are self-accounting on an accruals basis, and are regarded as Related Parties. During the year, each NDPB has had a material transaction with the Department, as listed below:

Fleet Air Arm Museum

Grant-in-Aid: £550,323 (2002-03: £527,578)
Commodore Naval Aviation (Deputy Chairman), Commanding Officer HMS Heron (RNAS Yeovilton), Commanding Officer HMS Seahawk (RNAS Culdrose), Director Support Operations (Rotary Wing), and Assistant Director Policy Co-ordination & Aviation (Director Naval Operations) are members of the Board of Trustees.

National Army Museum

Grant-in-Aid: £4,413,460 (2002-03: £4,747,800)
No Departmental representation.

Royal Air Force Museum

Grant-in-Aid: £6,810,815 (2002-03: £6,060,731)
No Departmental representation.

Royal Marines Museum

Grant-in-Aid: £688,061 (2002-03: £654,601)
Director Royal Marines, Corps Secretary Headquarters Royal Marines and Corps Regimental Sergeant Major, Royal Marines Stonehouse, Plymouth are members of the Board of Trustees.

Royal Naval Museum

Grant-in-Aid: £962,120 (2002-03: £882,286)

Naval Base Commander Portsmouth and Chief of Staff (Warfare) CinCFleet are members of the Board of Trustees.

Royal Navy Submarine Museum

Grant-in-Aid: £509,332 (2002-03: £488,008)

Rear Admiral Submarines is a member of the Board of Trustees.

Oil and Pipelines Agency

Agency Fees: £1,600,000 (2002-03: £1,523,000) VAT recovery £280,000 (2002-03: £266,525).
Director Defence Fuels Group is a member of the Board of Directors.

Other

Ian Andrews CBE TD, Second Permanent Under Secretary of State, is a trustee of the Imperial War Museum. Mr Charles Miller Smith is Chairman of Scottish Power. These entities are therefore related parties of the Ministry of Defence.

The payments made to these entities were:

		£000
Imperial War Museum	Various transactions	15
Scottish Power	Various transactions	5,443

During the year there were also various works of art and other items transferred to and from the Imperial War Museum. No value was attributed to these items.

Note:

i)   The Department also pays a number of grants to other bodies outside the Departmental Boundary. These include Grants-in-Aid to the Royal Hospital Chelsea and the Commonwealth War Graves Commission; and

ii) The museums are designated NDPBs under the National Heritage Act 1983. Each NDPB is required to produce annual accounts in accordance with the Charities (Accounts and Reports) Regulations 1995 (Statutory Instrument 1995 No. 2724). The Oil and Pipelines Agency is a corporate body established under the Oil and Pipelines Act 1985.

Joint Ventures and Collaborative Projects

11.2 European Transonic Windtunnel GmbH (ETW):

At 31 March 2004, the Department had no future involvement in ETW. Payments of £260,000 were made during the year.

The Department had a 31% interest in ETW, a non-profit making company, which was jointly owned by the governments of France, Germany, the Netherlands and the United Kingdom. ETW provided facilities for developments or research relating to air vehicles. Under a Memorandum of Understanding extended in January 2000, the Department was committed to making payments up to 31 March 2004. All of which was recoverable from the Department of Trade and Industry. The contributions made to ETW are charged to operating costs when incurred.

The Department is also involved in collaborative projects with various foreign countries for the development and production of fighting equipment. Costs capitalised represent the Department's proportion of the total cost of a project.

12. Stocks and Work in Progress

	31 March 2004 £000	31 March 2003 £000
Work in progress	60,058	39,116
Raw materials and consumables	6,255,211	5,294,617
Assets declared for disposal	2,955	3,392
	6,318,224	5,337,125

Note:

Raw materials and consumables at 31 March 2004 include some £750 million which was reclassified from fixed assets into stocks during the year.

13. Debtors

	31 March 2004 £000	31 March 2003 £000
Amounts falling due within one year		
Trade debtors	133,695	171,404
Deposits and advances	39,437	24,398
Value Added Tax	244,920	251,683
Amounts owed by other Government Departments	68,252	66,641
Amounts owed by entities in which the Department has a participating interest	7,446	10,517
Other debtors	209,570	211,480
Prepayments and accrued income	1,224,380	879,643
Amount due from Consolidated Fund	–	39,665
	1,927,700	1,655,431
Amounts falling due after one year		
Trade debtors	50,254	13,506
Other debtors	88,948	103,838
Prepayments and accrued income	608,457	428,451
Amounts owed by other Government Departments	–	299
Amounts owed by entities in which the Department has a participating interest	60	127
Total debtors amounts falling due after one year	**747,719**	546,221
Total Debtors	**2,675,419**	2,201,652

Note:

i)   Other debtors include loans for house purchase and other loans made to staff amounting to £91,317,714 (2002-03: £97,554,131). The number of staff with house purchase loans was 13,927 (2002-03: 14,452); and

ii) Prepayments, shown under amounts falling due within one year, include an amount of £343,500,000 paid into an Escrow account in 2002-03 in respect of an adjudication decision where an appeal is pending.

14. Cash at Bank and in Hand

	31 March 2004 £000	31 March 2003 £000
At 1 April	415,928	631,681
Net Cash Inflow/(Outflow):		
Received from Consolidated Fund	29,257,550	27,136,321
Utilised	(29,360,914)	(27,352,074)
Increase/(decrease) during year	(103,364)	(215,753)
At 31 March	**312,564**	415,928
Represented by:		
Balances at the OPG	279,166	147,197
Commercial Banks and Cash in Hand	33,398	268,731
	312,564	415,928
The balance at 31 March comprises:		
Consolidated Fund Extra Receipts received during the year and due to be paid to the Consolidated Fund (Note 15)	222,659	134,737
Amounts due from the Consolidated Fund for supply	(80,095)	144,956
Amount in respect of prior year payable to the Consolidated Fund	–	(39,665)
Net amount due to the Consolidated Fund	142,564	240,028
Amounts held in respect of Collaborative Projects (see note below)	170,000	175,900
Total	**312,564**	415,928

Note:

The cash at bank balance includes £170,000,000 (2002-03: £175,900,000) of sums advanced by foreign governments to the Department on various collaborative projects where the United Kingdom is the host nation. Advances made by foreign governments for the procurement of defence equipment on their behalf are also included in this amount. The corresponding liability for these advances is shown under creditors due within one year.

15. Creditors: amounts falling due within one year

	31 March 2004 £000	31 March 2003 £000
Trade creditors	472,930	608,803
Payments received on account	7,979	6,160
Other taxation and social security	203,939	164,041
Other creditors	357,592	400,635
Accruals and deferred income	4,216,352	3,736,625
Obligations under finance leases	4,853	549
Obligations under PFI contracts	10,418	6,105
Payable to the Consolidated Fund	142,564	279,693
Amounts owed to other Government Departments	5,281	2,561
Amounts owed to entities in which the Department has a participating interest	239,091	177,303
Loans	1,599	1,375
Total creditors due within one year	**5,662,598**	5,383,850

Note:

Amounts payable to the Consolidated Fund amounting to £142,564,000.00 (2002-03: £279,692,811.63) comprise:

	31 March 2004 £000	31 March 2003 £000
CFERs received during the year	19	1,110
CFER – proceeds on part sale of shareholding in QinetiQ	–	39,427
CFER – proceeds of certain fixed assets	–	44,300
CFER – loan repayments by QinetiQ	–	49,900
Excess Operating Appropriations-in-Aid	85,315	–
Excess Non-Operating Appropriations-in-Aid	137,325	–
	222,659	134,737
Amount repayable by Consolidated Fund in respect of prior year	–	(39,665)
Amount in respect of supply to be set off against CFER liability (Note iii)	(80,095)	144,956
Net amount payable to Consolidated Fund	142,564	240,028
Amount shown within debtors due within one year	–	39,665
	142,564	279,693

Note:

i) Loans are from the National Loans Fund in respect of the Armed Forces Housing Loans. These are fully repayable between years 2012 and 2028, with the last instalment due on 20 February 2028. Interest on the loans is payable at rates ranging from 4.25% to 7% per annum.

ii) Included in other creditors are amounts advanced by foreign governments to the Department in respect of various collaborative projects where the United Kingdom is the host nation and for the procurement of defence equipment on their behalf of £170,000,000 (2002-03 – £175,900,000).

iii) The amount comprises amounts drawn down from the Consolidated Fund £29,257,550,000 less net cash requirement (Schedule 1) of £29,337,645,000.

16. Creditors: amounts falling due after more than one year

	31 March 2004 £000	31 March 2003 £000
Other creditors	96,897	287,953
Accruals and deferred income	2,655	14,844
Obligations under finance leases:		
– Amounts payable between one and two years	5,372	360
– Amounts payable between two and five years	8,413	502
– Amounts payable over five years	6,528	3,163
Obligations under PFI contracts:		
– Amounts payable between one and two years	16,884	9,204
– Amounts payable between two and five years	43,837	21,470
– Amounts payable over five years	219,215	59,128
Amounts owed to other Government Departments	–	–
Amounts owed to entities in which the Department has a participating interest	21	283
Loans:		
– Amounts payable between one and two years	2,527	1,599
– Amounts payable between two and five years	8,500	5,396
– Amounts payable over five years	40,800	46,431
Total creditors due after more than one year	**451,649**	450,333

17. Provisions for Liabilities and Charges

	Nuclear Decommissioning £000	Other Decommissioning & Restoration costs £000	Early Retirement Commitments £000	Other £000	Total £000
At 1 April 2003	5,529,752	144,801	361,293	958,381	6,994,227
Increase in Provision	175,518	27,799	26,935	259,859	490,111
Unwinding of discounting	2,524,769	16,059	28,209	40,168	2,609,205
Amounts released	(29,010)	(2,979)	(8,851)	(24,570)	(65,410)
Reclassifications	140	2,344	(5,900)	3,416	–
Amounts capitalised	(99,276)	–	–	–	(99,276)
Utilised in year	(283,124)	(3,120)	(90,739)	(162,184)	(539,167)
At 31 March 2004	7,818,769	184,904	310,947	1,075,070	9,389,690

Analysis of amount charged/(credited) to Operating Cost Statement

	2003-04 £000	2002-03 £000
Charged/(credited) to:		
Staff costs	40,379	232,485
Nuclear and Other Decommissioning provisions	154,509	1,635,223
War Pensions and Allowances	866	–
Other costs	228,947	171,782
Net interest (receivable)/payable	2,609,205	247,703
	3,033,906	2,287,193
Made up of:		
Increase	490,111	2,345,459
Release	(65,410)	(305,969)
	424,701	2,039,490
Unwinding of discount	2,609,205	247,703
Net increase in provisions	3,033,906	2,287,193

Nuclear Decommissioning

17.1 HM Treasury issued instructions to reduce the rate used for discounting the value of provisions from 6% to 3.5% effective from 1 April 2003. This accounted mainly for the increase in the value of provisions at the Balance Sheet date of £2,384,868,000 and increased the operating costs by the same amount.

17.2 Nuclear decommissioning provisions relate principally to the cost of facility decommissioning and the treatment and storage of nuclear waste arising at British Nuclear Fuel plc (BNFL) sites, operations at United Kingdom Atomic Energy Authority (UKAEA) sites, operations at MoD sites, operations of Royal Navy submarines and for the Departmental share of planning and constructing a national repository for the eventual disposal of that waste.

17.3 A new body will be created called the Nuclear Decommissioning Authority (NDA) to take over the responsibility for certain nuclear clean up issues. The authority will sit within the DTI. It is expected the MoD will transfer to NDA our liabilities relating to civil nuclear sites and the associated value of our provisions and funding for decommissioning costs. The liability for the decommissioning of MoD sites and for the disposal of submarine waste will not be transferred at this stage. The initial transfer is expected to take effect from 1 April 2005.

Liabilities have arisen since the late 1940's and will continue well into the future as a result of ongoing production and operations associated with the manufacture and reprocessing of Special Nuclear Materials (SNM). The majority of the liability is historic and relates to facilities used for the production of SNM by BNFL and its predecessor the UKAEA. The Atomic Weapons Establishment is the other main source of MoD's liabilities.

The liabilities include the costs associated with decommissioning and care and maintenance of redundant facilities including submarines (the conditioning, retrieval and storage of contaminated materials), research and development and the procurement of capital facilities to handle the various waste streams. Calculation of the provision to cover the liabilities is based on schedules of information received by the MoD from major decommissioning contractors. These schedules are based on technical assessments of the processes and methods likely to be used in the future to carry out the work. Estimates are based on the latest technical knowledge and commercial information available, taking into account current legislation, regulations and Government policy. The amount and timing of each obligation are therefore sensitive to these factors. These sensitivities and their likely effect on the calculation and amount of the liabilities are reviewed on an annual basis.

The latest estimate of the undiscounted cost of dealing with the MoD's nuclear liabilities is £23,387,678,000 (2002-03: £21,947,363,000).

The estimate of £7,818,769,000 (2002-03: £5,529,752,000) at 31 March 2004 represents the liabilities discounted at 3.5% and expressed in 2003/4 money values.

The estimated timescale over which the costs will need to be incurred is as follows:

	2004 £bn	2003 £bn
Up to 3 years	1.5	1.2
From 4 – 10 years	2.1	1.9
Beyond 10 years	4.2	2.4
Total	7.8	5.5

The bulk of the earlier anticipated costs relate to pre and post 1971 liabilities allocated to the Department. The significance of pre and post 1971 refers to the formation date of BNFL. Specific liabilities refer to the BNFL Sellafield, Springfields, Capenhurst, Calder Hall and Chapelcross sites.

Later provisions have been made to cover the costs associated with the research, development and construction of the NIREX Deep Waste Repository (DWR). The provisions have been based on advice provided by NIREX.

However, the policy for the disposal of intermediate and high level waste has yet to be clarified following the previous government's rejection, in May 1997, of planning consent for the proposed DWR. Pending the current government's consideration of a House of Lords Sub Committee report on means of disposing radioactive waste, the UK holders of such waste are working on the assumption that a repository will not be available earlier than 2040. This will necessitate the continued provision of interim storage.

Other Decommissioning and Restoration

17.4 Other decommissioning and restoration provisions relate primarily to contaminated sites where the Department has a constructive or a legal obligation to restore the sites for normal use and for the decommissioning of certain fighting equipment and GWMB.

Early Retirement Pensions

17.5 Where the Department implements an early retirement scheme, provision is made for future liability payable to civilian early retirees. This includes provisions arising from the "80:20 Scheme" under which 20% of the cost was borne by the Department and 80% was borne by the Civil Superannuation Vote. This scheme was terminated in 1997 and the full cost of the obligations are now payable by CSP.

Other

17.6 Other provisions include costs arising from the disposal of fixed assets; redundancy and relocation costs associated with reorganisation and restructuring; and amounts payable under guarantees, litigation and contractual arrangements. Provisions include those concerning an adjudication decision where an appeal is pending.

18. Reconciliation of Net Operating Costs to changes in General Fund

	2003-04 £000	2002-03 £000
Net Operating Cost for the Year (Sch 2)	(34,530,547)	(41,793,591)
Paid and payable to the Consolidated Fund	(182,125)	(317,780)
Parliamentary funding from the Consolidated Fund (Sch 4)	29,257,550	27,136,321
Transfer to General Fund of realised element of:		
– Revaluation reserve (Note 19)	1,258,804	830,832
– Donated asset reserve (Note 19)	6,794	6,537
Non-cash charges:		
– cost of capital charge (Sch 2)	2,769,726	5,074,726
– auditors' remuneration (Note 3)	3,150	3,405
Net decrease in General Fund	(1,416,648)	(9,059,550)
General Fund at 1 April	65,445,156	74,504,706
General Fund at 31 March	**64,028,508**	65,445,156

19. Reserves

	Revaluation Reserve £000	Donated Asset Reserve £000
At 1 April 2003	14,181,634	1,811,327
Arising on revaluation during the year (net)	2,473,493	(36,386)
Additions during the year	–	3,733
Transfers and reclassifications	121	(49)
Transferred (to) / from Operating Cost Statement	–	(49,675)
Transferred (to) / from General Fund	(1,258,804)	(6,794)
At 31 March 2004	**15,396,444**	**1,722,156**

20. Capital Commitments

Capital Commitments for which no provision has been made in these financial statements, were as follows:

	31 March 2004 £000	31 March 2003 £000
Contracted but not provided for	**15,158,637**	17,824,501

21. Financial Commitments

Commitments under operating leases:

	Land and Buildings		Other	
	31 March 2004 £000	31 March 2003 £000	31 March 2004 £000	31 March 2003 £000
The Department was committed to making the following payments during the next year in respect of operating leases expiring:				
Within one year	7,883	6,284	15,178	12,844
Between two and five years	13,733	11,644	69,413	14,483
After five years	168,517	144,678	48,596	109,828
	190,133	162,606	**133,187**	137,155

22. Private Finance Initiative (PFI) Commitments

22.1 The payments made during the year in respect of on and off Balance Sheet PFI transactions were £605,139,000 (2002-03: £542,048,000).

22.2 The service payments which the Department is committed to make during the year 2004-05 are analysed below by time-bands specifying the period in which the individual commitment expires:

	31 March 2004 £000	31 March 2003 £000
In the 2nd to 5th years	181,324	225,325
In the 6th to 10th years	94,986	126,969
In the 11th to 15th years	49,693	3,820
In the 16th to 20th years	34,312	15,830
In the 21st to 25th years	185,566	127,451
In the 26th to 30th years	54,252	75,531
In the 31st to 35th years	1,300	–
In the 36th to the 40th years	30,060	–
In the 41st to the 45th years	–	6,250

The following information is provided for those schemes assessed as off Balance Sheet:

Project Description	Capital Value* £000	Contract Start**/ End Dates	
Training, Administration and Financial Management Information System (TAFMIS): Provision of training administration and financial management information systems to the Army Training and Recruiting Agency (ATRA)	41,000	Aug 1996	Aug 2007
Hazardous Stores Information System (HSIS): Provision of an information management service for hazardous stores safety datasheets with 2,000 users	1,000	Feb 1997	Dec 2007
Defence Fixed Telecommunications System (DFTS): Integration of 50 fixed telecommunications networks used by the Armed Forces and MoD, including the delivery of voice, data, LAN interconnect and other WAN services	70,000	Jul 1997	Jul 2007
Electronic Messaging Service: Interoperability of messaging services for the Army	33,000	Apr 1997	Apr 2007
Medium Support Helicopter Aircrew Training Facility (MSHATF): Provision of 6 flight simulator training facilities, covering three different types of helicopter, at RAF Benson	114,000	Oct 1997	Oct 2037
Hawk Synthetic Training Facility: Provision of replacement simulator training facilities at RAF Valley	19,000	Dec 1997	Dec 2015
Joint Services Command and Staff College (JSCSC): Design and delivery of a new tri-Service Command and Staff Training College infrastructure and supporting services, including single residential accommodation and married quarters (of which £29 million relates to on-balance sheet)	92,800	Jun 1998	Jun 2028
Attack Helicopter Training Service: Provision of full mission simulator, 3 field deployable simulators, ground crew, maintenance and armament training	165,000	Jul 1998	Sep 2027
Family Quarters Yeovilton: Provision of married quarters accommodation for 88 Service families at RNAS Yeovilton	8,200	Jul 1998	Jul 2028
RAF Lyneham Sewage Treatment: Refurbishment of existing sewage treatment facilities, serving a population of 7,000, to meet regulatory standards at RAF Lyneham	3,809	Aug 1998	Aug 2023
Tidworth Water and Sewerage: Pathfinder project providing water, sewerage and surface water drainage, serving a population of 12,000 military and dependants at Tidworth.	5,000	Feb 1998	Aug 2018
RAF Mail: Provision of informal messaging services for the RAF	12,000	Nov 1998	Nov 2008
Fire Fighting Training Units: Provision of fire fighting training for the Naval Recruiting and Training Agency (NRTA)	22,500	Apr 1999	Apr 2019
Light Aircraft Flying Training: Provision of flying training and support services for Air Experience Flying (AEF) and University Air Squadron (UAS) Flying Training	20,000	Apr 1999	Mar 2009

Project Description	Capital Value* £000	Contract Start**/ End Dates	
Tornado GR4 Synthetic Training Service: Provision of aircraft training service at RAF Marham and RAF Lossiemouth	61,700	Jun 1999	Jun 2031
Army Foundation College: Provision of teaching and training facilities for the further vocational education and military training of high-quality school leavers	73,400	Feb 2000	Dec 2029
RAF Cosford/RAF Shawbury Family Quarters: Provision of married quarters accommodation for 145 Service families at RAF Cosford and RAF Shawbury	15,100	Mar 2000	Jun 2025
Central Scotland Family Quarters: Provision of married quarters accommodation for 164 Service Families in Central Scotland	24,700	Aug 1999	Jan 2021
Tri-Service Material Handling Equipment: Provision of Tri-Service materials handling capability	35,000	Jun 2000	Jun 2010
Commercial Satellite Communication Service (INMARSAT): Provision of world-wide commercial satellite communication system for Royal Navy Ships to run for five years	2,600	Mar 2001	Mar 2006
E3D Sentry Aircrew Training Service: E3D Sentry simulators instructors and maintainers at RAF Waddington	6,900	Jul 2000	Dec 2030
Lynx MK 7 and 9 Aircrew Training Service: Provision for simulator training facility for Lynx MK 7 and 9 helicopter aircrew	15,400	Jul 2000	Jul 2025
Tri-Service White Fleet: Provision, management and maintenance of support vehicles in the UK	40,000	Jan 2001	Jan 2011
Family quarters at Wattisham: Provision of married quarters accommodation for 250 service families	34,200	May 2001	Mar 2028
Family quarters at Bristol / Bath / Portsmouth: Provision for married quarters accommodation for 317 service families	78,000	Nov 2001	Sep 2028
Defence Housing Executive Information Systems (DOMIS): Provision for a management information system for the Defence Housing Executive	11,600	Oct 2001	Sept 2010
Marine Support to Range and Aircrew Training: Provision of management, manning, operation and maintenance of Air Support Craft and Range Safety Craft	11,800	Dec 2001	Dec 2012
Astute Class Training: Provision of a training environment for crewmen and maintainers to support Astute Class submarines for 30 years	79,600	Sep 2001	Sep 2031
Strategic Sealift (RoRo): Provision of strategic sealift services based on six RoRo ferries in support of Joint Rapid Reaction Force (JRRF) deployments	175,000	Jun 2002	Dec 2024
Field Electrical Power Supplies (FEPS): Provision of generator sets to support operational electrical requirements in the field	73,500	Jul 2002	Jun 2022
Material Handling Equipment: Provision of tri-service material handling equipment for Army, Navy and RAF storage depots	12,300	Aug 2002	Jul 2010
Aquatrine Project A: Provision of water and waste water services	154,000	Apr 2003	Nov 2028
Hayes Records and Storage: Pan-Government Records Management and Archive Services	11,100	Sep 2003	Sep 2028
Defence Sixth Form College: Development of a sixth form college to help meet the future recruitment requirements in the Armed Forces and MoD Civil Service	20,000	Jun 2003	Aug 2033
Colchester Garrison: Redevelopment, rebuilding and refurbishment to provide accommodation and associated services (messing, education, storage, workshops)	539,000	Feb 2004	Feb 2039
Skynet 5: Range of satellite services, including management of existing Skynet 4 satellites	1,079,000	Oct 2003	Feb 2018

 * The capital value is based on private sector partners' capital investment, where known, or otherwise the capital value of the public sector comparator.

 ** The dates when the contracts were signed.

The following PFI projects, where service delivery has commenced, are treated as on balance sheet and their service payment commitments for the year 2004-05 are included in the table shown above: Lossiemouth FQs; RAF Fylingdales; Defence Helicopter Flying School; Defence Animal Centre; Naval Communication; Provision of storage facilities; Main Building Redevelopment, part of the Joint Services Command and Staff College, Heavy Equipment Transporter and Defence Electronic Commerce Services.

Since the year ended, the Department has signed a PFI contract for Devonport Support Services for a period of 25 years. The contract is for the provision of support services and Fleet accommodation centre services at Devonport Naval Base (HMS Drake).

No specific contingent liabilities have been identified in respect of the PFI contracts listed above.

23. Contingent Liabilities and Contingent Assets Disclosed Under FRS 12

Contingent Liabilities

Contingent liabilities estimated at some £1,127,000,000 (2002-03: £1,318,000,000) were identified. Indemnities issued to contractors and suppliers that were quantifiable as at 31 March 2004 amounted to £852,000,000 (2002-03: £1,162,000,000).

Contingent Assets

A US salvage company, Odyssey Marine Exploration, has found what is believed to be the wreck of HMS Sussex, which sank in the Western Mediterranean in 1694 carrying gold and silver coins estimated to be valued at the time at £1 million. If confirmed as HMS Sussex the wreck and its contents are legally the property of Her Majesty's Government.

A licensing agreement was signed on 27 September 2002 between the Disposal Services Agency of the Ministry of Defence, on behalf of Her Majesty's Government and Odyssey for further archaeological exploration of the wreck of HMS Sussex and recovery of artefacts et cetera. Under the agreement the net proceeds of the sale of coins and other marketable artefacts will be shared between the two parties. Insufficient certainty exists at present as to the presence or value of any potential recovery of artefacts to quantify the contingent asset.

24. Contingent Liabilities Not Required To Be Disclosed Under FRS 12 But Included For Parliamentary Reporting And Accountability

24.1 Quantifiable

MoD has entered into the following quantifiable contingent liabilities by offering guarantees, indemnities or by giving letters of comfort. None of these is a contingent liability within the meaning of FRS12 since the likelihood of a transfer of economic benefit in settlement is too remote.

	1 April 2003	Increase in year	Liabilities crystalised in year	Obligation expired in year	31 March 2004	Amount reported to Parliament by departmental minute
UNRESTRICTED						
Indemnities						
Residual liability for the remediation of unidentified contamination in parts of the former Rosyth Naval Base which has been sold to Rosyth 2000 plc.	Up to £1,000k				Up to £1,000k	n/a
Termination liabilities arising out of MoD's association with the Research Council under the Joint Grants Scheme.	£17,620k	NIL	NIL	NIL	£17,620k	£17,620k
Liabilities arising from insurance risk of exhibits on loan to the Army, Navy and RAF Museums.	£1,489k	£476k (1)	NIL	NIL	£1,965k	
RESTRICTED						
Details on restricted liabilities not given because they are sensitive due to commercial confidentiality, national security, or where public knowledge of a guarantee could prompt claims from third parties.						

Explanation of movement

(1) General Reassessment of risk.

Reconciliation between disclosed amount and amount reported to Parliament

The last comprehensive valuations were as reported in the 2001-02 Treasury return.

24.2 Unquantifiable

MoD has entered into the following unquantifiable contingent liabilities by offering guarantees, indemnities or by giving letters of comfort. None of these is a contingent liability within the meaning of FRS12 since the likelihood of a transfer of economic benefit in settlement is too remote.

Unrestricted Indemnities

- Indemnity given in relation to the disposal of Gruinard Island in the event of claims arising from the outbreak of specific strains of anthrax on the Island.

- Indemnity to Devonport Royal Dockyards Ltd (DRDL) in respect of nuclear risks under the Nuclear Installations Act 1965.

- Indemnity to the Babcock Group in respect of nuclear risks under the Nuclear Installations Act 1965.

- Indemnities to Devonport Royal Dockyards Ltd (DRDL) and the Babcock Group in respect of non-nuclear risks resulting from claims for damage to property or death and personal injury to a third party.

- Product liability to British Aerospace in respect of work carried out by third party contractors on aircraft for which BAe are Design Authority and for which BAe, at MoD's request provide the third party contractor with design advice and verification.

Restricted Indemnities

- Details on restricted liabilities are not given because they are sensitive due to commercial confidentiality and national security.

- Explanation as to why unquantifiable: These liabilities are unquantifiable due to the nature of the liability and the uncertainties surrounding them.

25. Post Balance Sheet Events

The Defence White Paper, published in December 2003, set out the Department's analysis of the future security environment, the implications for defence, strategic priorities and how it intends to adapt its planning and force structures to meet potential threats. Using the policy baseline established in the White Paper and following a rigorous examination of force structure, specific equipment requirements and supporting infrastructure, manpower and organisational structure, the Secretary of State set out, in July 2004, the changes the Department should make to the force structure and its key capacity requirements for the future.

26. Notes to Schedule 5

The net costs of the Departmental Objectives are determined as follows:

Objective 1: Achieving success in the tasks we undertake

This objective comprises the following:

	2003-04			2002-03		
	Gross £000	Income £000	Net £000	Gross £000	Income £000	Net £000
Operations	1,236,721	(3,566)	1,233,155	1,117,429	–	1,117,429
Other military tasks	1,733,706	(74,893)	1,658,813	1,658,433	(52,743)	1,605,690
Contributing to the community	419,977	(59,784)	360,193	564,923	(59,129)	505,794
Helping to build a safer world	427,868	(198,752)	229,116	411,562	(165,811)	245,751
Total	3,818,272	(336,995)	3,481,277	3,752,347	(277,683)	3,474,664

Costs are identified as follows:

- *Operations* comprises the additional costs incurred deploying the armed forces in military operations, e.g. in Iraq, over and above the costs of maintaining the units involved at their normal states of readiness;

- *Other military tasks* includes ongoing military commitments, e.g. to security in Northern Ireland and Overseas Commands, and the costs of identifying and countering the threat of terrorist attack on the UK mainland, and of maintaining the integrity of UK waters and airspace;

- *Contributing to the community* includes ongoing support activities, e.g. search and rescue, administration of cadet forces. In addition, it includes the costs of assistance to other Government Departments and agencies, e.g. in counter drugs operations; and

- *Helping to build a safer world* includes the costs of defence diplomacy undertaken to build confidence and security with our allies. It also includes the Department's support of wider British interests.

Objective 2: Being ready to respond to the tasks that might arise

The costs of delivering the military capability to meet this objective are analysed among force elements of the front line commands, including joint force units where these have been established, and a small number of centrally managed military support activities.

In addition to the direct operating costs of the front line units, they include the attributed costs of logistical and personnel support, identified by reference to the output costs of supplier Management Groupings.

In common with all Objectives, these also contain a share of the costs of advising ministers and accountability to Parliament, and apportioned overheads for head office functions and centrally provided services. The total comprises the full costs, including support services, of force elements grouped under the following headings:

	2003-04			2002-03		
	Gross £000	Income £000	Net £000	Gross £000	Income £000	Net £000
Royal Navy						
Aircraft carriers	299,679	(6,880)	292,799	421,865	(5,550)	416,315
Frigates and Destroyers	1,744,387	(35,195)	1,709,192	3,080,057	(51,136)	3,028,921
Smaller warships	293,095	(9,139)	283,956	504,617	(17,923)	486,694
Amphibious ships	344,496	(5,581)	338,915	436,480	(6,763)	429,717
Strategic sealift	2,691	(70)	2,621	15,283	(655)	14,628
Fleet support ships	360,029	(12,507)	347,522	474,224	(13,110)	461,114
Survey and other vessels	160,030	(3,249)	156,781	232,336	(8,923)	223,413
Naval aircraft	1,429,942	(37,403)	1,392,539	1,246,648	(25,599)	1,221,049
Submarines	4,904,164	(42,492)	4,861,672	5,662,233	(73,110)	5,589,123
Royal Marines	617,431	(13,078)	604,353	481,415	(4,615)	476,800
	10,155,944	(165,594)	9,990,350	12,555,158	(207,384)	12,347,774
Army						
Field units	6,585,112	(212,672)	6,372,440	7,613,358	(231,653)	7,381,705
Other units	2,519,327	(169,006)	2,350,321	3,031,434	(184,282)	2,847,152
	9,104,439	(381,678)	8,722,761	10,644,792	(415,935)	10,228,857
Royal Air Force						
Strike/attack and offensive support aircraft	2,464,139	(57,067)	2,407,072	3,212,034	(74,360)	3,137,674
Defensive and surveillance aircraft	2,140,241	(28,380)	2,111,861	2,772,787	(50,136)	2,722,651
Reconnaissance and maritime patrol aircraft	370,066	(19,639)	350,427	737,534	(26,796)	710,738
Tankers, transport and communications aircraft	1,079,959	(40,135)	1,039,824	1,257,826	(46,723)	1,211,103
Future capability	345,722	(6,515)	339,207	312,281	(6,003)	306,278
Other aircraft and RAF units	784,155	(30,982)	753,173	1,131,165	(40,584)	1,090,581
	7,184,282	(182,718)	7,001,564	9,423,627	(244,602)	9,179,025
Centre Grouping						
Joint and multinational operations	341,411	(193,658)	147,753	628,716	(55,623)	573,093
Centrally managed military support	310,388	(73,987)	236,401	549,567	(80,464)	469,103
Maintenance of war reserve stocks	700,089	(21,470)	678,619	909,204	(12,990)	896,214
	1,351,888	(289,115)	1,062,773	2,087,487	(149,077)	1,938,410
Total Objective 2	27,796,553	(1,019,105)	26,777,448	34,711,064	(1,016,998)	33,694,066

Note:

The 2003-04 and 2002-03 figures shown above are not comparable. 2002-03 was an exceptional year when, some £4,000 million in the value of fixed assets was written down as a direct impact of the Quinquennial Valuation of fixed assets. The impact of the substantial write down also had the effect of reducing the depreciation charge in 2003-04 by some £1,200 million. A further £1,700 million in exceptional charges were also made in last year's accounts in respect of nuclear decommissioning provisions following a strategic review and changes in methodology carried out by BNFL, and the Quinquennial review of AWE. The balance of the reduction is accounted for by various costs, as listed in Note 3.

Most groupings are self explanatory. The following however should be noted:

- *Smaller warships* includes mine hunting and offshore patrol vessels;

- *Amphibious ships* includes assault ships providing platforms for landing craft and helicopters, and Royal Fleet Auxiliary landing support ships;

- *Strategic sealift* is the Roll-On Roll-Off ferry facility supporting the Joint Rapid Reaction Force;

- *Fleet support ships* includes Royal Fleet Auxiliary ships providing tanker and replenishment support to warships;

- *Survey and other vessels* includes ocean and coastal survey and ice patrol ships;

- *Naval aircraft* include Sea King, Lynx and Merlin helicopters deployed in anti-submarine, airborne early warning, Royal Marine support, and reconnaissance and attack roles;

- *Submarines* includes the operating costs of submarines and support of nuclear propulsion and weapons systems, including nuclear decommissioning;

- *Army – Field units* includes 1 (UK) Armoured Division, 3 (UK) Division, Joint Helicopter Command and Theatre troops;

- *Army – Other units* includes Regional Divisions and Land support and training;

- *Strike/attack and offensive support aircraft* includes Tornado GR1/GR1A/GR1B/GR4/GR4A, Joint Force Harrier and Jaguar aircraft deployed in strike/attack and offensive support roles;

- *Defensive and surveillance aircraft* includes Tornado F3 and Sentry AEW1 aircraft deployed in UK air defence, and NATO and UN peacekeeping commitments;

- *Reconnaissance and maritime patrol aircraft* includes Canberra and Nimrod R1 aircraft deployed on reconnaissance, and Nimrod MR2 aircraft on maritime patrol. (Tornado GR1A/4A included in *strike/attack and offensive support aircraft* also undertake reconnaissance roles);

- *Tankers, transport and communications aircraft* includes C-17, Hercules, Tristar and VC10 aircraft providing air transport and air to air refuelling, and smaller transport aircraft (BAe 125/146 and Squirrel helicopters) used in a rapid communications role;

- *Future capability* includes primarily the preparatory costs for the introduction of the Typhoon aircraft;

- *Other aircraft and RAF units* includes ground forces (e.g. the RAF Regiment) and miscellaneous aircraft not included elsewhere;

- *Joint and multinational operations* includes Chief of Joint Operations HQ and the costs less receipts of UK participation in NATO;

- *Centrally managed military support* includes intelligence operational support and Special Forces; and

- *Maintenance of war reserve stocks* includes the holding costs and charges of munitions and other stocks, above the levels required for planned consumption.

Objective 3: Building for the future

This objective comprises the following elements:

	2003-04			2002-03		
	Gross £000	Income £000	Net £000	Gross £000	Income £000	Net £000
Research	1,007,082	(75)	1,007,007	972,089	–	972,089
Equipment programme	2,204,899	(56,131)	2,148,768	2,514,938	(60,547)	2,454,391
Total	3,211,981	(56,206)	3,155,775	3,487,027	(60,547)	3,426,480

- *Research* comprises the costs, including capital charges, of the Research Building Block, and research expenditure incurred by other TLBs; and

- *Equipment Programme* refers to the administration and programme costs, primarily of the Defence Procurement Agency, associated with specifying requirements for and procurement of fighting equipment and other assets. The values of fixed asset additions are shown in Note 9.

Attribution to Objectives

Gross expenditure of £27,155 million (75.6%) (2002-03 - 76.4%) and Operating Income of £692 million (49.0%) (2002-03 – 48.9%) were allocated to tasks, force elements or activities directly supporting the Objectives. The rest was apportioned in one of two ways:

i) by means of cost attributions to "customer" Management Groupings, using local output costing systems to identify the full local costs of services provided. Cost attributions from suppliers are analysed onward to final outputs on advice from the recipients. If specific advice is not given, attributed costs are assumed to follow the same pattern as locally incurred expenditure;

ii) as an element of central overhead, shared among Objectives in proportion to all other attributions. The force elements etc. described above receive a share of the expenditure and income components of these overheads, on the basis of their net costs. The central overheads comprised:

	2003-04			2002-03		
	Gross £000	Income £000	Net £000	Gross £000	Income £000	Net £000
Support for ministers and Parliament	18,971	(33)	18,938	9,380	(3)	9,377
Departmental corporate services	1,356,300	(91,033)	1,265,267	1,164,202	(279,767)	884,435
Strategic management	207,188	(11,911)	195,277	507,630	(9,562)	498,068

- *Support for ministers and Parliament* includes the central provision of advice to ministers and the costs, wherever incurred in the Department, of dealing with Parliamentary business;

- *Departmental corporate services* comprises internal support functions, e.g. payment of bills, payroll administration, and housing and medical care for service personnel; and

- *Strategic management* comprises Departmental policy making functions in strategic, personnel, scientific and medical matters.

Capital employed

The deployment of the Department's capital in support of its objectives does not follow the pattern of operating costs. Net assets totalling £61,252 million (75.5%) support the military capability required to meet Objective 2. The remainder comprises assets wholly attributable to tasks within Objective 1 (£3,689 million – 4.5%), and intangible assets, fighting equipment and other assets under construction, and assets related to equipment procurement within Objective 3 (£16,218 million – 20.0%), and payment of War Pensions and Allowances (-£12 million).

27. Segmental Analysis of Net Resource Outturn by Top Level Budget (TLB) Holders

	2003-04						2002-03
	Other Current Expenditure	**Grants**	**Operating Appropri-ations -in-Aid**	**Total Net Resource Outturn**	**Total Net Resource Estimate**	**Total Net Outturn Compared with Estimate**	**Total Net Resource Outturn**
	£000	**£000**	**£000**	**£000**	**£000**	**£000**	**£000**
TLB HOLDER							
Commander-in-Chief Fleet	3,383,418	–	(16,884)	**3,366,534**	3,439,409	72,875	4,998,342
General Officer Commanding (N Ireland)	654,891	–	(1,550)	**653,341**	656,399	3,058	717,454
Commander-in-Chief Land Command	5,077,714	83	(215,694)	**4,862,103**	5,110,107	248,004	5,483,101
Air Officer Commanding-in-Chief RAF Strike Command	3,497,856	–	(28,760)	**3,469,096**	3,569,005	99,909	4,829,141
Chief of Joint Operations	571,667	–	(36,182)	**535,485**	499,046	(36,439)	678,989
Chief of Defence Logistics	8,272,492	9,987	(331,891)	**7,950,588**	8,643,801	693,213	11,183,743
2nd Sea Lord/Commander-in-Chief Naval Home Command	743,638	–	(47,003)	**696,635**	691,566	(5,069)	740,124
Adjutant General	1,785,636	–	(28,500)	**1,757,136**	1,728,922	(28,214)	1,748,733
Air Officer Commanding-in-Chief RAF Personnel & Training Command	1,146,606	–	(142,337)	**1,004,269**	1,026,283	22,014	1,086,581
Central	3,052,370	120,927	(524,511)	**2,648,786**	2,591,628	(57,158)	2,766,889
Defence Procurement Agency	4,861,520	(1,717)	(42,198)	**4,817,605**	4,702,526	(115,079)	5,083,169
Major customers' research budgets*	419,842	–	(75)	**419,767**	422,904	3,137	414,578
Total (RFR 1)	33,467,650	129,280	(1,415,585)	**32,181,345**	33,081,596	900,251	39,730,844
Total (RFR 2) (Note 2)	1,233,155	–	–	**1,233,155**	1,413,610	180,455	1,117,429
Total (RFR 3) (Note 1)	1,116,047	–	–	**1,116,047**	1,158,005	41,958	1,165,411
Total	35,816,852	129,280	(1,415,585)	**34,530,547**	35,653,211	1,122,664	42,013,684
Income netted off against operating expenditure between TLB holders	(3,279)		3,279				
Items netted off against other operating costs but treated as Appropriations in Aid for Schedule 1 (Note 4)	84,201		(84,201)				
Excess Operating Appropriations-in-Aid			85,315	**85,315**		(85,315)	
Items treated as CFERs to be allocated	1,995		33,369	**35,364**		(35,364)	
	35,899,769	129,280	(1,377,823)	**34,651,226**	35,653,211	1,001,985	42,013,684
				Sch 1	Sch 1		Sch 1

* Major customers' research budgets is not a Top Level Budget (TLB) Holder.

Note 1: **War Pensions and Allowances – Programme Costs**
The Chief Executive of the Veterans Agency is not a Top Level Budget Holder, but exercises all the
responsibilities for the programme costs.

Note 2: **Conflict Prevention (RFR2)**
The analysis of the Conflict Prevention costs is as follows:

Operations	Operating Costs £000
BALKANS	103,584
AFGANISTAN (includes VERITAS, FINGAL and JACANA)	35,865
IRAQ	1,050,563
CONGO	1,003
SIERRA LEONE	735
EUFYROM	808
	1,192,558
Programme Expenditure	40,597
TOTAL	1,233,155

The Department's cost of operation in Iraq (Operation TELIC) forms the main component of the above costs.
Further details and assumptions used in arriving at these figures are as set out below:

General

1. The MoD had £1.539 bn (2002-03: £1bn), including £334 million (2002-03: £400 million) for capital
    expenditure, in voted provision for Operation TELIC in the Spring Supplementary Estimates 2003-04.

2. The resource outturn in 2003-04 for the operation was £1.051 bn (2002-03: £629 million), which reflects
    the costs for the period to 31 March 2004.

3. The capital expenditure for Operation TELIC paid and accrued in the financial statements amounted to
    £260 million (2002-03: £218 million)

4. Full details of the Department's aims and performance assessment for Operation TELIC are provided in
    the Departmental Performance Report.

Assumptions

The following assumptions have been used in arriving at the net resource Outturn figures for Operation TELIC:

1. In accordance with the accounting principles agreed with HM Treasury, the Department has identified the
    costs of Operation TELIC on the basis of net additional costs. Expenditure such as wages and salaries are
    not included as they would have been incurred in any event, and the costs of activities such as training
    and exercises, which have been cancelled because of the operational commitment, have been deducted;

2. There have been no fixed asset impairments resulting from the operation in Iraq, though cost of
    equipment destroyed in the conflict is included. It is likely that repair and refurbishment costs will need
    to be incurred in the future in order to bring the equipment back into full operational use; these costs
    will be reflected in the Operating Cost Statement in the year in which they are incurred;

3. Stock consumption was determined by taking the opening stock in Iraq on 1st April 2003, adding to it issues shipped during the year, deducting stock shipped back to the UK and the year-end stock figure; the latter amount was assessed on the basis of various stock returns received from Iraq. Stock consumption is charged at a gross cost and the related stock provision movements are shown under the stock provision line in the Operating Cost Statement.

4. Write offs of fighting equipment and GWMB, charged in the financial statements, are based on actual records.

28. Financial Instruments

FRS 13, Derivatives and Other Financial Instruments, requires disclosure of the role which financial instruments have had during the period in creating or changing the risks an entity faces in undertaking its activities. Because of the largely non-trading nature of its activities and the way in which government Departments are financed, the Department is not exposed to the degree of financial risk faced by business entities. Moreover, financial instruments play a much more limited role in creating or changing risk than would be typical of the listed companies to which FRS 13 mainly applies. Financial assets and liabilities are generated by day-to-day operational activities and are not held to change the risks facing the Department in undertaking its activities.

Liquidity risk

The Department's revenue and capital resource requirements are voted annually by Parliament and are therefore not exposed to significant liquidity risks.

Interest rate risk

A significant proportion of the Department's financial assets and liabilities carry nil or fixed rates of interest. The exposure to interest risk is therefore not significant.

Foreign currency risk

The Department enters into forward purchase contracts annually with the Bank of England to cover the majority of its foreign exchange requirements for the following year. The details of the outstanding foreign currency contracts were as follows:

Currency	Foreign Currency US$/Euro 000	Weighted Average Exchange Rate (=£1)	31 March 2004 Sterling £000	31 March 2003 Sterling £000
2004/ 2005 delivery (2003/ 2004 delivery)				
US Dollar	1,520,000	1.5677	969,581	(870,378)
Euro	1,350,000	1.4253	947,173	(696,466)
2005/ 2006 delivery				
US Dollar	1,558,000	1.7463	892,182	
Euro	1,278,000	1.4289	891,949	
Total			3,700,885	(1,566,844)
The 31 March 2004 mid-market closing rates for US Dollar and Euro were £/$ 1.8378 and £/Euro 1.4955 respectively.				

Fair values

Financial assets

The Department's financial assets include investments and loans made in Trading Funds, MoD agencies funded through a Trading Fund and QinetiQ, a Self Financing Public Corporation. The net assets of these bodies (excluding MoD loans) and the interest rates applicable to these loans are shown in Note 10. Other financial assets fair values approximates to their book values.

Financial liabilities

The Department's liabilities include loans from National Loans Fund Obligations under finance leases and PFI contracts and a loan from AWE amounting in total to £368.9 million (2002-03: £155.3 million). The fair values of these liabilities will be different from their book values but since these represent only 2.4% of the gross liabilities and provisions, the impact on the Department's net assets will not be material. The fair values of provisions for liabilities and charges are not materially different to their book values which are stated after discounting at the Treasury rate of 3.5%. Other liabilities fair values approximate to their book values.

29. Losses and Special Payments

Losses and Special Payments shown below fall within the following two categories:

A)   Closed cases where all the case work has been finalised and the cases have been formally signed off. These are reported below in accordance with Treasury's Resource Accounting Manual.

B)   Cases where formal sign off cannot, and has not, taken place until all the work necessary to establish the validity and the exact amount of the loss has been concluded. Where an individual loss or special payment exceeds £100,000, this is disclosed in the Accounts under "Advance Notification". The amounts stated under Advance Notification are the best estimates and are reflected in the Accounts where appropriate. Advance Notification also includes cases brought forward from the previous year. Where these cases have been formally signed off during the year, they are shown under the closed cases section of the Losses Statement.

CLOSED CASES	
Losses Statement	**£000**
Total (excluding gifts): 12,847 cases	460,945
Details (cases over £100,000)	
Cash Losses	
New premises were constructed for a non-synopsis welfare facility contrary to the rules on the provision of assistance to non-MoD agencies. The incident was subject to investigation and limitations on the use of property management funds reinforced. (LAND)	274
British Defence Staff Washington: Write off of a control account balance. (CENTRAL)	189
Property Management arrangements were erroneously used to refurbish non-synopsis welfare facilities in Germany. The incident was investigated by a Board of Inquiry which found mismanagement rather than any impropriety. (LAND)	148
A cash loss of £137,895 has been incurred as the result of the Navy Days event which took place in Devonport Naval Base during August 2002. A forecast of income and expenditure for the Navy Days 2002 assumed a breakeven position with 60,000 visitors attending. Although expenditure fell within the budget, income was lower than anticipated mainly due to reduced visitor numbers (44,551). (DLO)	138
Claims Waived or Abandoned	
Treasury approval has been obtained to abandon a £49.987M claim against the contractor following cancellation of project VIXEN in February 1997. The MoD received £14.550M in compensation but agreed to pay £3.504M in Treasury Solicitor costs. (DPA)*	38,941

Losses Statement	£000
In February 2002 HM Treasury agreed to waive a claim of £2.3 million in respect of Edinburgh House. Subsequently, this transfer has been included in an agreement signed with the Government of Gibraltar (GOG), the "Lands Memorandum", gifting a number of properties to GOG. (CJO)	2,339
Treasury approval has been granted to write off £309,405.76 as a claim abandoned/waived. This loss of revenue occurred as a result of incorrect charging for Operational Sea Training between October 1995 and March 1998. Operational Sea Training is provided to foreign navies in return for full payment, but at the time of the loss the rules for charging were not clearly expressed. (DLO)	309
A contract was placed with Dieselpart Ltd on the 1st February 1995 for a contract period of three years for the reconditioning of pumps and water pumping equipment. Dieselpart Ltd went into liquidation in March 1997, causing the net loss of £230,448.45 for rejected work and additional cost. (DLO)	230
Claim against EDS in respect of payroll services waived in accordance with AFPAA Amended Contract FY03/04. (CENTRAL)	131
Stores and other Losses	
Following the closure of the Defence Storage and Distribution Centre, Sub Depot (formerly ABSDA Sub Depot) Thatcham in March 2000, finalisation of the Sub Depot's equipment and stores accounts revealed that, in a number of instances, accounting procedures covering movement of equipment and stores had not been fully complied with. As a result the audit trail was incomplete and, whilst no physical loss has been proven, the value of all stores unaccounted for on closure must be written off as a loss. (DLO)*	1,889
A Ptarmigan Radio Relay vehicle crashed during an Exercise and was damaged beyond repair. The accident was fully investigated by a Board of Inquiry and Accident Investigation teams. (LAND)	1,055
Water seeped through the seals on laptop cases following their storage, in the open, resulting in the loss of JFACHQ laptops. (STC)	160
Fire in a workshop building at School of Electrical and Mechanical Engineering, Bordon on 26 Sep 02. Investigation by the Defence Fire Service determined that the cause of the fire was an accident. There were no injuries or fatalities. (AG)	159
Constructive Losses	
The Departmental Resource Accounts (DRAc) for 2002/03 identified the impact of reviewing the accounting treatment for the Submarine facility at Devonport to reflect planned workload. The impact of this change in accounting treatment was a write down of £287 million which is classified as a Constructive Loss. (DLO)*	287,000
A decision was taken in taken in 2003 to withdraw from the Multi Role Armoured Vehicle (MRAV) programme. The strategic environment had changed markedly, with much greater emphasis on rapid deployability and expeditionary operations. The design of MRAV could not effectively meet this change in requirement. A constructive loss of £48M was incurred covering the UK costs of participating in the multilateral collaborative programme up to the point of withdrawal. (DPA)	48,000
The in service date for the Astute Class Training Service (ACTS) PFI project will be delayed as a consequence of slippage to the Astute submarine programme. This has resulted in a constructive loss. (DPA)	31,373
Write-off of equipment that, owing to the recent closure of a number of security force bases in Northern Ireland and reductions in operational activity, is no longer of use. (GOCNI)	18,088
Following the decision to cancel project PASCO a contract termination agreement was signed in July 2003. Costs incurred up to this period have been written off as a constructive loss. (DPA)	12,245
A constructive loss was incurred following a performance/cost trade decision in 2003 not to pursue a digital integration of the Rangeless Airborne Instrumented briefing System (RAIDS) training system onto Tornado F3. The decision was made on grounds of value for money in the light of the significant capability improvements already delivered by RAIDS at the lesser level of integration. (DPA)	5,269
A constructive loss has been incurred in relation to equipment purchased under an Urgent Operational Requirement (UOR) in June 1999. The equipment was never fully accepted in to service. Disposal action was delayed in light of further conflicts but in June 2003 it was confirmed that there had been no requests for the equipment in theatre. (DPA)	1,022
A project to design a suitable trailer to carry specialist equipment has been cancelled due to technical difficulties identified during trials. (DPA)	644
A fruitless payment of £355,033.31 was made for work initiated by Defence Clothing Integrated Project Team. A contract was agreed with NITECH Ltd to produce 40,000 Personal Combat Torches to issue to Special Forces. The work was started in 1993. However, when the torches were tested, they were found to be noisy due to the loose-fitting of the battery. Although this criterion was not mentioned in the contract, it made the torches unsuitable for Special Forces operations. (DLO)	355
The Defence Transport and Movements Agency (DTMA) Airlift Planning System (DAPS) was to introduce IT support to the military Air Transport planning process with the aim of ensuring the maximum possible usage of the Air Transport Force (ATF). Following the initial introduction of the system in July 02, a user evaluation was carried out and it was found that the DAPS operation was too slow to be useable. In addition, there were interface problems between DAPS and the Integrated Air Transport System (IATS). Further work may have overcome the DAPS / IATS interface problems. However, HQ 2 Gp (RAF) had decided to replace IATS with the Boeing Operational Command System (BOCS) and an interface between DAPS and BOCS was not possible. These problems resulted in a constructive loss of £204,760. (DLO)	205
RNAS Culdrose – Clean up costs incurred in 2003-04 following discharge of aviation fuel in June '02. Total amount incurred: £652,000. (FLEET)	66

Losses Statement	£000
Gifts	
International Courtesy Rules	
Supplies and services provided on a reciprocal basis to Commonwealth and Foreign Navy vessels during visits to British ports at Clyde, Portsmouth, Devonport and Gibraltar. (CENTRAL)	2,246
Other	
Ebrington Barracks, a Non-Core MoD site in Northern Ireland, transferred to the Office of the First Minister/ Deputy First Minister of the Northern Ireland Executive. (CENTRAL)	13,000
Spitfire TB752 and Hurricane LF751 transferred to the Royal Air Force Museum for onward loan to the Spitfire and Hurricane Memorial Building Trust. (DLO)	375
Combat Support Vehicles Support IPT (now known as General Support Vehicles) was instructed by the AL Hussein Project Team in 2003-04 that a number of Scammel Commanders were to be sold to the Jordanian Armed Forces. This had ministerial approval. The equipments were sent to IRAQ and then on to Jordan once they had been replaced by the new Heavy Equipment Transporter (HET). The write off of these equipments occurred in 03/04 and was £760,076.22. The receipt of monies for these equipments will be received into MoD Centre in 04/05 and is approximately £598k. The net loss to the MoD will be approximately £162k.(DLO)	162
De-mining equipment transferred to the Government of Kenya. (CJO)	156
Special payments	
Total: 284 cases	98,124
The Court of Appeal ruled against the Department and in favour of pensioners and widows affected by the Hulme judgement. In addition to reviewing attributable pension entitlement decisions made on the original basis of 'the balance of probabilities' and paying the cost of past pensions, the Department has set up provision for payment of compensation amounting to £77.2 million. (CENTRAL)	77,200
Compensation for loss of interest on Income Tax wrongly deducted from invalidity pensions. (CENTRAL)	12,600
An extra-contractual payment was approved arising from failure to provide fully working government furnished equipment in a timely manner for the Automated Message Switch Comcen Equipment Replacement Programme. (DPA)*	4,294
An extra-contractual payment was approved in relation to a submarine programme in June 2003. This followed a claim from the contractor that failure to supply submarine and threat data resulted in additional costs being incurred. (DPA)	3,700
Ex-gratia payments have been made during 2003-04 on account to British Nuclear Fuels plc and the United Kingdom Atomic Energy Authority towards the cost of treating and disposing of nuclear wastes and decommissioning plant at British Nuclear Fuels plc sites. The total amount paid to date: £1,341,000.(DPA)	166
An ex-gratia payment was made to a civilian employee, in respect of a complaint against the Department that was upheld. (DLO)	150
ADVANCE NOTIFICATION	
Previously notified in 2002-03	
A constructive loss arose from the UK Government decision not to proceed into production for either long range (loss £205 million) or medium range (loss £109 million) anti-tank guided weapons system. (DPA)*	314,000
DSMS formed part of the DLO Business Change Programme. During development, doubts surfaced about the programme's ability to deliver the expected benefits and its affordability leading to the programme being suspended and a potential constructive loss of £118 million. Work is still going on to finalise the case which is expected to be formally reported in 2004/05. (DLO)*	118,000
Re-negotiation of a contract for the Nimrod reconnaissance aircraft project has resulted in a possible claim abandoned (£39 million) and a constructive loss (£36 million). (DPA)*	75,000
Increased development costs relating to the Brimstone project arising from the non-availability of trial platforms. (DPA)*	9,165
A delay in the production of helicopter training course material has resulted in a potential write-off. (CJO)*	8,500
Communication equipment located on a remote hilltop site was stolen resulting in a possible stores loss	573
Metropole Building re-wire project (fraud); an alleged fraud during 1990-1995 which is still being investigated. (CENTRAL)*	500
A depletion and disposal of surplus stock has arisen due to improved processes and procedures as a result of the Strategic Defence Review and the formation of the Defence Logistics Organisation. It is not possible at this time to separate out the associated value from that arising as a result of ongoing activity but when the value has been determined it will be noted in the future year's Resource Accounts. (DLO)*	
Not previously notified	
Cash Losses	
British Defence Staff Washington: Net write off to regularise the various control accounts used to manage Foreign Military Sales in the USA. (CENTRAL)	8,332

Losses Statement	£000
A review of the Overseas Leave Travel Scheme and the Welfare Warrants Scheme Allowances indicated that a possible over payment has arisen at one of the Department's establishments. Initial assessment of the loss is £850,000 but investigations are proceeding. (PTC)	850
A combined cash loss of £199,263.24 relating to 4 un-reconciled control accounts emanating from the Anglo/French FRUGAL agreement on the development and production phases of the Jaguar aircraft is being investigated. This will result in write off action. (DLO)	199

Claims Waived or Abandoned

Debts for the training of the Pakistan Navy during the period 1989 to 1991 are awaiting final write off authorisation; a provision for the full amount of the debt is reflected in the accounts. (2SL)	117

Stores and other Losses

Loss as a result of a fire on an AS90 (self-propelled artillery gun) during Ex Saif Sareea 2 (Oman). Work is ongoing and the case is expected to be formally reported in 2004-05. (LAND)	2,202
Renegotiations in respect of the Hydrographic and Oceangraphics Survey Vessels (SVHO) contract has resulted in a possible claim abandoned. (DPA)	1,034
Part of an accommodation block in Clive Barracks, Tern Hill was destroyed as a result of arson. Work is ongoing to finalise the case and is expected to be completed in 2004-05. (LAND)	500
Loss, through fire, of miscellaneous equipment during Operation TELIC. Investigations are ongoing and will be formally reported when the case work has been completed. (LAND)	375
Although no physical loss occurred, incomplete documentation on ammunition movements during an Operation in Afghanistan resulted in paper deficiencies in stock holding. The case will be finalised in 2004-05. Measures have been taken to prevent any recurrence. (LAND)	241
A constructive loss of £147,683.14 occurred in February 2001. It represents the write off of two C130J right-hand main undercarriage shock struts: the faulty struts were mislaid between the unit staffs and the CRILS team at RAF Lyneham. An urgent inquiry was convened between January and April 2002. (DLO)	148
A stores loss identified during a stock check when a signal squadron disbanded. A full investigation is ongoing and will formally be reported when the case work has been completed. (LAND)	132
A fire involving stores, fuel products and munitions destroyed buildings, tents and other property during an Operation. Investigations were conducted and found that the accident was not attributable to a single individual or specific act of negligence. (LAND)	104

Constructive Losses

A loss of £205 million has arisen following the impairment of Chinook MK3 helicopters. (DPA)	205,000
A loss of £65 million has been incurred following impairment of an operational building (DPA)	65,000
The extended range ordnance modular charge system has been cancelled as a result of technical difficulties and could result in a possible write-off. (DPA)	34,540
The decision to suspend and now seek cancellation of the Remote Ammunitioning Facility Tamar at Devonport Naval Base will result in a constructive loss of £25M. The project was suspended in May 2002 following a Defence Ordnance Group study showing that the effects of potential ammunition explosions would be more localised than originally predicted. It was concluded that a satisfactory facility could be provided at the submarines' current berths within the Naval Base, without the need to construct a remote facility. Since then Devonport has established confidence that existing facilities can be used and full costs of the cancellation have become clearer. Ministerial approval is now being sought to cancel the project. Once this is received, the constructive loss will be formally reported in the 2004-05 accounts. (DLO)	25,000
Retrospective notification of a constructive loss of £18 million incurred as a result of the write off of Project ACCESS. A strategic Options Study, involving all stakeholders, identified the need for more joined up IS support to Attack Helicopter and agreed that further development of Project ACCESS should be cancelled. (DLO)	18,000
A contract to provide a centrifuge required to train aircrew for modern agile fast jet aircraft at high G force has been cancelled resulting in a potential write-off. (DPA)	14,400
There is the possibility of a loss in relation to the Harrier Night Bombing System. (DLO)	12,896
Advance notification that an estimated loss of £6.5M has been incurred through the procurement of new aircraft lifts that were to be fitted to Royal Naval Aircraft Carriers. A more cost effective solution has been found which takes advantage of technical advances and the lifts are no longer required. There were various expressions of interest in buying the aircraft lifts from the MoD, but none of these have resulted in a sale so far. A constructive loss write off case is now being prepared. (DLO)	6,500
Advance notification that an estimated loss of £1.5M has been incurred by the cancellation of the Oasis Stores and Engineering Project (OSEE). The development of the IT project was subject to delays and was not deemed fit for purpose in its current form when trials were undertaken in mid 2002. At the same time a review of DLO projects carried out by McKinsey & Co found that OSEE did not meet the new recommended criteria for the continuation of IT projects. It was therefore recommended that the project should be suspended. There has been some mitigation of the loss through an arrangement to purchase licences for a different product in use in the MoD and a constructive loss write off case is now being prepared. (DLO)	1,500

Losses Statement	£000
This loss relates to a settlement payment made to a service provider as a result of a termination of contract due to technical reasons relating to Defence Information Infrastructure (C) requirements. (DLO)	850
A constructive loss has arisen as a result of the need to re-design the roof at RNAS Yeovilton after it was found that the recently constructed roof obscured the view of the end of the runway from the Aircraft Control Tower. (FLEET)	618
The loss represents a settlement payment made to Elonex as a result of a technical breach of contract. (DLO)	600
A constructive loss arose in respect of the Voice Monitoring and Analysis Facility (VMAF) due to several factors including a limited capability and a change in policy placing the onus on contractors to provide their own capability testing. (DLO)	434
The Defence Communication Services Agency (DCSA) incurred training costs for infrastructure managers, in respect of the PASCO contract which was terminated; the costs in respect of the main contract were written off by DPA. (DLO)	290
A payment of £170,000 incurred due to the need to recover terminal boxes sent to a third party for disposal could result in a possible fruitless payment. (DLO)	170
Retrospective notification is given of a constructive loss, currently estimated at £151,000, incurred as a result of accidental scrapping of 45 Lynx Metal Tail Rotor Blades in October 2002, that were originally destined for recovery by industry. (DLO)	151
Special Payments	
Delays in supplying design information and equipment has resulted in a claim on the MoD relating to additional delay and dislocation costs. (DPA)	40,000
*Reported as an Advance Notification in 2002-03.	

30. Non-Operational Heritage Assets

The Department owns a range of non-operational heritage assets from historically significant defence equipment, through archive information, to museum and art collections. In accordance with HM Treasury policy non-operational heritage assets are normally valued except where:

a)   The cost of the valuation outweighs the benefits that the knowledge of the valuation would deliver; or

b)   it is not possible to establish a sufficiently reliable valuation.

On the above basis, no non-operational heritage assets, except land, were valued at the year-end.

30.1 The scope and diversity of the holdings of non-operational heritage assets which are not valued is illustrated by the examples detailed in the table below:

Item	Location	Description
HMS Victory	Portsmouth	HMS Victory is a 100 gun, first rate ship of the line, most famous for her role as Lord Nelson's Flagship at the Battle of Trafalgar. Victory was commissioned into the fleet in 1778 and serves today as flagship to 2nd Sea Lord/Commander-in-Chief Naval Home Command. Open to the public since 1928, Victory now attracts around 400,000 visitors a year.
Army Historic Aircraft Flight	Middle Wallop	Formed in the late 1980s, the flight consists of eight aircraft and makes about 14 public appearances between Easter and October.
Historic Gun Collection	DSDC Donnington	The museum currently holds a collection of 749 small arms of British and foreign origin together with a small number of larger weapons.
Battle of Britain Memorial Flight	RAF Coningsby	Formed in 1973 the Memorial Flight operates 11 mainly World War 2 aircraft that appear at in excess of 250 airshows, public events and state occasions. Memorial Flight aircraft can also be viewed by the public at their hangar at RAF Coningsby.
MoD Art Collection	Various locations	The MoD Art Collection comprises approximately 800 works of fine art and 250 antiques such as clocks and furniture. Many other miscellaneous items, such as photographs and manuscripts are contained in the archive. At the core of the collection are works commissioned by (and bequeathed to) the Admiralty during the 19th century, and those given to the Admiralty and to the War Office by the War Artists Commission at the end of Second World War. Items from the MoD art collections are displayed in conference rooms and senior officers' accommodation throughout the defence estate. The most important items are on permanent public display in the National Maritime Museum and on temporary loan to many other public museums and galleries.
Records and artworks	London, Taunton	The Admiralty and Institute of Naval Medicine Libraries and the Air Historical Branch (London) comprise text and records of historical and research items. Although not open to the public, access is available on application.
Artefacts, records and artworks	Various locations	Some 69 Regimental and Corps Museums exist across the country. Ownership of the buildings and contents of the museums varies between the MoD, local authorities and regimental associations. The museums, which are open to the public, trace the history of the regiments and comprise displays of uniforms, weapons, medals and records.

31. Entities within the Departmental Boundary

The entities within the boundary during 2003-04 were as follows:

Executive Agencies	**Advisory Non-Departmental Public Bodies**
Armed Forces Personnel Administration Agency	Advisory Committee on Conscientious Objectors
Army Personnel Centre	Animal Welfare Advisory Committee
Army Training and Recruitment Agency	Armed Forces Pay Review Body
British Forces Post Office	Dartmoor Steering Group
Defence Analytical Services Agency	Defence Nuclear Safety Committee
Defence Bills Agency	Defence Scientific Advisory Council
Defence Communication Services Agency	Independent Board of Visitors for Military Corrective Training Centres
Defence Dental Agency	National Employers' Liaison Committee
Defence Estates	Review Board for Government Contracts
Defence Geographic and Imagery Intelligence Agency	Royal Military College of Science Advisory Council
Defence Housing Executive	
Defence Intelligence and Security Centre	
Defence Medical Education Training Agency	**Other Entities**
Defence Procurement Agency	The Reserve Forces and Cadet Associations (formerly TAVRA)
Defence Storage and Distribution Agency	
Defence Transport and Movements Agency	
Defence Vetting Agency	
Disposal Services Agency	
Duke of York's Royal Military School	
Medical Supply Agency	
Ministry of Defence Police	
Naval Manning Agency	
Naval Recruiting and Training Agency	
Pay and Personnel Agency	
Queen Victoria School	
RAF Personnel Management Agency	
RAF Training Group Defence Agency	
Service Children's Education	
Veterans Agency	
Warships Support Agency	

32. Actual Outturn – Resources and Cash

Actual Outturn – resources:

Request for resources 1: Provision of Defence Capability.
Actual amount net resources Outturn £32,302,024,114.93.
Actual amount of savings in resources over Estimate £779,571,885.07.

Request for resources 2: Conflict Prevention.
Actual amount net resources Outturn £1,233,155,000.00.
Actual amount of savings in resources over Estimate £180,455,000.00.

Request for resources 3: War Pensions and Allowances, etc
Actual amount net resources Outturn £1,116,047,094.00.
Actual amount of savings in resources over Estimate £41,957,906.00.

Actual Outturn – cash:

Net cash requirement: Outturn net cash requirement was £29,337,645,888.93

The amount surrenderable to the Consolidated Fund was £142,563,607.45.

33. Votes A Statement – Statement of Approved Maximum Armed Forces Numbers

33.1 Votes A Statement is presented annually to Parliament to seek authority for the maximum numbers of personnel to be maintained for service with the Armed Forces for the year and is audited by the National Audit Office.

33.2 Maximum numbers of personnel to be maintained for service with the Armed Forces:

	Numbers voted by the House of Commons	Maximum numbers maintained	Peak dates
Officers, Men & Women for NAVAL SERVICE	46,025	41,553	1 April 2003
Officers, Men & Women for ARMY SERVICE	128,195	121,207	1 October 2003
Officers, Men & Women for AIR FORCE SERVICE	57,415	53,775	1 March 2004

33.3 Maximum numbers of personnel to be maintained for service with the Reserve Forces:

	Numbers voted by the House of Commons	Maximum numbers maintained	Peak dates
Reserve Naval and Marine Forces	17,600	15,466	1 Feb 2004
Special Members of the Reserve Naval Forces	300	163	1 July 2003
Reserve Land Forces	84,000	71,861	1 May 2003
Special Members of the Reserve Land Forces	6,000	58	1 March 2004
Reserve Air Forces	23,050	16,293	1 April 2003
Special Members of the Reserve Air Forces	550	66	1 Jan 2004

Annexes

ANNEX A:
Organisation and Management of Defence

Secretary of State and Ministers

1.   The Secretary of State for Defence is responsible for the formulation and conduct of defence policy. On 31 March 2004, the Secretary of State was supported by a Minister of State for the Armed Forces, and two Parliamentary Under-Secretaries of State (one for Defence Procurement and one for Veterans).

The MoD Head Office

2.   Beneath Ministers lies the top management of the MoD, comprising ten senior officials and Service officers (as shown in Figure 8 below). The Secretary of State has two principal advisers: the Permanent Secretary (PUS), and the Chief of the Defence Staff (CDS). They share responsibility for much of the Department's business, reflecting the input that both military and civilian personnel make to political, financial, administrative and operational matters. The PUS has primary responsibility for policy, finance and administration in the Department. He is the MoD's Principal Accounting Officer and is personally accountable to Parliament for the expenditure of all public money voted for Defence purposes. CDS is the professional head of the Armed Forces and the principal military adviser to the Secretary of State and the Government.

3.   PUS and CDS each have a deputy; the Second Permanent Secretary (2nd PUS), and the Vice Chief of the Defence Staff (VCDS). They jointly head the Central Staff, the policy core of the Department.

4.   The role of the MoD Head Office is:

* The strategic and policy context (what our stakeholders require from Defence);

* Military strategic command of operations;

* Direction through high level plans, associated balance of investment and resource allocation required to achieve defence objectives (where we are going);

* The framework of objectives and targets against which the major management/delivery areas in the department should be held accountable (how we will get there);

* Setting departmental standards, including on key departmental processes and process owners, and ways of working in order to drive continuous performance improvement (the way we do things);

* The machinery of a Department of State.

5.   Also within the head office in London sit the Chief of Staff of each of the three Services, The Chief of the Naval Staff (CNS), Chief of the General Staff (CGS), and Chief of the Air Staff (CAS). Together with the Chief of Defence Procurement (CDP), the Chief of Defence Logistics (CDL) and the Chief Scientific Adviser (CSA), they sit on the Defence Council and its executive arm, the Defence Management Board.

The Defence Council

6.   The Defence Council is the senior Departmental committee. Chaired by the Secretary of State it provides the formal legal basis for the conduct of defence in the UK through a range of powers vested in it by statute and Letters Patent.

The Defence Management Board

7.   The Defence Management Board (DMB) is the highest, non-ministerial committee in the MoD. Chaired by PUS, it is essentially the main corporate board of the MoD, providing senior level leadership and strategic management of Defence. Its role is to deliver the Defence aim set out in the Public Service Agreement. Its executive membership for 2003-04 is shown in Figure 8. It also includes two non-executive members. The DMB is responsible for:

- **The role of Defence** – providing strategic direction, vision and values;

- **Objectives and targets** – establishing the key priorities and defence capabilities necessary to deliver the MoD's Departmental objectives;

- **Resource allocation and strategic balance of investment** – to match Defence priorities and objectives; and

- **Performance management** – managing and driving corporate performance.

The Service Boards

8.   Whilst the Management Board is responsible for managing the delivery of the key Departmental outputs, the administration of the single Services and their personnel is delegated to the Service Boards (the Admiralty, Army and Air Force Boards) from the Defence Council. The Service Boards are chaired by Ministers, with 2nd PUS acting as the Secretary.

Service Executive Committees

9.   The day to day business of managing the single Services is formally conducted through the Service Executive Committees. They are:

- The Navy Board;

- The Executive Committee of the Army Board; and

- The Air Force Board Standing Committee.

10.   These Committees bring together, under their respective single Service Chief of Staff, the operational and personnel commanders for each Service. The Committees support the respective Chiefs of Staff in his executive role, his management and operational advisory roles, and as the professional head of the Service.

The Chiefs of Staff Committee

11.   The Chiefs of Staff (COS) Committee is chaired by the CDS and is the main forum in which the collective military advice of the Chiefs is obtained on operational issues. The PUS attends the COS Committee.

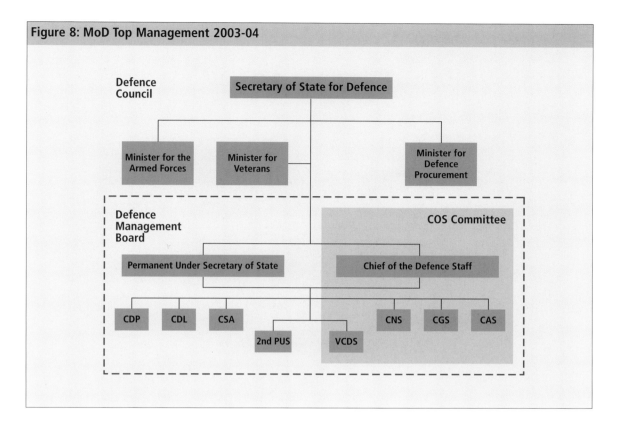

Figure 8: MoD Top Management 2003-04

Top Level Budgets

12. Most Defence activity takes place outside the MoD head office and is managed through eleven Top Level Budget (TLB) holders (twelve from 1 April 2004), (shown in Figure 9), and five Trading Funds not included in the TLB structure. PUS grants each TLB holder extensive delegated powers over personnel, infrastructure and budget. The Navy, Army and Air Force each has two separate TLBs for its Operational and Personnel commands, and the Army has a third TLB for Northern Ireland.

13. The other TLBs are Defence rather than single Service organisations. These are:

- The Defence Procurement Agency, which procures equipment for all three Services;

- The Defence Logistics Organisation, the sole authority for providing logistics support to the armed forces;

- The Permanent Joint Headquarters at Northwood, headed by the Chief of Joint Operations, who is responsible for the planning and execution of joint (tri-Service) operations; and

- The Central TLB, includes the MoD head office and provides corporate services to other TLBs.

- The Corporate Science and Technology TLB, headed by the Chief Scientific Adviser was formed on 1 April 2004 from a merger of two existing budgetary areas. The prime outputs of this area are expert advice and the development of scientific and technological solutions to satisfy MoD's needs and problems.

14. Each TLB holder has a 'contract' with MoD head office, known as a Service Delivery Agreement, which specifies the outputs required of that TLB, the resources they are given to deliver these outputs, and the authority delegated to TLB holders by the PUS. Within the TLB structure are a range of agencies, spanning the bulk of Defence support activity, including logistics, training and corporate services such as bill paying and policing (see Annex C). The Secretary of State owns and is ultimately accountable for the performance of Defence agencies and Trading Funds.

Figure 9: Top Level Budget Structure of the MoD

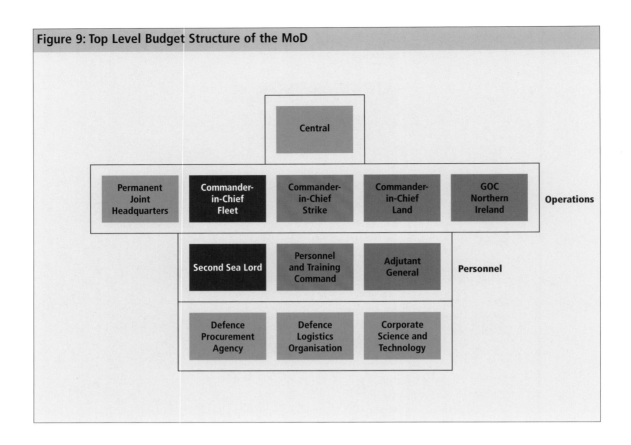

ANNEX B:

Summary of Progress Against Public Service Agreement Objectives and Targets

Table 22: Spending Review 2000 Public Service Agreement, 1 April 2001 to 31 March 2004 Final Assessment of MoD Performance			
PSA Target	**Performance Indicator**	**Assessment**	**Further Detail**
Objective I – Provide and direct Armed Forces able to undertake successfully a major operation on a similar scale and duration to the Gulf War, or two medium scale operations (of similar size to that in Kosovo), one involving warfighting, and sustain them simultaneously for up to six months, whilst meeting long standing commitments and being able to rebuild a bigger force should a major threat to Europe emerge.			
1. To achieve the above, by 2005 ensure that a minimum of 90% of rapidly available military units are at required states of readiness. **Overall Assessment: Met**	Assessment, against specified standards, of the ability of high and medium readiness forces to deploy ready for operations. Assessment, against specified standards, of the ability to transport above forces to required location.	**Met** As set out in the *MoD Annual Report and Accounts 2002-03*, from 1 April 2003 performance has been measured against the more demanding target that 90% of all forces are at their required state of readiness. By 31 March 2004 93% of all forces were at their required readiness levels with no critical weaknesses. Performance across the period varied depending on operational commitments. Operations in Iraq and elsewhere in 2003/2004 demonstrated our ability to deploy and sustain forces on operations of a similar scale and duration to the Gulf War, and recover them thereafter. A range of lessons learned during operations have already been addressed and we are looking carefully at how we can improve our ability to prepare in advance of commitment to specific deployments.	*MoD Performance Report 2001-02* paragraphs 37-41 *MoD Annual Report and Accounts 2002-03* paragraphs 40-44 *MoD Annual Report and Accounts 2003-04* paragraphs 32-36
	Establish the operational capability of the Joint Rapid Reaction Forces by late 2002-03.	**Met – Slippage** The requirement was largely met by the end of 2002-03, although it was assessed then that it would not be possible to generate and sustain some specialist JRRF force elements within planned timescales. However, operations in Iraq and elsewhere in 2003/2004 effectively demonstrated the ability to mount and sustain a single, non-enduring medium scale warfighting operation despite continuing shortfalls in some specialist areas.	*MoD Performance Report 2001-02* paragraphs 43-44 *MoD Annual Report and Accounts 2002-03* paragraph 47 *MoD Annual Report and Accounts 2003-04* paragraph 41
	Provide the strategic lift capability provided by four large aircraft, by 2002.	**Met** The fleet of four C-17 aircraft entered service on 30 September 2001, and have been used extensively since. Acquisition of a 5th C-17 was announced in July 2004.	*MoD Performance Report 2001-02* paragraph 43. *Delivering Security in a Changing World: Future Capabilities,* paragraph 2.26

Table 22 continued...			
PSA Target	**Performance Indicator**	**Assessment**	**Further Detail**
Objective I *(continued)* – **Provide and direct Armed Forces able to undertake successfully a major operation on a similar scale and duration to the Gulf War, or two medium scale operations (of similar size to that in Kosovo), one involving warfighting, and sustain them simultaneously for up to six months, whilst meeting long standing commitments and being able to rebuild a bigger force should a major threat to Europe emerge.**			
2. Recruit, retain and motivate the personnel needed to meet the manning requirement of the Armed Forces, so that by March 2004, the Royal Navy and RAF achieve full manning, and the Army meets 97% of its manning requirement. (Full manning is defined as falling within a tolerance band of +1/-2% to reflect the temporary impact of ongoing structural and organisational change within the Armed Forces). **Overall Assessment: Partly Met**	Royal Air Force at full manning from 2001-02. Royal Navy/Royal Marines at full manning by 2002-03. Army at 97% of requirement by March 2004, as progress towards full manning by 2005.	**Partly Met** Improvements in all three Service. From April 2001 to April 2004 • RN increased from 96.6% to 97.7% of requirement, remaining just below manning balance. • Army increased from 92.7% to 97.2% of requirement, remaining just below manning balance. • RAF increased from 97.1% to 98.5% of requirement, achieving manning balance by April 2002 and maintaining it thereafter. All three Services continued to experience critical shortages in certain specialised areas.	*MoD Performance Report 2001-02* paragraphs 80-92 *MoD Annual Report and Accounts 2002-03* paragraphs 80-83 *MoD Annual Report and Accounts 2003-04* paragraphs 73-75
	Achieve the single Service guidelines for deployed service.	**Not Met** Although all three Services met their guidelines in 2001-02, very heavy subsequent operational commitments meant that they were not always able to do so thereafter. In particular in 2003-04, Army tour intervals for some units were well below the 24 months guideline.	*MoD Performance Report 2001-02* paragraphs 81-83 *MoD Annual Report and Accounts 2002-03* paragraphs 158 *MoD Annual Report and Accounts 2003-04* paragraph 160
	New investment in family accommodation in Great Britain to improve the living conditions of Service personnel and their families to Standard 1 for condition by 2005/06.	**Met – Ongoing** Over the period the Defence Housing Executive upgraded 6,712 Service Family houses to Standard 1 for Condition, against overall in-year targets of 4,800. Proportion of long-term housing stock at Standard 1 for Condition increased from about 31% on 31 March 2001 to about 55% on 31 March 2004.	*MoD Performance Report 2001-02* paragraph 96 *MoD Annual Report and Accounts 2002-03* paragraphs 107 *MoD Annual Report and Accounts 2003-04* paragraph 96-97
	Implement from April 2001 a new pay system for Regular forces which will enable better recognition of the skills and experience gained by individuals as they progress through a rank and align pay more closely with job weights.	**Met** Pay 2000 was successfully implemented for the vast majority of regular personnel on 1 April 2001, and the transition to all Service personnel completed in October 2003.	*MoD Performance Report 2001-02* paragraph 134 *MoD Annual Report and Accounts 2002-03* paragraph 156

Table 22 continued...			
PSA Target	**Performance Indicator**	**Assessment**	**Further Detail**
Objective I *(continued)* – **Provide and direct Armed Forces able to undertake successfully a major operation on a similar scale and duration to the Gulf War, or two medium scale operations (of similar size to that in Kosovo), one involving warfighting, and sustain them simultaneously for up to six months, whilst meeting long standing commitments and being able to rebuild a bigger force should a major threat to Europe emerge.**			
	Implementation of the Armed Forces Overarching Personnel Strategy (AFOPS) as guided by its supporting Action Plan.	**Met** The implementation of AFOPS provided the framework to take forward the key personnel themes of Attract, Recruit, Retain, Sustain and Remember and such policies such as Joint Personnel Administration (JPA), and the Defence Housing Policy. From 1 April 2004 AFOPS has been replaced by the Service Personnel Plan.	*MoD Performance Report 2001-02* paragraph 133 *MoD Annual Report and Accounts 2002-03* paragraph 154 *MoD Annual Report and Accounts 2003-04* paragraph 167
3. Achieve the objectives established by Ministers for military operations that arise in which the United Kingdom's Armed Forces are involved. **Overall Assessment: Met**	Successful fulfilment of Operations as measured through achievement of Operational Objectives.	**Met** The Armed Forces achieved a high degree of success against the military objectives set in all Operations overseas, including in Afghanistan, Bosnia, the Democratic Republic of Congo, Iraq, Kosovo, Macedonia, and Sierra Leone. In addition they maintained a minimum nuclear deterrent capability; maintained the security of the UK's Overseas Territories; supported the civil authorities at home, including in Northern Ireland, in civil emergencies (particularly in response to Foot and Mouth and in provision of emergency fire cover across the UK), in routine provision of Search and Rescue and of Fisheries Protection services, and in the investigation and disposal of suspected explosive devices.	*MoD Performance Report 2001-02* paragraphs 8-30 *MoD Annual Report and Accounts 2002-03* paragraphs 11-31 *MoD Annual Report and Accounts 2003-04* paragraphs 7-28
Objective II – **In order to achieve the above, provide an effective defence policy, planning and management structure.**			
4. Working with NATO Allies, implement the decisions of the NATO Washington Summit, including the new Strategic Concept and the Defence Capabilities Initiative, and help to adapt NATO to the new strategic environment.	A more effective and efficient NATO, including through the implementation of the measures agreed at the Washington Summit.	**Met** NATO has transformed its structures, procedures and capabilities in order to adapt to new threats and challenges. A streamlined NATO command structure was approved, the NATO Response Force reached interim operating capability, NATO leaders committed to transform the Alliance to meet new threats, including terrorism and Weapons of Mass destruction.	*MoD Performance Report 2001-02* paragraphs 57-58 *MoD Annual Report and Accounts 2002-03* paragraphs 50-53 *MoD Annual Report and Accounts 2003-04* paragraphs 43-47
Overall Assessment: Met	NATO enlargement is in line with UK interests.	**Met** Bulgaria, Estonia, Latvia, Lithuania, Romania, Slovakia and Slovenia acceded to NATO on 29 March 2004.	

Table 22 continued...			
PSA Target	**Performance Indicator**	**Assessment to End of 2002-03**	**Paragraph**
Objective II *(continued)* – **In order to achieve the above, provide an effective defence policy, planning and management structure**			
5. Work with partners so that the European Union (EU) can, by 2003, deploy forces of up to Corps level (50-60,000 personnel) within 60 days, capable of undertaking the full range of Petersberg tasks (from disaster relief to large scale peace-support operations) in and around Europe. **Overall Assessment: Met**	By 2003, EU able to deploy forces of up to Corps level within sixty days, capable of undertaking the full range of Petersberg tasks.	**Met** Defence Ministers confirmed in May 2003 that the EU had attained operational capability across the full range of Petersberg Tasks, albeit limited and constrained by recognised shortfalls.	*MoD Performance Report 2001-02* paragraphs 59-60 *MoD Annual Report and Accounts 2002-03* paragraphs 54-57 *MoD Annual Report and Accounts 2003-04* paragraphs 15, 19, 43-47
	Effective political/military decision-making apparatus established within the EU. Minimum duplication with NATO and national machinery.	**Met** EU political and military decision making structures became fully operational in 2001-02 and continued to develop. The EU conducted its first two military operations in 2003-04. European Defence Agency established. UK successfully ensured that NATO capabilities are not duplicated.	
	Effective EU relationships with NATO acceptable to all members.	**Met** 'Berlin Plus' arrangements agreed between EU and NATO whereby EU has access to some common NATO assets and capabilities. Successful EU operation carried out under these in Macedonia. Reciprocal liaison arrangements agreed between EU Military Staff and SHAPE.	
6. Improved effectiveness of the UK contribution to conflict prevention and management as demonstrated by a reduction in the number of people whose lives are affected by violent conflict and by a reduction in potential sources of future conflict, where the UK can make a significant contribution. JOINT TARGET WITH DFID AND FCO. **Overall Assessment: [Not yet assessed]**	In all countries and regions in which activities are funded by resources from the joint pools, reduced rate in the: • Incidence, or likelihood, of new conflicts; • Incidence of conflict-related displacement; and • Incidence of war-related casualties.	**Not yet assessed** Formal analysis of statistics on deaths, refugees and internally displaced people not yet available. Successful range of cross-Departmental activities in support of agreed priorities in Africa and rest of the world continued to develop. MoD working to support conflict prevention initiatives across Africa, the Middle East, Europe, Central America and Asia, as well as undertaking wider-ranging conflict-prevention work under the Defence Diplomacy Programme. Further development and refocusing of defence relations programmes and initiatives in 2003-04.	*MoD Performance Report 2001-02* paragraphs 65-66 *MoD Annual Report and Accounts 2002-03* paragraphs 58-61 *MoD Annual Report and Accounts 2003-04* paragraphs 48-50
Objective III – **Provide fighting equipment for the Armed Forces using Smart Procurement principles, so that they maintain the military capability to conduct the operational tasks required of them.**			
7. Develop and deliver battle-winning equipment to time, cost and capability requirement targets that will enable the Armed Forces to provide the military capability required of them now and in the future **Overall Assessment: Partly Met**	On average, in-year slippage to in-service date of fewer than 10 days for new major projects.	**Not Met** Average in-year slippage of 15 days in 2001-02, 54 days in 2002-03, 2.2 months in 2003-04.	*MoD Performance Report 2001-02* paragraphs 65-66 *MoD Annual Report and Accounts 2002-03* paragraphs 58-61 *MoD Annual Report and Accounts 2003-04* paragraph 123
	On average, in-year slippage to in-service date of fewer than 4 weeks for existing major projects.	**Not Met** Average in-year slippage of 6 weeks in 2001-02, 62 weeks in 2002-03, 2.8 months in 2003-04.	
	97% of customer's key requirements to be attained.	**Met** 98.8% of customers' key requirements met in 2001-02, 99.5% in 2002-03, 98.8% in 2003-04.	
	On average, no increase in major project costs.	**Partly Met** No increase on average in 2001-02, Average growth against approval of 5.4% in 2002-03 and 2.7% in 2003-04.	

Table 22 continued...

PSA Target	Performance Indicator	Assessment to End of 2002-03	Paragraph
Value for Money			
8. Achieve value for money through delivering efficiency savings of 3% a year, benefits of the Smart Procurement Initiative of £750 million over the period 2001-02 to 2003-04, and continuing the drive for the optimum utilisation of the Defence asset base, with disposals of over £600M of assets by March 2004. **Overall Assessment: Met**	Reduce the output costs of the DLO by 20% in resource terms by 2005, whilst ensuring that it continues to deliver and, where appropriate, improves the quality of its outputs. (Target rebased in 2002-03 to 14% savings by April 2006 against April 2002 baseline, reflecting change in cost of capital rate in April 2003)	**On Course** • 5.6% reduction in output costs from April 2000 to March 2002; • 3.1% reduction in output costs 2002-03 against revised baseline; • 3.7% reduction in output costs 2003-04 against revised baseline (subject to validation); • Cumulative reduction of 6.8% by April 2004 against cumulative target of 6% towards revised 14% reduction baseline.	*MoD Performance Report 2001-02* paragraph 110 *MoD Annual Report and Accounts 2002-03* paragraphs 146-47 *MoD Annual Report and Accounts 2003-04* paragraph 138
	Identify by 2002 those core Defence Estate sites required for continued use by the Department and Armed Forces.	**Met** • Categorisation of sites agreed by 31 December 2002. • Implementation plan approved February 2004.	*MoD Performance Report 2001-02* paragraph 97 *MoD Annual Report and Accounts 2002-03* paragraph 111 *MoD Annual Report and Accounts 2003-04* paragraph 98
	Achieve asset disposals of over £600M by March 2004.	**Met** Total asset disposals £748M: • 2001-02 £184M Estate, £28M equipment; • 2002-03 £278M Estate, £29M equipment; • 2003-04 £207M Estate, £22M equipment.	*MoD Performance Report 2001-02* paragraphs 78-79 *MoD Annual Report and Accounts 2002-03* paragraphs 77-78 *MoD Annual Report and Accounts 2003-04* paragraphs 101 and 149
	Deliver £750M Smart Acquisition savings over the period 2001/2002 to 2003/2004.	**Met** Estimated reductions of some £2Bn were made to the MoD's planned equipment programme between 1998 and 2008. However, Smart Acquisition is now normal practice and data to support notional Smart Acquisition savings proved to be unreliable. The MoD is discussing with the NAO how to establish reliable performance metrics. Currently the most reliable metrics are those in the annual Major Projects Report which indicate that for equipment, SA programmes currently have less slippage and cost overrun than legacy programmes.	*MoD Performance Report 2001-02* paragraph 118 *MoD Annual Report and Accounts 2002-03* paragraph 129 *MoD Annual Report and Accounts 2003-04* paragraphs 124-125
	Efficiency Savings: Develop new approach to efficiency, subject to agreement between the MoD and HMT.	**Met** • New system agreed in SR2002 and implemented from 1 April 2002. • 2.3% savings under new system in 2002-03; • 2.9% savings in 2003-04 (subject to validation); • cumulative savings of 5.2% by April 2004 against cumulative target of 5%.	*MoD Performance Report 2001-02* paragraph 77 *MoD Annual Report and Accounts 2002-03* paragraphs 143-44 *MoD Annual Report and Accounts 2003-04* paragraphs 150-152
	Subject to value for money considerations, complete the Defence Evaluation and Research Agency Public Private Partnership by April 2002.	**Met – Slippage** Given market conditions it was decided to delay the initial QinetiQ transaction to the end of 2002. The agreement was signed on schedule on 5 December 2002.	*MoD Performance Report 2001-02* paragraphs 149-50 *MoD Annual Report and Accounts 2002-03* paragraph 191

Table 23: 2004 Spending Review Public Service Agreement Targets

AIM

Deliver security for the people of the United Kingdom and the Overseas Territories by defending them, including against terrorism, and act as a force for good by strengthening international peace and stability.

OBJECTIVES AND PERFORMANCE TARGETS

Objective I: Achieve success in the military tasks we undertake at home and abroad.

1. *Achieve the objectives established by Ministers for operations and military tasks in which the United Kingdom's Armed Forces are involved, including those providing support to our civil communities.*

2. *By 2008, deliver improved effectiveness of UK and international support for conflict prevention by addressing long-term structural causes of conflict, managing regional and national tension and violence, and supporting post-conflict reconstruction, where the UK can make a significant contribution, in particular Africa, Asia, Balkans and the Middle East.* JOINT WITH THE FOREIGN AND COMMONWEALTH OFFICE AND THE DEPARTMENT FOR INTERNATIONAL DEVELOPMENT.

Objective II: Be ready to respond to the tasks that might arise.

3. *Generate forces which can be deployed, sustained and recovered at the scales of effort required to meet the Government's strategic objectives.*

4. *Play a leading role in the development of the European Security Agenda, and enhance capabilities to undertake timely and effective security operations, by successfully encouraging a more efficient and effective NATO, a more coherent and effective European Security and Defence Policy (ESDP) operating in strategic partnership with NATO, and enhanced European defence capabilities.* JOINT WITH THE FOREIGN AND COMMONWEALTH OFFICE.

5. *Recruit, train, motivate and retain sufficient military personnel to provide the military capability necessary to meet the Government's strategic objectives.*

Objective III: Build for the future.

6. *Deliver the equipment programme to cost and time.*

WHO IS RESPONSIBLE FOR DELIVERY?

The Secretary of State for Defence is responsible for the delivery of this PSA. The Secretary of State for Foreign and Commonwealth Affairs is jointly responsible for delivery of target 4 and, together with the Secretary of State for International Development, target 2. The Secretary of State for Defence is also responsible for delivering the agreed efficiency target set out in the Ministry of Defence chapter of the 2004 Spending Review White Paper (see below).

A reconciliation of SR2002 and SR2004 targets can be found on the Treasury website at www.hm-treasury.go.uk.

EFFICIENCY TARGET

The Ministry of Defence will realise total annual efficiency gains of at least £2.8 billion by 2007/08, of which three-quarters will be cash releasing, to be re-invested in defence capability and further modernisation initiatives.

ANNEX C:
Defence Agency Performance

Table 24: Defence Agency Performance							
Agency	Key Targets 2002-03		Key Targets 2003-04					
	Targets Met/ Targets Set[1]	Proportion Met	Targets Met/ Targets Set[1]	Proportion Met	Marginal Miss[2]	Better Performance[3]	Significantly Better Performance[4]	Targets not directly comparable to 2002-03[5]
Armed Forces Personnel Administration Agency	8/9	89%	9/9	100%	0	0	0	5
ABRO (Trading Fund)	4/5	80%	5/5	100%	0	1	0	2
Army Personnel Centre[6]	3/4	75%	2/4	50%	2	0	2	0
Army Training and Recruiting Agency	2/5	40%	4/5	80%	1	3	1	0
British Forces Post Office	2/3	67%	10/11	91%	1	4	0	2
Defence Analytical Services Agency	4/7	57%	7/8	88%	1	2	1	5
Defence Aviation Repair Agency (Trading Fund)	4/4	100%	4/4	100%	0	2	2	0
Defence Bills Agency	7/7	100%	6/6	100%	0	0	0	0
Defence Communication Services Agency	6/7	86%	6/7	86%	1	5	1	0
Defence Dental Agency	4/8	50%	3/6	50%	1	0	3	0
Defence Estates	3/5	60%	10/11	91%	0	0	0	4
Defence Geographic and Imagery Intelligence Agency	3/8	38%	6/8	75%	2	0	0	3
Defence Housing Executive[7]	5/8	63%	2/9	22%	4	0	1	0
Defence Intelligence and Security Centre	5/7	71%	2/4	50%	1	0	0	1
Defence Medical Education and Training Agency	–	–	7/7	100%	0	1	1	4
Defence Procurement Agency	3/5	60%	2/5	40%	0	2	0	0
Defence Science and Technology Laboratory (Trading Fund)	4/4	100%	7/7	100%	0	1	2	4
Defence Storage and Distribution Agency	4/4	100%	2/6[8]	33%	1	0	0	4
Defence Transport and Movements Agency	6/6	100%	3/3	100%	0	2	0	1
Defence Vetting Agency	7/17	41%	8/17	47%	0	0	14	0
Disposal Services Agency	4/4	100%	4/4	100%	0	0	0	0
Duke of York's Royal Military School[9]	6/8	75%	5/8	63%	1	3	0	1
Medical Supplies Agency	2/7	29%	1/5	20%	2	0	0	2
Met Office (Trading Fund)	4/7	57%	6/7	86%	0	3	2	2
MoD Police[10]	2/6	33%	2/8	25%	2	1	0	4
Naval Manning Agency[6]	6/12	50%	6/10	60%	1	5	1	0

Table 24 continued...							
Agency	Key Targets 2002-03		Key Targets 2003-04				
	Targets Met/ Targets Set[1]	Proportion Met	Targets Met/ Targets Set[1]	Proportion Met	Marginal Miss[2]	Better Performance[3]	Significantly Better Performance[4]	Targets not directly comparable to 2002-03[5]
Naval Recruiting and Training Agency	5/7	71%	4/7	57%	0	1	1	0
Pay and Personnel Agency	7/7	100%	5/6[11]	83%	1	0	2	4
Queen Victoria School	4/5	80%	5/5	100%	0	1	3	0
RAF Personnel Management Agency[6]	4/5	80%	5/5	100%	0	4	0	0
RAF Training Group Defence Agency	5/7	71%	5/7	71%	0	0	0	0
Service Children's Education	7/16	44%	5/16	31%	5	4	0	2
UK Hydrographic Office (Trading Fund)	7/12	58%	9/11	82%	1	0	3	8
Veterans Agency	6/6	100%	5/6	83%	1	3	1	1
Warships Support Agency	10/11	91%	5/8	63%	0	1	1	1
Total		70%		72%	29	49	42	60

Notes:

[1] Where there are multiple elements to a Key Target these have been counted separately.

[2] Where a target is judged to be narrowly missed, by a shortfall of under 2%.

[3] Where outturn against a measure, or commentary on performance, indicates improvement over the previous year. Only applicable to Key Targets that have remained the same since 2002-03.

[4] Where there were large changes in possible performance against comparable measures for the previous year. These have generally been taken as at least a 5% increment in performance, usually more. Only applicable to Key Targets that have remained the same since 2002-03.

[5] Since the formation of the Directorate of Business Delivery in 2003, Agencies have been encouraged to re-assess key targets in order to make them more relevant/challenging.

[6] De-agencified April 2004.

[7] De-agencified and merged with Defence Estates in April 2004.

[8] KT 2 (unit cost of output) results not available at time of print.

[9] One key target to be verified by Defence Internal Audit.

[10] Renamed Ministry of Defence Police and Guarding Agency in April 2004 after merging with the Ministry of Defence Guarding Service.

[11] Customer satisfaction target not measurable until 2004-5 therefore not included.

Background

1.   Despite the obvious pressures and disruption caused by Op TELIC and other commitments, Defence Agencies generally performed well in 2003-04. Ten agencies met all their key targets, an increase over the previous year. Overall the average number of targets met also increased from 70% to 72% compared to 2002-03. Since the formation of the Directorate of Business Delivery in MoD headquarters in August 2003, Trading Funds and agencies have also been actively encouraged to review their target-setting processes with a view to exchanging best practice and setting more relevant and challenging targets in the future.

Organisational Changes

2.   On 1 April 2003, the number of on-vote Defence Agencies reduced from 31 to 30 with the merger of the Defence Secondary Care Agency and Defence Medical Training Organisation to form the Defence Medical Education and Training Agency. From 1 April 2004 three agencies – the Naval Manning Agency, the Army Personnel Centre and the RAF Personnel Management Agency were de-agencified as a result of the Service Personnel Process Review. In addition the Defence Housing Executive Agency was merged into Defence Estates and the MoD Police Agency was renamed the Ministry of Defence Police and Guarding Agency after merging with the MoD Guarding Service.

Trading Funds

3.   MoD has five Trading Fund Agencies. **ABRO**, the **Defence Aviation Repair Agency (DARA)** and the **Defence Science and Technology Laboratory (Dstl)** met all their key targets in 2003-04. For ABRO the average equipment repair price reduced by 8% against a 4% target (following a 9% reduction in 2002-03). The agency has been proactive in securing new business direct from the defence industry, through partnering with prime contractors and diversifying into the fleet services and rail markets, resulting in £17.9M additional sales. In DARA, overheads were reduced, workload volumes were maintained, and the Agency offered its customers price reductions in real terms. They achieved their order intake target of £160M, recorded pre-tax profits of £6M whilst securing a three year average Return on Capital Employed in excess of the 6% target.

4.   Dstl's Return on Capital Employed was 11.9% against a target of 6.5%, representing a significant improvement against an achievement of 9.6% in 2002-03. This was combined with an increase in overall levels of customer satisfaction of 7%.

5.   **Met Office** achieved 6 out of 7 of its key targets. Their staff skills index target was missed mainly owing to the fact that Met Office lost many of its most experienced staff upon its relocation to Exeter. The **UK Hydrographic Office (UKHO)** achieved 5 out of 7 key targets. Although there was slippage in some elements of the plans to put in place enablers for the expansion into Wider Markets, sales in the Hydrographic Office were strong: up £5.7M compared to budget and costs contained. The Return on Capital Employed was 16.4% against a target of 7.5%.

On-Vote Agencies

Logistics

6.   New and ongoing operations continued to have a significant impact on demand, causing some MoD agencies to fail to meet their set targets despite the fact that performance in many areas had improved. For example, whilst the **Defence Storage and Distribution Agency (DSDA)** narrowly failed to meet its key target against non explosive issues (93.24% against a target of 95%), this hides the fact that demand increased significantly and the agency actually met some 13% more issues than originally planned. Examples of key developments in other agencies are as follows:

7.   The **Defence Communications Services Agency (DCSA)** played a pivotal role in the UK's largest ever Communication Information Systems deployment – Op TELIC. This included the provision of 48 land-based satellite ground terminals carrying some 1000 channels of services and a combined bandwidth of 54 megabits.

8.   **British Forces Post Office (BFPO)** activities reached a peak when nearly 3000 bags of mail were despatched in relation to Op TELIC in a single day with a monthly total of 70,000 bags in April 2003.

9.   The **Warship Support Agency (WSA)** failed to deliver ambitious targets for numbers of vessels that were either materially available for their current operational tasking or materially fit to meet their readiness criteria and further work is continuing with customers to ease the situation. However, it made significant improvements to installing priority capability upgrades to warships: for example, the Agency returned *HMS Invincible*, now the Fleet Flagship, with 100% of the planned improvements to time and cost. In addition the Agency once again exceeded its target improvement in the quality of Single Living Accommodation.

10.   At the same time as supporting operations and achieving all its key targets, the **Defence Transport and Movements Agency (DTMA)** made significant progress with its e-business strategy, the introduction of a new Freight Transport Clearing House concept that uses the irreducible spare capacity of MoD in-house freight assets to greater effect, and delivered strategic efficiencies of some £2.8M.

11.   Whilst it missed the majority of its key targets, the **Medical Supplies Agency (MSA)** made a major contribution to Op TELIC, delivering the same number of medical items and amount of equipment as for the 1991 Gulf conflict in only half the time. The Agency is currently undergoing a major transformation programme to make further improvements to its performance. This aims to build on the Department's capability to provide "whole life" support to medical equipment by integrating technical staff currently employed elsewhere in the DLO, and will develop the MSA into a true 'decider' organisation, will improve customer service, and reduce costs.

Recruiting, Training, and Manning

12.   There were a number of notable successes in those agencies involved with personnel, recruiting and training. For example, the **Army Training and Recruitment Agency (ATRA)** provided 622 commissioned officers against a target of 600, and 9794 soldiers against a target of 9475. The Agency narrowly missed (by half a percent) its target for improving pass rates for soldiers made available to undergo career or professional development. This was principally due to the impact of operational requirements, which resulted in personnel having to be withdrawn from courses part way through. For the Navy, the partnering arrangements with Flagship Training Ltd in the **Naval Recruiting and Training Agency (NRTA)** delivered in-year benefits of £17.43M against a target of £15M.

13.   The **Defence Medical Education and Training Agency (DMETA)** made significant progress in demanding circumstances in its inaugural year. The key achievement was the provision of 100% of the requirement for secondary care personnel needed for operational deployments. This included some 750 people deployed to Iraq at the height of Op TELIC. At the same time, the Agency also made a number of improvements to medical education and training, a highlight being the development of a Foundation Modern Apprenticeship Scheme for Allied Health Professionals and advances to the development of Clinical Governance (CG) policy together with a supporting quality management framework and CG audit protocol.

14.   Demands for intelligence training from all three services continued to rise and the **Defence Intelligence and Security Centre (DISC)** is evolving to meet changing customer requirements and technologies. New additions to the Agency include the Defence School of Photography at RAF Cosford and the Defence School of Languages at Beaconsfield. In addition, the Agency's flagship course for overseas students, the International Intelligence Directors course, continues to attract high-level interest from all continents and provides a significant opportunity for intelligence diplomacy at the highest levels.

15.   The removal of agency status from the three service **manning agencies** from 1 April 04 will enable the three Services to respond more effectively to customers' strategic and operational requirements in relation to manning, through-career drafting and appointing, and terms and conditions of service in the future.

Personnel Administration

16. In the last months of FY 03/04, the **Defence Vetting Agency (DVA)** began to meet its Developed Vetting Targets for the first time, and overall performance improved against 82% of the key targets. Further initiatives are in hand including the greater use of technology to streamline processes with the aim of making further improvements to the Agency's performance.

17. The **Pay and Personnel Agency (PPA)** continued to maintain high levels of average accuracy (97.9%) and timeliness (97.5%) for salary payments, expenses payments and pension awards, as well as reducing unit costs associated with these transactions. The Agency also gained ISO 9001 quality accreditation for 100% of its corporate service areas.

18. The **Armed Forces Personnel Administration Agency (AFPAA)** faced the challenge of maintaining current services and their associated legacy systems whilst preparing the Agency for the huge transformation that will be necessary for AFPAA to be at the heart of service delivery in the new, modern Joint Personnel Administration environment.

19. In June 2003, the **Veterans Agency (VA)** was a category winner in the Chartered Institute of Public and Financial Accounting (CIPFA)/PricewaterhouseCoopers Public Reporting and Accountability awards. The Agency was particularly praised for "displaying in its website and printed materials an admirable concern to assist its clients through the thickets of bureaucracy and attain their rights", and customer ratings were high. The VA has also reduced sick absence levels among staff by over 20%.

Education

20. Despite missing a number of its key targets, **Service Children's Education (SCE)** again outstripped the UK (English) National performance in all 10 of the academic subject areas covering key stages 1-3 by an average of 5.5%. In addition, the notional positions of the agency in the English Local Education Authority (LEA) League tables were highly respectable (second at Key Stage 1, twenty-third at Key Stage 2 and fourteenth at Key Stage 3 – of 150 LEAs). Both **Queen Victoria School** and the **Duke of York's Royal Military School** also saw notable improvements in academic performance in many areas.

Specialist Service Provision

21. The **Defence Analytical Services Agency (DASA)'s** two long-running key targets on service delivery and customer satisfaction were both met, having been failed in 2002-03, and a number of major pieces of work were concluded, for example the creation of the Op TELIC research database. The Agency also won the National Council for Work Experience award in the public sector category for the quality of placements offered to students.

22. The **Defence Geographic and Imagery Intelligence Agency (DGIA)** was successful in meeting its commitments to support operations. This did, however, require the diversion of some resources away from the Strategic and Contingency planning areas, which meant there was a small reduction in performance against these targets.

23. Despite extensive efforts, the **MoD Police Agency** (now the MoD Defence Police and Guarding Agency) was not able to meet its target of recruiting 6% of new recruits from ethnic minorities. However, recruitment of female staff doubled and now stands at 15.4%. Solvency for crime classified as "primary", i.e. directly against MoD interests, was 56.9% against a target of 48%.

24.   The **Disposal Services Agency (DSA)** exceeded its gross cash receipts target of £20M to achieve £22M worth of sales in 2003-04.

25.   The **Defence Dental Agency (DDA)** met all demands for operationally deployable dental teams. On other targets there was a significant reduction in treatment needs for RN and RAF personnel although difficulties with the Army meant this target was missed largely owing to the difficulties in providing treatment to the large numbers of troops involved with operational activities.

26.   Further details on Defence Estates, the Defence Housing Executive and the Defence Procurement Executive can be found in the body of the MoD Annual Report.

Non Departmental Public Bodies (NDPBs)

27.   The Department has seven Executive and twelve Advisory NDPBs. Further details on their purpose, size and funding can be found on the MoD website at http://www.mod.uk/issues/open_government/ndpbs.htm Six of the Department's sponsored Executive NDPBs are museums, which contribute to the broader government agenda relating to heritage, education and social inclusion. For example, some 30,000 activity places were arranged at the RAF Museum for children as part of organised school parties in 2003-04. The other Executive NDPB, the Oil and Pipelines Agency, achieved all its 2003-04 business targets within budget.

28.   Further details about the activities and performance of MoD's agencies and NDPBs can be found in individual organisations' reports and accounts, and in the supplementary documents to the MoD Annual Report.

ANNEX D:
Government Standards

Fraud

1. A re-launch of the joint Defence Fraud Analysis Unit (DFAU) and MoD Police fraud awareness programme, which included the provision of 115 presentations during the year, sustained the rising trend of whistleblowing disclosure identified in previous years. This contributed to the total of 356 suspected cases of irregularity, fraud, theft and corruption recorded by the DFAU in 2003-04 with an estimated value of £2.11M. Suspected contract fraud accounted for 49 cases; the large increase over previous years was primarily accounted for by theft of assets related to Op TELIC. The increase in reported suspected fraud was marginal. Further initiatives included the launch of the DFAU internal website and the development of an interactive electronic learning module, designed to teach risk awareness. To support new initiatives and a more proactive role, including full interaction between all business areas and the development of data-mining techniques, the DFAU began the process of recruiting additional staff.

Table 25: Bill Paying Performance – Proportion of Bills Settled Within Thirty Calendar Days				
	2002-03		2003-04	
	Target	Achieved	Target	Achieved
Defence Bills Agency[1]	100%	99.93%	99.90%	99.98%
ABRO	100%	100%	100%	99.90%
Defence Aviation Repair Agency[2,3]	100%	90.60%	100%	91.00%
Defence Science and Technology Laboratory	100%	97.00%	100%	98.00%
Met Office[3]	100%	99.80%	100%	99.79%
UK Hydrographic Office	100%	98.70%	100%	99.10%

Notes:

(1) Representing all MoD bills with the exception of those paid by Trading Funds.

(2) There have been some transitional payment delays as DARA have introduced changes to their internal invoice approvals processes.

(3) Standard payment terms are 30 days, however other pre-arranged terms may on occasion be agreed with customers.

Open Government

2.   Preparations for the introduction of full access rights under the Freedom of Information (FOI) Act were well advanced by the end of 2003-04. The FOI Programme established in 2002 continued to promote awareness of the Act and to develop Department-wide policies and procedures for compliance with the obligations placed on public authorities. As part of the Programme, an FOI "Toolkit" is being developed. This will allow requests for information to be tracked and overall performance to be monitored from January 2005.

3.   During 2003-04, information continued to be added to the MoD's Publication Scheme, launched at the end of 2002. Much of the information can be accessed directly from the electronic version of the Publication Scheme (http://www.foi.mod.uk). We have also continued to use MoD's website to provide more dynamic information. In particular, regular headline reports have been posted to chart the progress of major deployments such as Op TELIC, and to provide a range of supporting background material such as maps, photographs, speeches, statements, reports and links to related sites.

4.   The programme of FOI preparations included an audit exercise to review the information we hold. In parallel with this, the re-review of records that have been closed for more than thirty years continued into the first quarter of 2004. A small number of records were released to the National Archives during this period, bringing to 12,150 the total number of records released since inception of the review programme in 1992. Further progress in this area has been hampered by the potential contamination with asbestos of a large number of records held in the Old War Office Building (OWOB). In addition, as part of an exercise coordinated by the National Archives, the MoD has undertaken a comprehensive re-review of files already transferred to the National Archives with a view to opening them before the date originally set.

5.   In advance of full implementation of the FOI Act, MoD continues to respond to requests for information in accordance with the Code of Practice on Access to Government Information. A summary of the key statistics for 2003, compared with 2002 is provided below:

Table 26: Requests in 2003 for Information Under the Code of Practice on Access to Government Information[1]

Category	2002	2003
Number of Code requests dealt with over the period	1,941	2,156
Number of Code requests answered within twenty working days	1,867	2,140
Number of Code requests for which charges were made	1,324	1,416
Number of Code requests where some information was withheld	67	8[2]
Number of internal reviews completed	3	9
Number of internal reviews completed within twenty working days	1	3
Number of internal reviews where the original decision was upheld	0	5
Number of internal reviews where additional information was disclosed	3	1
Number of investigations completed by the Parliamentary Ombudsman	3	1
Number of Ombudsman investigations where MoD's decision was upheld	0	0
Number of Ombudsman investigations where additional information was disclosed	3	1

Notes:

(1) These figures include MoD agencies, Trading Funds and Non-Departmental Public Bodies for the calendar year 2003.

(2) The significant decrease between 2002 and 2003 is largely due to: (a) a high number of requests in 2002 for the same file (the information withheld has now been released and the complete file is included in the Publication Scheme); (b) requests for information relating to procurement projects that were at a sensitive stage in 2002.

Accountability to Parliament

6. Since 1 April 2003, the Ministry of Defence has given evidence to the House of Commons Defence Committee on a number of occasions covering a wide range of issues, and the Government has responded to a number of the Committee's reports. Committee publications, including published evidence given to the Committee, are summarised below and are available at www.parliament.uk/parliamentary_committees/defence_committee.cfm.

Session 2003-04

Reports (Government Responses are listed in brackets after the report they relate to)

First Report
HC 96-i & ii   *Armed Forces Pensions and Compensation*
(Cm 6109)

Second Report
HC 293   *Annual Report for 2003*

Third Report
HC 57-i, ii & iii   *Lessons of Iraq*
(HC 635)

Fourth Report
HC 390   *Strategic Export Controls: Annual Report for 2002, Licensing Policy and Parliamentary Scrutiny*

Fifth Report
HC 465-i & ii   *The Defence White Paper 2003*
(HC 1048)

Sixth Report
HC 572-i & ii   *Defence Procurement*

MoD Evidence

Annual Report and Accounts 2002-03
HC 589-i   Oral Evidence given by Sir Kevin Tebbit, KCB CMG, Permanent Under Secretary of State, and Mr Trevor Woolley, Finance Director, 12 May 2004

Iraq
HC 721-i   Oral Evidence given by Mr Martin Howard, Director General, Operational Policy, and Major General Nick Houghton, ACDS(Operations), 23 June 2004

Duty of Care
HC 620-i   Oral Evidence given by Lieutenant General Anthony Palmer, Deputy Chief of Defence Staff (Personnel), Rear Admiral Simon Goodall, Director General Training and Education, Colonel David Eccles, Chief of Staff, Army Training and Recruitment Agency, and Mr Julian Miller, Director General of Service Personnel Policy, 26 May 2004

Session 2002-03

Reports (Government Responses are listed in brackets after the report they relate to)

Third Report
HC 321   *Arms Control and Disarmament (Inspections) Bill*
(HC 754)

Fourth Report
HC 620   *The Government's Proposals for Secondary Legislation under the Export Control Act*
(Cm 5988)

Fifth Report
HC 474   *Strategic Export Controls: Annual Report for 2001, Licensing Policy and Parliamentary Scrutiny*
(Cm 5943)

Sixth Report
HC 93-i & ii   *A New Chapter to the Strategic Defence Review*
(HC 975)

Seventh Report
HC 557   *Draft Civil Contingencies Bill*
(Cm 6078)

Eighth Report
HC 694   *Defence Procurement*
(HC 1194)

MoD Evidence

European Security and Defence
HC 1165-i   Minutes of oral evidence presented by Mr Simon Webb CBE, Policy Director, Ministry of
                Defence, Dr Sarah Beaver, Director for EU and UN, Ministry of Defence, and Mr Paul
                Johnston, Head of Security Policy Department, Foreign and Commonwealth Office,
                15 October 2003

Armed Forces Pension and Compensation
HC 1255   Minutes of oral evidence presented by Mr Ivor Caplin, Under-Secretary of State and Minister
                for Veterans, and Mr Jonathan Iremonger, Director, Service Personnel Policy (Pensions),
                5 November 2003

The Appointment of the New Chief of the Defence Staff
HC 771-i   Minutes of oral evidence presented by General Sir Michael Walker, GCB CMG CBE ADC,
                Chief of the Defence Staff, 11 June 2003

The Army Training and Recruiting Agency
HC 124-i   Minutes of oral evidence presented by Major General A D Leakey CBE, Chief Executive, and
                Mr Martyn Piper, Deputy Chief Executive, Army Training and Recruiting Agency, 1 May 2003

7.   Since 1 April 2003, the Ministry of Defence has given evidence to the House of Commons Public Accounts Committee on value for money issues on a number of occasions, and the Government has responded to a number of the Committee's reports. Committee publications, including published evidence given to the Committee, are summarised below and are available at www.parliament.uk/parliamentary_committees/committee_of_public_accounts.cfm.

Session 2003-04

Reports (Government Responses are listed in brackets after the report they relate to)

Thirty-ninth Report

HC 273   *Operation TELIC: United Kingdom military operations in Iraq*

Twentieth Report

HC 551   *Improving service delivery: the Veterans Agency*

(Cm 6271)

MoD Evidence

Major Projects Report 2003

HC 383-i   Oral Evidence given by Sir Kevin Tebbit, KCB CMG, Permanent Under-Secretary of State, Sir Peter Spencer, KCB, Chief of Defence Procurement, and Lieutenant Rob Fulton, Deputy Chief of Defence Staff (Equipment Capability), 23 February 2004

HC 383-ii   Oral Evidence given by Sir Peter Spencer, KCB, Chief of Defence Procurement, and Lieutenant Rob Fulton, Deputy Chief of Defence Staff (Equipment Capability), 25 February 2004

Session 2002-03

Reports (Government Responses are listed in brackets after the report they relate to)

Forty-sixth Report

HC 533   *Building an air manoeuvre capability: the introduction of the Apache Helicopter*

(Cm 6105)

Thirty-seventh Report

HC 636   *The construction of nuclear submarine facilities at Devonport*

(Cm 6016)

Thirteenth Report

HC 566   *Progress in Reducing Stocks*

(Cm 5849)

8.   Ministers have also accounted to Parliament in other ways during 2003-04 on all aspects of the Department's business. 4,801 Parliamentary Questions were tabled, Defence Ministers led 12 debates on defence issues in the House of Commons and 6 in the House of Lords, responded to 14 Adjournment Debates and one urgent question in the House of Commons, and made 5 oral statements to the House of Commons and 3 to the House of Lords. They also made 152 written statements to the House of Commons and (from introduction of Lords Written Statements in January 2004) 40 to the House of Lords. Details are published in Hansard, and a full list of defence debates and oral and written statements is available on www.mod.uk.

Ministerial Correspondence

9.   Ministers have engaged in widespread correspondence with Members of Parliament, Members of Devolved Legislatures, Members of the European Parliament, and Peers. The table below shows Departmental and agency performance in replying to correspondence from during 2003-04.

Table 27: Ministry of Defence Ministers and Agency Chief Executives' Performance in Replying to Ministerial Correspondence

	Target set for despatch (working days)	Number of letters received for answer	Percentage of replies within target
Ministry of Defence (excluding Defence Agencies)	15	5,313	73
Defence Agencies			
ABRO	15	4	100
Armed Forces Personnel Administration Agency	15	93	99
Army Personnel Centre	15	17	94
Army Training and Recruiting Agency	15	2	100
British Forces Post Office	15	6	66.7
Defence Analytical Services Agency	15	–	–
Defence Aviation Repair Agency	15	7	100
Defence Bills Agency	10	1	100
Defence Communication Services Agency	15	–	–
Defence Dental Agency	15	9	100
Defence Estates	15	10	91
Defence Geographic and Imagery Intelligence Agency	15	–	–
Defence Housing Executive	15	13	92
Defence Intelligence and Security Centre	15	–	–
Defence Medical Education and Training Agency	15	–	–
Defence Procurement Agency	7	4	50
Dstl	14	–	–
Defence Storage and Distribution Agency	15	5	100
Defence Transport and Movements Agency	15	1	100
Defence Vetting Agency	7	4	100
Disposal Services Agency	15	1	100
Duke of York's Royal Military School	3	–	–
Medical Supplies Agency	15	1	100
Ministry of Defence Police	15	3	100
Naval Manning Agency	15	–	–
Naval Recruiting and Training Agency	15	–	–
Pay and Personnel Agency	10	6	100
Queen Victoria School	15	1	100
RAF Personnel Management Agency	15	–	–
RAF Training Group Defence Agency	15	–	–
Service Children's Education	15	–	–
Met Office	15	3	100
UK Hydrographic Office	15	15	93
Veterans Agency	15	236	99.6
Warship Support Agency	15	11	91

Notes:

(1)   Defence Housing Executive merged with Defence Estates on 1 April 2004.

(2)   Army Personnel Centre, Naval Manning Agency and RAF Personnel Management Agency all de-agencified from 1 April 2004.

Sponsorship

10. As part of the Government's response to the Sixth Report of the Committee on Standards in Public Life, the MoD compiles a summary of all sponsorship of MoD activities by the private or voluntary sector valued at over £5,000. Table 28 shows the information for 2003-04.

Table 28: Commercial Sponsorship Within MoD During 2002-03		
Activity	**Individual Sponsors**	**Company Contribution £ VAT EX**
RAF Aerobatic Display Team	BAE Systems	22,128
	Breitling	10,638
	Total/Fina/Elf	6,809
	BP Air	14,893
RAF Falcons Parachute Display Team	Avia Match Company	12,000
	Vauxhall	37,447
	Sonic Communications	5,000
Blue Eagles Helicopter Display Team	BAE Systems	5,000
	Breitling	10,731
Battle of Britain Memorial Flight	MG Rover	7,658
Royal Naval Presentation Team	Jaguar	25,532
Road safety promotion within British Forces Germany	Land Rover Deutschland GmbH	7,660
RRW Regimental Promotion	Brains Brewery	12,766
RNAS Culdrose Air Days	Lockheed Martin	17,021
Exercise Cambrian Patrol	Red Bull	10,213
RA – The Flying Gunners	Wurth	8,511
The Rheindahlen & Elmpt Bulletin	Mitsubishi Motors Bruggen	15,915
Yeovilton Air Day	Rolls Royce	17,500
Bowman Video	GD (UK)	20,000
Rolling Rock	Cotswold	8,500

Better Regulation

11. There was no MoD sponsored legislation and the Department neither conducted nor proposed any Regulatory Impact Assessments or Regulatory Reform Orders during 2003-04. The Department held one public consultation, on the Interim Storage of Laid-Up Submarines. Copies of consultation documents are published on www.mod.uk. This ran from 12 September to 24 December 2003, complying with the 12 weeks consultation period.

12. On 1 April 2004, the Cabinet Office announced the extension of the Regulatory Impact Assessment process to include all substantial policies and proposals which affect the public sector and to incorporate sustainable development outcomes. We are working with the Cabinet Office Regulatory Impact Unit on how to incorporate this requirement into the MoD's processes with the minimum added bureaucracy while taking account of the operational and security constraints governing the business of Defence.

Safety, Health, Environment and Fire

13. In 2003-04, the Department were involved in a wide range of Safety, Health, Environment and Fire (SHEF) initiatives and achievements. For example we:

- Responded in detail to a NAO report on Compensation Claims in MoD. A major recommendation was that more should be done to strengthen the links between those parts of the MoD that deal with risks, incidents and claims. In response, MoD combined its Claims and SHEF Policy organisations at the beginning of 2004 to form the Directorate of Safety and Claims;

- Reviewed the process of incident reporting, recording and investigation and are setting up a more robust process for learning and communicating lessons from incidents to prevent re-occurrence. Part of this process is to set up a linked database accessible across the Department;

- Provided military personnel, managed by professional MoD Firefighters, for emergency fire-fighting and rescue during industrial action by the Fire Brigades Union;

- Followed up the success of combining safety, health, environment and fire into a single audit methodology, by including other aspects of safety (e.g. nuclear, explosives, fuel, equipment) in a single organisation audit. The audit was partially successful but more work is required to develop a single set of audit system requirements that can fully assess the effectiveness of an entire safety management system;

- Successfully completed a major emergency response exercise, testing the ability of joint UK/US military and civilian staff to respond to a nuclear weapon accident. This involved some 100 UK and US Agencies and nearly 2000 people;

- Continued to develop the arguments to inform a ministerial decision on which of two options – the Airfield Support Services Project or Fire Study 2000 – should be chosen to re-organise the existing Defence Fire Service;

- Continued to provide support to Legal Advisor in relation to the cases currently under consideration by the European Court of Justice relating to application of the Euratom Treaty to military activities;

- Completed the environmental surveys of UK accommodation sites in Bosnia and Kosovo for depleted Uranium and a number of other contaminants;

- Provided the Committee on Radioactive Waste Management with details of MoD's radioactive wastes, spent fuel and fissile materials to ensure these are properly considered when the Government decides the way forward for the long term management and disposals of these materials;

- Provided advice, through the Department for International Development, to the interim Iraqi Government on hazards from depleted uranium and other radioactive materials associated with battlefield scrap;

- Continued work on complete review of JSP418, the MoD's Environmental Manual, aimed at a publication date of January 2005;

- Continued work on development of MoD's Sustainable Development strategy which will be launched later in 2004;

- Commenced a programme to deliver environmental improvements in procurement including timber;

- Continued to promote joint working by enhanced liaison with Government departments and agencies, NATO and other Defence departments.

ANNEX E:
Defence Equipment Programme and Collaborative Procurement

1.   The following tables show the numbers of deliveries accepted in 2003-04 and/or planned for 2004-05, on 31 March 2004, for major equipment programmes. This includes all current projects on which, at 31 March 2004, development expenditure of over £50M or production expenditure of over £100M had been approved, or for which an Invitation to Tender had been issued where procurement costs are expected to exceed £100M. The precise definition of in service date varies with different equipment although, in general terms, it can be taken to refer to the date on which the equipment is expected to be available and supportable in service in sufficient quantity to provide a usable operational capability. The dates quoted for ships and submarines are based on the acceptance date from the contractor of the First of Class, not the date by which the equipment (or specified number of pieces of equipment) will contribute to the operational capability of the Royal Navy.

Battlespace Manoeuvre

2.   The Battlespace Manoeuvre area incorporates capabilities designed to provide direct battlefield engagement, tactical mobility, expeditionary logistics support, nuclear, biological and chemical defence, battlefield engineering, special projects and combat service support. While most of the equipment will be utilised by the Army, it also covers other Services and joint organisations, for example assets that will belong to the Joint Helicopter Command.

Table 29: Capability Manager Battlespace Manoeuvre Equipment Programme

Equipment	Number Ordered Before 1 April 2003	Number Ordered During 2003-04	Number Delivered Before 1 April 2003	Number Delivered During 2003-04	Deliveries Planned During 2004-05	Balance Outstanding	In Service Date (Year Only)
Ground Manoeuvre							
Future Command and Liaison Vehicle (FCLV)	0	401	0	0	0	401	2007
Battlegroup Thermal Imaging (BGTI)[1]	601	0	0	6	323	272	2004
Trojan & Titan	66[2]	0	0	0	0	66	2006
Terrier[3]	65	0	0	0	0	65	2008
Light Forces Anti-Tank Guided Weapon (LF ATGW)	[4]	[4]	[4]	[4]	[4]	[4]	2005
Next Generation Light Anti-armour Weapon (NLAW)	[4]	[4]	[4]	[4]	[4]	[4]	2006
Air and Littoral Manoeuvre							
Attack Helicopter	67	0	43	23	1	0	2001
Chinook MSH HC3	8	0	8	0	0	0	2007[5]

Table 29 continued...							
Equipment	Number Ordered Before 1 April 2003	Number Ordered During 2003-04	Number Delivered Before 1 April 2003	Number Delivered During 2003-04	Deliveries Planned During 2004-05	Balance Outstanding	In Service Date (Year Only)
Theatre Airspace							
Typhoon (Eurofighter)	55[8]	0	0	6[6]	11[6]	38	2003[7]
Typhoon ASTA							
(Aircrew Synthetic Training Aids)	1[8]	0	0	0	0	1	2004[9]
ASRAAM (Advanced Short Range Air-to-Air Missile)	4	4	4	4	4,10	4	2002
BVRAAM (Beyond Visual Range Air-to-Air Missile):							
Meteor	4	0	0	0	0	4	2012
AMRAAM11	4	0	0	0	0	4	2007
Expeditionary Logistics & Support							
A400M	0	0	0	0	0	12	2011
Landing Platform Dock	2	0	0	1	1	0	2003
Auxiliary Oiler	2	0	1	1	0	0	2003
Landing Ship Dock (Auxiliary)	4	0	0	0	0	4	2006[13]

Notes:

(1) Delivery numbers refer to systems delivered and fitted to vehicles.

(2) 33 of each vehicle.

(3) The replacement for the Combat Engineer Tractor.

(4) Weapon numbers are classified.

(5) The in-service date of Chinook Mk3 is currently under review.

(6) Includes instrumented production aircraft and fatigue specimen, which will not be delivered to the RAF.

(7) Date of delivery of first aircraft to the Royal Air Force.

(8) Relates to the first of three envisaged tranches.

(9) Date of provision of initial training capability at RAF Coningsby for Cockpit Trainer.

(10) Deliveries will be complete in early 2005.

(11) AMRAAM 120C is being procured as an interim AAM solution for Typhoon pending the introduction of Meteor, and is included within the Meteor/BVRAAM approval.

(12) The UK requirement for 25 aircraft was confirmed in May 2003.

(13) The In Service Date has slipped from 2004 owing to underestimation of the work involved in producing the LSD(A) design. This has resulted in rework on LSD(A)01 and delays to outfitting of the vessel, which has impacted on the whole programme.

Precision Attack

3.   The Precision Attack area covers the above-water and under-water battlespaces, and deep target attack. It therefore contains programmes ranging from Storm Shadow stand off missile to the nuclear submarines to artillery systems. Although most programmes will subsequently be delivered to the Royal Navy, it also includes substantial Army and Royal Air Force equipment. The table below does not reflect several major equipment programmes where orders have not yet been placed – for example, the future aircraft carriers, Joint Combat Aircraft, additional Astute Class Submarines, and Future Surface Combatants.

Table 30: Capability Manager Precision Attack Equipment Programme

Equipment	Number Ordered Before 1 April 2003	Number Ordered During 2003-04	Number Delivered Before 1 April 2003	Number Delivered During 2003-04	Deliveries Planned During 2004-05	Balance Outstanding	In Service Date (Year Only)
Above-Water Battlespace							
Type 45 Destroyer	6	0	0	0	0	6	2009[1]
Seawolf Block 2	[2]	[2]	[2]	[2]	[2]	[2]	2005
Seawolf Mid-Life Update	44	0	0	0	0	44	2007
Under-Water Battlespace							
Sonar 2087	6	0	0	0	0	6[3]	2006
Astute Class Submarine	3	0	0	0	0	3	2009
Swiftsure and Trafalgar Class Update	4	0	1	1	1	1	2005[4]
Nimrod MRA4 Aircraft[5]	3 (with option for additional 15)	0	0	0	0	3	2009
Stingray Torpedo Mod 1	0	[2]	0	0	0	[2]	2006
Deep Target Attack							
Brimstone anti-armour weapon	[2]	[2]	[2]	[2]	[2]	[2]	2005[6]
COBRA (Counter Battery Radar)	7	0	0	1	2	4	2004
Extended Range Ordnance/ Modular Charge System (ERO/MCS) for AS90 Self-Propelled Howitzer[7]							
Tornado GR Mid-Life Update	142	0	137	5	0	0	1998
PGB (Precision Guided Bomb)	0	[2]	0	0	0	[8]	2007
Conventionally Armed Stand Off Missile (Storm Shadow)	[2]	[2]	[2]	[2]	[2]	[2]	[9]
Guided Multiple Launch Rocket Systems (GMLRS)	0	0	0	0	0	[10]	2008
Tomahawk Block III Missiles	107	0	85	22	0	0	1998

Notes:

(1) In service date slipped to reflect late start of manufacture and re-assessment of baseline programme.

(2) Weapon numbers are classified.

(3) Planned total of ship systems required was reduced from sixteen to twelve in the 2002 planning round and a contract has been placed for six sets with an option for a further six. The requirement for the additional six sets is subject to review. Two part sets, the industrial reference set and the integration testing set, have been ordered. S2087 are providing Ships Staff training for the first 2 ship platforms. A decision on future Ships Staff training strategy is imminent.

(4) Date dependant on host submarine's separate maintenance programme, which has been revised since the previous reporting period.

(5) Following MoD/BAE SYSTEMS Agreement in February 2003, the contract now covers the supply of the first 3 aircraft and long lead item investment for a further 15, procurement of which will be subject to acceptable design maturity and price.

(6) The in service date has been delayed owing to the guidance and control software for the missile requiring an update.

(7) During 2003-04, we decided to terminate the ERO/MCS contract. The way ahead is subject to a 155mm Systems Study.

(8) Contract placed December 2003. Numbers are classified.

(9) In Service Date slipped from 2002 owing to technical problems. New In Service Date currently being reviewed.

(10) 6204 munitions to be bought, dependent on signature of Memorandum of Understanding (MoU), expected in late 2004.

Information Superiority

5.   This capability area covers intelligence, surveillance, target acquisition and reconnaissance, and command, control and information infrastructure. Most projects are inherently tri-service in nature.

Table 31: Capability Manager Information Superiority Equipment Programme

Equipment	Number Ordered Before 1 April 2003	Number Ordered During 2003-04	Number Delivered Before 1 April 2003	Number Delivered During 2003-04	Deliveries Planned During 2004-05	Balance Outstanding	In Service Date (Year Only)
Intelligence, Surveillance, Target Acquisition and Reconnaissance							
ASTOR (Airborne Stand-off Radar)[1]							
Aircraft	5	0	0	0	0	5	2005
Ground	8	0	0	0	0	8	
Soothsayer	0	5	0	0	0	5	2006[2]
Communications							
Skynet 5	0	1	0	0	1	0	2005[3]
NEST[4]	0	1	0	0	0	1	2007
Bowman (Combat Radio System)[5]	1	0	0	1	0	0	2004
CIP[6]	1	0	0	0	1	0	2004
Royal Navy Joint Tactical Information Distribution System and Satellite Tactical Data Links[7]							
Increment 1	7	3	8	2	0	0	2003
Increment 2	11	0	0	0	0	11	2005
Increment 3	16	0	0	0	0	16	2005
Increment 4	11	0	0	0	0	11	2006
Increment 5	11	0	0	0	0	11	2008
CORMORANT[8]	1	0	0	0	1	0	2004

Notes:

(1)   ASTOR comprises five Sentinel R Mk 1 aircraft and eight ground exploitation facilities. The ASTOR in service date is defined as the operational availability of two air platforms, two ground stations, a corresponding support capability and the availability of sufficient trained manpower. This would enable a basic operational capability for a brigade-level deployment.

(2)   Soothsayer, an integrated Land Electronic Warfare system, will be delivered in capability increments with ISDs from 2006.

(3)   Skynet 5 PFI subsumes current Skynet 4 capability and will deliver the next generation of military satellite communication services to support UK peacekeeping and military operations, including, in due course, the replacement of the Skynet 4 constellation of satellites. The programme includes ground infrastructure and terminals for static and mobile users in the land and sea environments. Skynet 5 PFI contract was awarded to Paradigm Secure Communications Ltd in October 2003. Paradigm will be purely responsible for the delivery of services. No assets will be acquired by the Department.

(4)   Naval EHF/SHF Satcom Terminal (EHF = Extremely High Frequency. SHF = Super High Frequency). Enhanced communications capability for naval platforms. Capability introduced from 2007.

(5)   Tactical data and voice communications system deliveries continue until 2007. Scope for 48,000 radios (not including 45,000 Personal Role Radios).

(6)   A Common Battlefield Application Toolset (ComBAT), Infrastructure (I) and armoured Platform Battlefield Information System Application (PBISA) to support Command and Battlespace Management for the Land Component.

(7)   A total of 10 Increment 1 platforms have been fitted and are operational. However, only 8 ships are fully supported at any one time, the remaining 2 ships being Fit To Receive (FTR).

(8)   CORMORANT communication system is designed to meet the needs of the Joint Rapid Reaction Force. It provides high capacity, secure communications within and between the deployed headquarters of the Joint Task Force.

International Equipment Co-operation

6. We continued to make a major contribution towards the development and expansion of our strong relationships with the UK's international partners within the armaments framework. The most notable achievements in the year 2003-04 were:

European Defence

- The MoD Centre and the Defence Procurement Agency played a proactive role in the shaping and establishment of a new **European Defence Agency (EDA)**. We provided a valuable contribution towards the Agency Establishment Team's working papers and put forward the UK's stance at the various EU meetings with conviction, including the need for the Agency to be focussed on harnessing and strengthening defence capabilities;

- We have worked closely with the **European Commission** during its preparatory work for a Green Paper on defence procurement, with the aim of improving the openness and transparency of the European Defence and Equipment Market whilst ensuring that the UK's defence industrial policy principles are preserved. This has included close co-operation with industry to influence the Commission's work, including the preparation of a joint policy paper. Work on the Green Paper and its aftermath will continue in 2004-05;

- We ensured that the UK continued to play a leading role in the **Western European Armaments Group (WEAG)** and worked closely with the Dutch Presidency of WEAG in drawing up plans for WEAG's eventual incorporation into the EDA;

United States of America

- Building on the Declaration of Principles we have continued our efforts to facilitate the flow of relevant information between the US and UK, both in the interest of programmes involving the procurement of US origin defence equipment and for UK industry looking for business opportunities in the US. We have also established a **Bilateral Defence Acquisition Committee (BDAC)**, which aims to develop and co-ordinate efforts to improve information and technology exchange. Initial signs are encouraging, but its success will ultimately be gauged by what real benefits are delivered. Its first meeting was held in February 2004;

OCCAR (Organisation Conjoint de Cooperation en matiers d'Armement)

- As a result of our extensive efforts as OCCAR Chair during 2003, OCCAR is now better placed to **deliver cost-effective and efficiently managed collaborative defence equipment programmes**. Results from last year's effectiveness review are now being put in place and are helping OCCAR to be a leading player in European defence acquisition, with the organisation being regarded as the main, but not only, port of choice for the management of co-operative programmes under the EDA. Despite the need for close links between the two organisations, we have successfully argued that OCCAR should not be formally incorporated into the EDA at this stage. We have also championed the importance of retaining OCCAR's founding principles, whilst stressing that OCCAR is open to membership by all European nations. We played an influential role in the A400M programme, the contract for which was signed between OCCAR and industry in May 2003;

Letter of Intent (LoI)

- During 2003/2004, the six LoI nations (France, Germany, Italy, Spain, Sweden and the UK) ratified the Framework Agreement, and signed four Implementing Arrangements (IA) covering Security of Supply, Research & Technology, Treatment of Technical Information and the Harmonisation of Military Requirements. The UK played a pivotal role in this process, which is aimed at fostering **more efficient equipment and industrial co-operation** with our European partners.

ANNEX F:
List of Further Sources

MoD Reports/Papers (some are available on www.mod.uk)

ABRO *Annual Report and Accounts 2003-04*

Armed Forces Personnel *Administration Agency Annual Report and Accounts 2003-04*

Army Personnel Centre *Annual Report and Accounts 2003-04*

Army Training and Recruiting Agency *Annual Report and Accounts 2003-04*

Civilian Attitude Survey, Paperclips, September 2004

CRE Partnership Agreement

Defence Academy *Annual Report 2003-04 (to be published in October 04)*

Defence Aviation Repair Agency *Annual Report and Accounts 2003-04*

Defence Communication Services Agency *Annual Report and Accounts 2003-04*

Defence Dental Agency *Annual Report and Accounts 2003-04*

Defence Estates Agency *Annual Report & Accounts 2003-04*

Defence Estates Framework Document

Defence Housing Executive Annual Report and Accounts 2003-04

Defence Housing Executive Corporate Plan 2003

Defence Medical Education and Training Agency *Annual Report and Accounts 2003-04*

Defence Procurement Agency Annual Report and Accounts 2003-04

Defence Procurement Agency Business Plan 2003

Defence Procurement Agency Corporate Plan 2003

Defence Science and Innovation Strategy

Defence Science and Technology Laboratories (Dstl) *Annual Report and Accounts 2003-04*

Defence Storage and Distribution Agency *Annual Report and Accounts 2003-04*

Defence Transport and Movements Agency *Annual Report and Accounts 2003-04*

Delivering Security in a Changing World (Defence White Paper and supporting essays)

Delivering Security in a Changing World: Future Capabilities

Director of Operational Capability's *Appraisal of Initial Training* (February 2003), *Departmental Progress Report* (July 2003) and Director of Operational Capability's *Re-Appraisal of Initial Training* (July 2003)

Disposal Services Agency *Annual Report and Accounts 2003-04*

Excellence in Defence Procurement 2004: Equipping the Armed Forces

Lessons for the Future (assessment of performance on Op TELIC)

Major Projects Report 2003

Medical Supplies Agency *Annual Report and Accounts 2003-04*

Ministry of Defence Departmental Resource Accounts 2003-04

Ministry of Defence Policy Papers no.4: *Defence Acquisition*

Ministry of Defence Policy Papers no.5: *Defence Industrial Policy, and* First Review of Defence Industrial Policy

Ministry of Defence Policy Paper no. 6: *Individual Training and Education in the Armed Forces*

MoD Sustainable Development Report 2003/2004

Modernising Defence Training: Report of the Defence Training Review

Naval Manning Agency *Annual Report and Accounts 2003-04*

Naval Recruiting and Training Agency *Annual Report and Accounts 2003-04*

Nov 2002 Missile Defence public discussion paper

Operations in Iraq: First Reflections

Opinion Surveys

Quarterly PSA reports to HM Treasury
(also available at www.hm-treasury.gov.uk/performance/MOD.cfm)

Papers supplied to *The Hutton Inquiry*

Pay and Personnel Agency *Annual Report and Accounts 2003-04*

RAF Personnel Management Agency *Annual Report and Accounts 2003-04*

RAF Training Group Defence Agency *Annual Report and Accounts 2003-04*

The Defence Health Programme 2003/2007

The Stewardship Report on the Defence Estate 2003

UK Defence Statistics 2004

Unified Diversity Strategy

Veterans Agency *Annual Report and Accounts 2003-04*

Warship Support Agency *Annual Report and Accounts 2003-04*

Session 2003-04

MoD Evidence to the HCDC and the PAC, and Government Responses to Committee Reports, as published on Parliament's website (www.parliament.uk)

HCDC Reports (Government Responses are listed in brackets after the report they relate to)

First Report
HC 96-i & ii   *Armed Forces Pensions and Compensation*
(Cm 6109)

Second Report
HC 293   *Annual Report for 2003*

Third Report
HC 57-i, ii & iii   *Lessons of Iraq*
(HC 635)

Fourth Report
HC 390   *Strategic Export Controls: Annual Report for 2002, Licensing Policy and Parliamentary Scrutiny*

Fifth Report
HC 465-i & ii   *The Defence White Paper 2003*
(HC 1048)

Sixth Report
HC 572-i & ii   *Defence Procurement*

PAC Reports (Government Responses are listed in brackets after the report they relate to)

Thirty-ninth Report
HC 273   *Operation TELIC: United Kingdom military operations in Iraq*

Twentieth Report
HC 551   *Improving service delivery: the Veterans Agency*
(Cm 6271)

MoD Evidence to HCDC

Annual Report and Accounts 2002/2003
HC 589-i   Oral Evidence given by Sir Kevin Tebbit, KCB CMG, Permanent Under Secretary of State, and Mr Trevor Woolley, Finance Director, 12 May 2004

Iraq
HC 721-i   Oral Evidence given by Mr Martin Howard, Director General, Operational Policy, and Major General Nick Houghton, ACDS(Operations), 23 June 2004

Duty of Care
HC 620-i   Oral Evidence given by Lieutenant General Anthony Palmer, Deputy Chief of Defence Staff (Personnel), Read Admiral Simon Goodall, Director General Training and Education, Colonel David Eccles, Chief of Staff, Army Training and Recruitment Agency, and Mr Julian Miller, Director General of Service Personnel Policy, 26 May 2004

MoD Evidence to PAC

Major Projects Report 2003
HC 383-i   Oral Evidence given by Sir Kevin Tebbit, KCB CMG, Permanent Under-Secretary of State, Sir Peter Spencer, KCB, Chief of Defence Procurement, and Lieutenant Rob Fulton, Deputy Chief of Defence Staff (Equipment Capability), 23 February 2004

HC 383-ii   Oral Evidence given by Sir Peter Spencer, KCB, Chief of Defence Procurement, and Lieutenant Rob Fulton, Deputy Chief of Defence Staff (Equipment Capability), 25 February 2004

Session 2002-03

HCDC Reports (Government Responses are listed in brackets after the report they relate to)

Third Report
HC 321   *Arms Control and Disarmament (Inspections) Bill*
(HC 754)

Fourth Report
HC 620   *The Government's Proposals for Secondary Legislation under the Export Control Act*
(Cm 5988)

Fifth Report
HC 474   *Strategic Export Controls: Annual Report for 2001, Licensing Policy and*
(Cm 5943)   *Parliamentary Scrutiny*

Sixth Report
HC 93-i & ii   *A New Chapter to the Strategic Defence Review*
(HC 975)

Seventh Report
HC 557   *Draft Civil Contingencies Bill*
(Cm 6078)

Eighth Report
HC 694   *Defence Procurement*
(HC 1194)

PAC Reports (Government Responses are listed in brackets after the report they relate to)

Forty-sixth Report
HC 533   *Building an air manoeuvre capability: the introduction of the Apache Helicopter*
(Cm 6105)

Thirty-seventh Report
HC 636   *The construction of nuclear submarine facilities at Devonport*
(Cm 6016)

Thirteenth Report
HC 566   *Progress in Reducing Stocks*
(Cm 5849)

MoD Evidence to HCDC

European Security and Defence
HC 1165-i   Minutes of oral evidence by Mr Simon Webb CBE, Policy Director, Ministry of Defence,
                  Dr Sarah Beaver, Director for EU and UN, Ministry of Defence, and Mr Paul Johnston, Head of
                  Security Policy Department, Foreign and Commonwealth Office, 15 October 2003

Armed Forces Pension and Compensation
HC 1255   Minutes of oral evidence by Mr Ivor Caplin, Under-Secretary of State and Minister for
                  Veterans, and Mr Jonathan Iremonger, Director, Service Personnel Policy (Pensions),
                  5 November 2003

The Appointment of the New Chief of the Defence Staff
HC 771-i   Minutes of oral evidence by General Sir Michael Walker, GCB CMG CBE ADC,
                  Chief of the Defence Staff, 11 June 2003

The Army Training and Recruiting Agency
HC 124-i   Minutes of oral evidence by Major General A D Leakey CBE, Chief Executive, and
                  Mr Martyn Piper, Deputy Chief Executive, Army Training and Recruiting Agency,1 May 2003

Central Government Supply Estimates 2003-04 Main Supply Estimates (HC 648)

Central Government Supply Estimates 2003-04 Spring Supplementary Estimates (HC 350)

National Audit Office report on *Through Life Management* (HC 698)

National Audit Office report on *Operation Telic – United Kingdom Military Operations in Iraq* (HC 60)

National Audit Office report on *The Management of Defence Research and Technology* (HC 360)

Review of Logistics to the Armed Forces, Hansard, Columns 26-27WS

Other

1990/1991 Gulf Conflict – UK Gulf Veterans Mortality Data: Cause of Death (http://www.dasa.mod.uk)

CBI survey: Room for Improvement: CBI Absence and Labour Turnover 2004, in association with AXA (available from The Stationery Office)

CIPD survey: Employee Absence 2004: A Survey of Management Policy and Practice
http://www.cipd.co.uk/subjects/hrpract/absence/empabs04.htm

Clinical Findings in 111 Ex-Porton Down Volunteers, Lee et al, Journal of the Royal Army Medical Corps, 2004, 150, 14-19

Council Joint Action 2004/551/CFSP of 12 July 2004 on the establishment of the European Defence Agency at http://ue.eu.int/uedocs

Draft Civil Contingencies Bill at http://www.ukresilience.info/ccbill/index.htm

European Council NATO-EU Planning, Consultation and Operations Document SN 307/03 of 11 December 2003 at http://ue.eu.int/uedocs

Final Report of the Lyons Review: *Well Placed to Deliver? – Shaping the Pattern of Government Service*
http://www.hm-treasury.gov.uk/consultations_and_legislation/lyons/consult_lyons_index.cfm

Gulf War Illness – Better, Worse, or Just the Same?, Hotopf et al, British Medical Journal, 2003, 327, p1370

Incidence of Cancer Among UK Gulf War Veterans, Macfarlane et al, British Medical Journal, 2003, 327, p1373

Istanbul Summit Communiqué, issued by the Heads of State and Government participating in the meeting of the North Atlantic Council, 28 June 2004 at http://nato.usmission.gov/News/ISUM_Communique_ 062804.htm

Miscarriage, Stillbirth and Congenital Malformation in the Offspring of UK Veterans of the First Gulf War, Doyle et al, International Journal of Epidemiology, 2004, 33, 74-86

Papers for the 2003 CWC Review Conference at www.opcw.org

Papers for the 2004 NPT Prepcom at www.fco.gov.uk

Protocol V on Explosive Remnants of War at www.gichd.ch/ccw

Psychiatric Disorder in Veterans of the Persian Gulf War of 1991, Stimpson et al, British Journal of Psychiatry, 2003, 182, 391-403

Race Equality Scheme (RES) 2002-2005
(www.mod.uk/linked_files/racial_equality.pdf)

Releasing Resources to the Front Line: Independent Review of Public Sector Efficiency
http://www.hm-treasury.gov.uk

RES first progress report
(www.mod.uk/linked_files/issues/personnel/2003_race_equality_report.pdf)

Strategy for Veterans (http://www.veteransagency.mod.uk/vasec/strategy.pdf)

The G8 Global Partnership: Progress Report on the UK's Programme to address nuclear, chemical and biological
legacies in the Former Soviet Union published jointly by FCO, DTI and MOD in Nov 03 and available at
www.dti.gov.uk/energy/nuclear/fsu/news/First_annual_report.pdf

Treaty establishing a Constitution for Europe at
http://ue.eu.int/igcpdf/en/04/cg00/cg00087.en04.pdf

Printed in the UK for The Stationery Office Limited
on behalf of the Controller of Her Majesty's Stationery Office
10/04, 171636
Printed on recycled paper containing 75% post consumer waste and 25% ECF Pulp